LIBRARY OF HEBREW BIBLE/
OLD TESTAMENT STUDIES

685

Formerly Journal for the Study of the Old Testament Supplement Series

Editors
Claudia V. Camp, Texas Christian University, USA
Andrew Mein, University of Durham, UK

Founding Editors
David J. A. Clines, Philip R. Davies and David M. Gunn

Editorial Board
Alan Cooper, Susan Gillingham, John Goldingay,
Norman K. Gottwald, James E. Harding, John Jarick, Carol Meyers,
Daniel L. Smith-Christopher, Francesca Stavrakopoulou,
James W. Watts

WATER AND WATER-RELATED PHENOMENA IN THE OLD TESTAMENT WISDOM LITERATURE

An Eco-Theological Exploration

Kivatsi Jonathan Kavusa

t&tclark
LONDON • NEW YORK • OXFORD • NEW DELHI • SYDNEY

T&T CLARK
Bloomsbury Publishing Plc
50 Bedford Square, London, WC1B 3DP, UK
1385 Broadway, New York, NY 10018, USA

BLOOMSBURY, T&T CLARK and the T&T Clark logo
are trademarks of Bloomsbury Publishing Plc

First published in Great Britain in 2020
Paperback edition first published 2021

Copyright © Kivatsi Jonathan Kavusa, 2020

Kivatsi Jonathan Kavusa has asserted his right under the Copyright,
Designs and Patents Act, 1988, to be identified as Author of this work.

For legal purposes the Acknowledgements on p. xiii constitute
an extension of this copyright page.

All rights reserved. No part of this publication may be reproduced or
transmitted in any form or by any means, electronic or mechanical,
including photocopying, recording, or any information storage or retrieval
system, without prior permission in writing from the publishers.

Bloomsbury Publishing Plc does not have any control over, or responsibility for,
any third-party websites referred to or in this book. All internet addresses given
in this book were correct at the time of going to press. The author and publisher
regret any inconvenience caused if addresses have changed or sites have
ceased to exist, but can accept no responsibility for any such changes.

A catalogue record for this book is available from the British Library.

A catalog record for this book is available from the Library of Congress.

ISBN: HB: 978-0-5676-8727-2
PB: 978-0-5677-0145-9
ePDF: 978-0-5676-8728-9
eBook: 978-0-5676-9227-6

Series: Library of Hebrew Bible/Old Testament Studies, 2513-8758, volume 685

Typeset by Forthcoming Publications Ltd

To find out more about our authors and books visit
www.bloomsbury.com and sign up for our newsletters.

To my beloved wife,
KAHINDO KYAKIMWA Maguy,
מעין גנים באר מים חיים ונזלים מן לבנון (Song 4:15)

Contents

List of Tables	ix
Foreword by Willie van Heerden	xi
Acknowledgements	xiii
Abbreviations	xv

Chapter 1
INTRODUCTION 1
   1.1. Water as an Interdisciplinary Subject 1
   1.2. Formulating the Problem 2
   1.3. Stating the Thesis 4
   1.4. The Relevance of Wisdom Books to Eco-theology 4
   1.5. Theoretical Framework 6
   1.6. Methodological Considerations 7
   1.7. Delimitation and Selection of Biblical Texts 11
   1.8. Difficulties and Limitations of the Study 12
   1.9. Division of Chapters 13

Chapter 2
PREVIOUS STUDIES ON WATER AND WATER-RELATED PHENOMENA IN THE OLD TESTAMENT 14
   2.1. Introduction 14
   2.2. Old Testament Studies on Water and Water-related Phenomena 14
   2.3. Eco-theological Studies about Water and Water-related Phenomena ... 20
   2.4. Studies on Wisdom Texts Containing Water and Water-related Phenomena ... 22
   2.5. Conclusion 31

Chapter 3
WATER AND WATER-RELATED PHENOMENA IN THE BOOK OF JOB 33
   3.1. Introduction 33
   3.2. Introduction to the Book of Job 33
   3.3. Water and Water-related Phenomena in Job 14:7-12 36
   3.4. Water and Water-related Phenomena in Job 36:26–37:13 43
   3.5. Water and Water-related Phenomena in Job 38:22-38 53
   3.6. Comparative Conclusion 66

Chapter 4
WATER AND WATER-RELATED PHENOMENA IN THE BOOK OF PROVERBS — 68
4.1. Introduction — 68
4.2. References to Water in the Metaphorical Texts of Proverbs — 68
4.3. Water and Water-related Phenomena in
   Proverbs 3:19-20 and 8:22-31 — 96
4.4. Comparative Conclusion — 105

Chapter 5
WATER AND WATER-RELATED PHENOMENA IN THE BOOK OF QOHELETH — 107
5.1. Introduction — 107
5.2. Introduction to the Book of Qoheleth — 107
5.3. Water and Water-related Phenomena in Qoheleth 1:4-11 — 110
5.4. Water and Water-related Phenomena in Qoheleth 2:4-6 — 121
5.5. Water and Water-related Phenomena in Qoheleth 11:1-6 — 128
5.6. Conclusion — 134

Chapter 6
WATER AND WATER-RELATED PHENOMENA IN THE DEUTERO-CANONICAL WISDOM BOOKS — 136
6.1. Introduction — 136
6.2. Water and Water-related Phenomena in
   Sirach 24:23-34 and 43:13-26 — 136
6.3. Water and Water-related Phenomena in Wisdom 11:2-14 — 156
6.4. Conclusion — 168

Chapter 7
CONCLUSIONS: ECO-THEOLOGICAL IMPLICATIONS OF THE STUDY — 170
7.1. Introduction — 170
7.2. Substantial Contributions to Eco-theology — 170
7.3. Ecological Implications of the Study for Today — 176
7.4. Remaining Questions for Further Research — 180

Appendix A:
REFERENCES TO WATER AND WATER-RELATED PHENOMENA IN THE OLD TESTAMENT WISDOM BOOKS — 181

Appendix B:
REFERENCES TO THE LIFE-GIVING AND LIFE-THREATENING POTENTIAL OF WATER AND WATER-RELATED PHENOMENA — 204

Bibliography — 206
Index of References — 216
Index of Authors — 225

List of Tables

Table 1: The Structure of Job 14:7-12   37
Table 2: The Literary Structure of Job 36:26–37:13   46
Table 3: The Rhetorical Structure of Proverbs 5:15-20   71
Table 4: The Structure of Proverbs 25:23-26   90
Table 5: The Rhetorical Structure of Proverbs 3:19-20   98
Table 6: The Structure of Proverbs 8:22-31   102
Table 7: The Literary Structure of Sirach 24:23-29   140
Table 8: The Structure of Sirach 24:29   145
Table 9: The Literary Structure of Sirach 24:30-34   146

Foreword

In 2014 the author of this book and I were discussing a possible topic for his doctoral studies at the University of South Africa. He wanted to explore the field of ecological interpretations of biblical texts. When he spoke about water issues in his home country, the Democratic Republic of the Congo, his eyes lit up. We realised that a study focusing on water and water-related phenomena would not only ground his study in personal experiences and concerns, but also contribute to the motivation doctoral students need to successfully complete their projects.

Kivatsi Jonathan Kavusa has had first-hand experience of both the life-giving and the life-threatening potential of water. We agreed that his study, which would focus on water and water-related phenomena, would be an attempt to address two problem areas in eco-theological discourses: first, an overly romantic view of nature in most eco-theological studies; and secondly, a tendency to focus on a number of favourite biblical texts, often excluding biblical wisdom literature. That is how the idea for this book, based on Kavusa's doctoral thesis, which was completed in 2016, originated.

At the time, a few prominent contributions to discourses on ecological hermeneutics set the agenda for many scholars who were exploring this relatively new field in biblical scholarship. The Earth Bible Project, which gained momentum around the year 2000, offered a hermeneutics of suspicion and retrieval (later extended to also include the element of identification). In practice this hermeneutical framework involved the application of six ecojustice principles, namely the principles of intrinsic worth, interconnectedness, voice, purpose, mutual custodianship, and resistance.

A second project was the Green Bible Project, which involved offering the complete text of the Bible (in English, the New Revised Standard Version), with thousands of passages claimed to speak directly about the earth and caring for creation printed in green. The Green Bible also contains a dozen essays by conservationists and theologians that highlight, in the words of the editors, 'important themes related to God's care of creation and show how to read the Bible through a "green lens".'

Another project shows appreciation for, but also offers a critique of both the above approaches. Participants in the University of Exeter project on 'Uses of the Bible in Environmental Ethics' developed a position somewhat between the stance of 'recovery' represented in some evangelical writing and in The Green Bible on the one hand, and the critical ecojustice hermeneutic offered by the Earth Bible team.

Professor Kavusa experiments with the hermeneutical model of the Earth Bible Project, adopting a general hermeneutic of suspicion and retrieval, applying also some of the ecojustice principles, particularly the principles of intrinsic worth, interconnectedness, voice, and purpose to fifteen biblical texts on water and water-related phenomena, all found in the Hebrew Bible wisdom literature. Three texts are from the book of Job, five from the book of Proverbs, three from Qoheleth (Ecclesiastes), and four from the Deutero-canonical wisdom books.

The book convincingly shows that biblical wisdom texts do not offer 'thin', romantic portrayals of nature. Instead, nature is viewed as rich and complex, life-giving and life-threatening. A surprising number of texts that have not yet featured in eco-theological studies have been shown to offer rewarding perspectives on the issue.

Through the completion of his doctoral project that culminated in the publication of this book, Prof. Kavusa offers a well-researched, original contribution to this exciting field of scholarship. It was a privilege to be part of this research journey in my capacity as promoter of his doctoral project.

Willie van Heerden
Pretoria, 12 November 2018

Acknowledgements

This book started as a doctoral thesis submitted to the Department of Biblical and Ancient Studies of the University of South Africa (UNISA) in September 2015. After its examination by a jury of three renowned scholars, the thesis was recommended for publication by the Senate of UNISA as one of the best theses of the year. Given that no major theological publications on water in the wisdom books have been issued to date, this book is a slight revision of that thesis.

I am thankful to the Ecumenical Theological Education desk of the World Council of Churches and Langham Partnership International for the financial grants I received to do my doctoral studies. In addition, Langham Partnership and Nagel Institute funded my research sojourn in Grand Rapids (Michigan) from September to November 2016 in order to convert the thesis into this book. The huge facilities of Calvin College's Hekman Library were helpful in the process.

I am particularly indebted to my thesis promoter, Professor Willie van Heerden, whose careful listening, guidance and updated insights in the field of ecological hermeneutics shaped and inspired the core body of this study. I am also grateful for the hospitality of Joel Carpenter, Donna Romanowski and Nellie Kooistra of the Nagel Institute during my stay at the Prophet's Chamber in Grand Rapids. Likewise, I am thankful to the management committee of my home university (ULPGL) for having granted me three months research leave to work on this book in the USA.

Finally, I am deeply thankful to my wife and best friend, Kahindo Kyakimwa Maguy, for her continuous support, and mostly for forgiving my absence in person and mind while I was working on this project. This book is dedicated to her with love.

Grand Rapids, MI, 10 October 2016

ABBREVIATIONS

AJSL	American Journal of Semitic Languages and Literatures
ATF	Australian Theological Forum
AUS	American University Studies
AWRA	*American Water Resources Association* (Water Resources Bulletin)
BA	*Biblical Archaeologist*
BAR	*Biblical Archaeologist Review*
BASOR	*Bulletin of the American Schools of Oriental Research*
BCE	Before Common Era
BETS	Bulletin of the Evangelical Theological Society
BFC	Bible Français Courant
BSac	*Bibliotheca Sacra*
BT	*Bible Translator*
CBAA	Catholic Biblical Association of America
CBQ	*Catholic Biblical Quarterly*
CBQMS	Catholic Biblical Quarterly Monograph Series
CE	Common Era
CJB	Complete Jewish Bible
EMJ	*Encounters Mission Journal*
GI	Greek Translation of Ben Sira's Grandson
GII	The Expended Greek Translation of Ben Sira
HTI	Hebrew Original of Ben Sira
HTII	Expanded Hebrew Text of One or More Recensions of Ben Sira
HTR	*Harvard Theological Review*
HUCA	*Hebrew Union College Annual*
IDB	G. A. Buttrick, ed. *The Interpreter's Dictionary of the Bible*. 4 vols. New York/Nashville: Abingdon, 1962
IEJ	*Israel Exploration Journal*
inscr.	Inscription
JARCE	*Journal of the American Centre in Egypt*
JBL	*Journal of Biblical Literature*
JBQ	*Jewish Bible Quarterly*
JNSL	*Journal of the Northwest Semitic Languages*
JPS	Jewish Publication Society
JR	*Journal of Religion*
JSJ	*Journal for the Study of Judaism*
JSOT	*Journal for the Study of the Old Testament*

JTS	*Journal of Theological Studies*
KJV	King James Version
LXX	The Septuagint
MT	The Masoretic Text
NIB	L. E. Keck, ed. *The New Interpreter's Bible*. 12 vols. Nashville: Abingdon, 1994–2004
NIDOTTE	Willem A. VanGemeren, ed. *New interpreter's Dictionary of the Old Testament Theology and Exegesis*. 5 vols. Grand Rapids: Zondervan, 1997
NIV	New International Version
NJPS	The New Jewish Publication Society (Bible Version)
NRSV	The New Revised Standard Version
OTE	*Old Testament Essays*
4QQoh[a]	The Earliest Qoheleth Scroll Fragments at Qumran
RB	*Revue Biblique*
RSV	The Revised Standard Version
s.a.	*Sine anno* (No date)
SBL	Society of Biblical Literature
SCM	Student Christian Movement
TANAK	*Torah Nebiim Ketubim* (i.e. Acronym for the Hebrew Bible)
TDOT	G. J. Botterweck, H. Ringgren, and H.-J. Fabry, eds. *Theological Dictionary of the Old Testament*. 8 vols. Grand Rapids: Eerdmans, 1974–1997
TEV	Today's English Version (Good News Bible)
TOB	Traduction Œcuménique de la Bible
TWOT	R. L. Harris, G. L. Archer and B. K. Waltke, eds. *Theological Wordbook of the Old Testament*. 2 vols. Chicago: Moody, 1980
UCT	University of Cape Town
UF	*Ugarit Forschungen*
ULPGL	Université Libre des Pays des Grands Lacs
UNESCO	United Nations Educational, Scientific and Cultural Organisation
UNISA	University of South Africa
VT	*Vetus Testamentum*
VTSup	Supplements to *Vetus Testamentum*
ZDPV	*Zeitschrift des Deutschen Palästina-Vereins*
ZAW	*Zeitschrift für die Alttestamentliche Wissenschaft*

Chapter 1

INTRODUCTION

1.1. *Water as an Interdisciplinary Subject*

Water is essential for all life. Covering nearly 70 per cent of the earth, it is uncertain that life on earth would have arisen without water, since no organism can live without it. Water is predominant in all living things: water makes up 60 per cent of a tree's weight; most animals contain an average of 50–60 per cent water.

And yet, while water is a basic condition of life, it is also an agent of destruction across the globe. For many readers of this book, water is an everyday commodity. The global demand for water is increasing at such significant rates that experts in international relations and conflict studies think that the major wars of this century will be fought not over oil but water. In many parts of our world, water is increasingly becoming a matter of life and death. In many developing countries, women and children spend hours walking to fetch clean water from distant sources.

For all its life-giving and life-preserving importance, water is involved in the death of many people. In Africa, roughly 600,000 people die every year from unsafe water, while water-related diseases kill millions more. Water is thus a valuable treasure and a potential threat that can both give and threaten life through its variable and complex aspects. It is not surprising that water has long been revered and feared. Wells and springs/fountains have been and still are (by some) regarded as sacred places, as places where deities reside and as sources of healing and refreshment (Prov. 5:15-20); seas, great lakes and rivers have, it seems, always had the ability to induce fear.

For this reason, the modern discussion of water has become a subject involving interdisciplinary approaches. UNESCO argues that the sustainable future of the planet requires cross-disciplinary investigation.[1]

---

1. UNESCO. Water issues. Available online from: http://www.unesco.org/water/water_links/Water_Issues/ (accessed 6 June 2013).

The present study is a theological perspective on the subject of water. It examines the life-giving and life-threatening potential of water and related phenomena in the Old Testament wisdom books.

1.2. *Formulating the Problem*

The crisis of water, which is a current and pressing problem of our time, was already one of the most important issues in the biblical world. As such, the subject of water occurs in the Bible broadly and in multivalent ways either as a metaphor for a given reality or a real physical domain. However, since Lynn White alleged that Western Christianity is liable for the current ecological crisis in 1967, biblical scholars and eco-theologians have tried to prove the contrary. Notably, their responses have been too narrow, as they favoured certain biblical texts about nature (water) and leaned towards the romantic view of nature (water) in the Bible.

Many publications exploring water and water-related phenomena select texts from the Pentateuch, Prophets and Psalms[2] that *expressis verbis* deal with water as a physical reality. These biblical loci have evolved as a kind of 'canon within the canon',[3] one that entails ignoring texts that do not present themselves as having ecological wisdom. As a result of this, the Old Testament wisdom books have not gained enough attention in the study of water and related phenomena. In the early 1980s, Loader[4] observed that very little or no attention is given to the Old Testament wisdom books in eco-theological studies. This tendency continues to date in studies about water in the Old Testament.

The 2011[5] volume of the journal *Interface*, entitled *Water: A Matter of Life and Death*, is one of the most noteworthy biblical and eco-theological studies on water in the Bible. This volume provides a series of contributions from biblical scholars and scientists who seriously engage with the concept of water as a spiritual and physical entity. However, even in this

---

2. Genesis 1–9, Deutero-Isaiah, Job 38–42 and Ps. 104 are the most dominant texts of eco-theological studies.

3. Dianne Bergant, 'The Wisdom of Solomon', in *Reading from the Perspective of Earth*, ed. Norman C. Habel (Cleveland: Pilgrim; Sheffield: Sheffield Academic, 2000), 138.

4. James A. Loader, 'Image and Order: Old Testament Perspectives on the Ecological Crisis', in *Are We Killing God's Earth? Ecology and Theology*, ed. W. S Vorster (Pretoria: UNISA, 1987), 22.

5. Normal C. Habel and Peter Trudinger, eds., *Water: A Matter of Life and Death* (Adelaide: ATF, 2011).

volume, which was explicitly entitled to highlight the opposing aspects of water in the Bible, the Old Testament wisdom books were ignored.

Another prominent example of the lack of interest in the wisdom books is the recently published scholarly book entitled *Thinking of Water in the Early Second Temple Period*.[6] This work clearly favours texts from the Pentateuch and prophetic books. Despite the fact that the books of Proverbs, Qoheleth, Sirach and Wisdom of Solomon belong to the Second Temple period, their views on water are simply ignored. The book contains only 'a brief overview' about thinking related to water in the book of Job.

As for the subject of water itself, many publications have a reductionist romanticist view of nature and, therefore, display a one-sided outlook. For the romanticist ecologists, the view of 'nature' needs not be confined to settings of Big Wilderness – as a negative entity – but must be perceived through eyes of wonder and beauty. This is the perspective that always animates tourists as they visit national parks and reserves. In this way, many eco-theological studies approach biblical texts about water and related phenomena with the aim of only retrieving the eco-friendliness of elements of nature.

To my knowledge, thorough study of water and water-related phenomena in general, and water as bearing life-giving and life-threatening potential in particular, in the Old Testament wisdom literature has not been done before, especially not from an eco-theological point of view. In addition, the romanticist view of nature is dominant in eco-theological Old Testament scholarship, which does not do justice to the global perception of elements of nature as depicted in the Old Testament texts.

Although there is a scarcity of scholarly works on water and water-related phenomena in these books, the Old Testament wisdom books overflow – pun intended – with references to waters that deserve a thorough exploration.[7] If we agree that the biblical texts can be the basis on which modern thoughts can be drawn for inspiration, then we need to discern the complexity of the subject of water as it occurs in the different parts of the Bible.

Therefore, after years of viewing the 'subject of water' primarily through the lenses of the Pentateuch, Psalms and prophetic literature, biblical scholars and eco-theologians are here invited to embrace a new

---

6. Ehud Ben Zvi and Christoph Levin, eds., *Thinking of Water in the Early Second Temple Period* (Berlin: de Gruyter, 2014).

7. The Old Testament wisdom books contain more than 600 references to water and water-related phenomena (see Appendix A).

way of thinking and acting imbued by the wisdom books' focus and observations that may provide a useful means of formulating realistic and practical answers to contemporary water crises.

This book attempts to address not only the issue of favouring certain texts by taking up the challenge of offering an eco-theological interpretation of water and related phenomena in the Old Testament wisdom books, but it also critically explores this subject of water in its complexity in terms of its life-giving and life-threatening potential. We need to analyse what the wisdom literature has preserved about ancient Israel's views on water, this significant and indispensable element of life, and yet a potential threat on earth.

Therefore, the following are the main guiding questions of this book:

1. How often do references to water occur in the Old Testament wisdom books?
2. Do the Old Testament wisdom texts where the waters of life and death occur offer ecological wisdom?

1.3. Stating the Thesis

Through its analyses, this book shows how, despite a shortage of scholarly interest in water in the Old Testament wisdom books, this part of the Bible contains a rich variety of references to water and water-related phenomena relevant for an eco-theological analysis. Additionally, this book's explorations into the positive and negative potential of water exemplifies how the romantic view of nature does not do justice to the biblical texts themselves. I hope that the insights of this book will shed light on contemporary attitudes towards water.

1.4. The Relevance of Wisdom Books to Eco-theology

Firstly, it is necessary to clarify what the word 'wisdom' means. There is a difference between (1) wisdom as a human faculty and (2) wisdom as wisdom literature with its characteristic ideas and literary forms. The faculty of wisdom is designated through a number of expressions in the Old Testament, most prominently חָכְמָה. The distinctive feature for חָכְמָה in all its occurrences is a high degree of knowledge and skill in any domain, in other words, expertise.[8]

---

8. Michael V. Fox, 'Joseph and Wisdom', in *The Book of Genesis: Composition, Reception and Interpretation*, ed. C. A. Evans, J. N. Lohr and D. L. Petersen (Leiden: Brill, 2012), 232.

The wisdom books are literary constructs that seek to instil this wisdom. In Prov. 8:22-31, Wisdom claims to have been personally present at creation: it is the principle in which God established creation. Thus, the main teaching of the wisdom books is that one recognises the order, which God put in creation from the beginning, and lives according to it.[9] This optimistic sapiential idea is clearly stated in the book of Proverbs, which suggests that if one desires happiness and success then one needs to adjust his/her life with the creation order. Failure to abide by this order/wisdom (*ma'at* in Egypt) will lead *inter alia* to calamity.

Seen in this way, the wisdom books would seem to be relevant when addressing the current ecological crisis. This is not surprising, since the wisdom literature might best be understood as storing and preserving observations and experiences accumulated by humans over a long period of time.[10] Water is both a basic need of living beings, and sometimes a destructive factor that is present in the daily life of human beings. For this reason, the subject of water and water-related phenomena extensively occur in the wisdom books in multivalent ways.

Surprisingly, very little or no attention has been paid to their vision on water. The Old Testament wisdom books teach wisdom 'not incidentally, not as one aspect among many (more) important things, but as the very fundamental cornerstone of *all* human culture'.[11] In this part of the Bible, there is no polarity between humans and nature, but a quest for order.

It is interesting that there is a self-criticism within the sapiential literature. The books of Job and Qoheleth argue that the created order is made up of both life-giving and life-threatening entities that are beyond human knowledge. Therefore, chs. 38–42 of Job conclude with the harmony of the cosmic order in a poetic symmetry, while Qoh. 11:1-6 depicts the human incapacity to master the mysteries of nature (also Sir. 24:29).

Fundamentally, the wisdom books provide such a realistic vision that, without being anachronistic, they offer the potential for re-defining and re-questioning our relationship with nature. They offer insightful wisdom that we can use to address our contemporary ecological crisis, including water issues.

---

9. James L. Crenshaw, 'Prolegomenon', in *Studies in Ancient Israelite Wisdom*, ed. James L. Crenshaw (New York: Ktav, 1976), 34.

10. Roumyana Petrova, 'Comparing Proverbs as Cultural Texts', *Proverbium: Yearbook of International Proverb Scholarship* 20 (2003): 331–44.

11. Loader, 'Image and Order', 22.

1.5. *Theoretical Framework*

This study is approached within the eco-theological framework, informed by a hermeneutics of suspicion and retrieval/trust as well as insights from the six eco-justice principles of the Earth Bible Project, namely intrinsic worth, interconnectedness, voice, purpose, mutual custodianship and resistance. According to the Earth Bible Team,[12] readers of the Bible may not find all these principles useful in reading a given biblical text afresh. This study is an attempt at reading the wisdom texts containing water as a life-giving or life-threatening entity in the framework of four eco-justice principles, namely the principles of *intrinsic worth, interconnectedness, voice* and *purpose.*

Additionally, this study makes use of a hermeneutics of suspicion and retrieval/trust. With regard to the element of suspicion, we suspect that biblical texts, written by human beings for human readers, reflect primarily the interests of humans. Briefly, the Bible has long been understood as God's book for humans in that all its passages are normally interpreted from the perspective of humans. The new ecological awareness requires that we begin reading the biblical text with the suspicion that it is likely to be inherently anthropocentric and/or has traditionally been read from a human-focused perspective.

However, ecological wisdom might also be retrieved from biblical texts. Many texts give voice to more than just the human members of the Earth community. In some cases, human actions and thoughts reflect remarkable ecological insight. Biblical texts also deserve the trust of their readers, as dialogue partners in search of ecological wisdom.

By applying a hermeneutics of suspicion and retrieval/trust, an attempt will be made in this study to detect instances where water and water-related phenomena are being used in the service of anthropocentrism, but also to be aware of instances where ecological wisdom can be retrieved from the texts. The mere selection of texts portraying both the life-giving and life-threatening potential of water and water-related phenomena shows that this study hopes to find ecological wisdom in the Old Testament wisdom books. These elements of the text may have been unnoticed, silenced or hidden through human-centred reading lenses.

Ecological hermeneutics should not be confused with exegetical methods or with the wide range of approaches to biblical exegesis. Similar to feminist or liberation readings, ecological hermeneutics is an interpretative strategy referring to techniques of re-appropriation used by readers

---

12. The Earth Bible Team, 'Guiding Ecojustice Principles', in Habel, ed., *Reading from the Perspective of Earth*, 39.

to overcome the historical gap between the text and a modern problem. Basically, ecological hermeneutics enables the interpreters to read the Bible afresh in the context of ecological crises, and to create doctrinal keys that function as *critical keys* with which to interact with the text.[13]

This interpretative strategy assumes that there is no *absolute truth* in the text, but that interpreting a text involves the *fusion of horizons* – that of the text and that of the reader – from which emerges a new meaning.[14] Ricoeur calls this result the 'surplus of meaning', in the sense that the text can yield an array of diverse meanings without compromising its literary integrity.[15] Therefore, while the historical setting and literary structure of our selected wisdom texts will be considered, we assume that their meaning can be brought beyond cultural and generational boundaries to convey various messages in diverse contexts, such as contemporary water issues.

With its ecological awareness and the use of the selected four eco-justice principles as *doctrinal keys*, along with the hermeneutics of suspicion and retrieval/trust, the framework of this book will lead us to the Old Testament wisdom literature's critical power and continuing stimulus in interaction with our modern ecological water crisis. Indeed, adopting insights from the six eco-justice principles of the Earth Bible Project does not mean that our hermeneutics will view these principles as a kind of 'canon' alongside which the 'validity' of biblical texts can be judged, as is the case in the Earth Bible series.

The eco-justice principles used in this book are simply interpretative constructs that will help us to unlock the significance of the Old Testament wisdom books' references to water in relation to our context of ecological crises. This reading posture assumes that biblical texts, written in a premodern society, might freely reveal their character as something unique and insightful to our contemporary issues. Yet, our questions and analysis will never confuse the world of the texts with our contemporary realities.

1.6. *Methodological Considerations*

The present study will rely on elements of historical criticism and literary approaches. When applied to biblical texts, these methods bring illumination of a holistic understanding of the text. Rather than viewing them as opposites, the two methods complement and enrich one another. Thus,

---

13. Ernest Conradie, *Christianity and Ecological Theology: Resources for Further Research* (Stellenbosch: Sun, 2006), 13.

14. Hans G. Gadamer, *Truth and Method* (New York: Seabury, 1975), 341.

15. Paul Ricoeur, *Interpretation Theory: The Surplus of Meaning* (Fort Worth: Texas Christian Press, 1976), 45–6.

this book examines how the historical and literary methods can assist in retrieving ecological insights in the selected wisdom texts that contain the life-giving and life-threatening potential of water and water-related phenomena.

1.6.1. *Historical Critical Methods*

Through historical criticism, the author examines and interprets selected wisdom texts in relation to their historical and literary contexts. In this hermeneutical process, the reader examines how insights from the socio-historical and geographical contexts of a given text can contribute to its understanding. In this study, the approach aids in utilising relevant information about culture, mentality, religion, meteorology and hydrological concerns that prevailed in the socio-historical setting of certain wisdom texts.

In this case, the various wisdom texts on water of life or death are studied not only in relation to their geographic context, their Palestinian, Mesopotamian, Egyptian or Hellenistic settings, but also to other sapiential literatures of Judaism during the same period. Given its ecological awareness, the study will ask questions that transcend previous anthropocentric historical analysis of the texts. In fact, one of the defining clues of historical-critical methods is their emphasis on asking free and critical questions about the meaning of the text, regardless of church traditions or dogma.

Special attention will be given to the meaning of waters of life and death in relation to historical and social changes experienced by Israel. Perdue[16] observed that creation, including the מַיִם (cosmic waters), was the centre of sapiential theologies that were produced over more than eight centuries, and that the variety of its expression altered in response to the historical, social/cultural events of subsequent periods of ancient Israel and early Judaism.

Thus, the wisdom texts cannot be dissociated from the social and historical context and geographical settings of Israel. The physical context of the Old Testament wisdom books is marked by real-world climactic conditions, be they arid or well-watered. The wisdom books that originated in dry places paid special attention to the life-giving function of the rain (Job 36:27), while those informed by destructive floods viewed water as a life-threatening aspect of existence. As such, the analyses focus on specific key words or metaphors in order to uncover the ecological world that informed the text.

---

16. Leo G. Perdue, *Wisdom Literature: A Theological History* (London/Louisville: Westminster John Knox, 2007), 326.

1.6.2. *Literary Analyses*

Given the didactic focus of the wisdom literature, it would not be appropriate to limit our analyses of the texts to historical criticism, but also to involve the internal dynamics of the texts in order to generate meaning. The self-critical, epigrammatic and reflexive nature of the wisdom literature lends to its work a character of versatility and transferability of literary form and rational insights, which may sometimes reveal more insight beyond the literary contexts.[17]

The selected texts for this study comprise various literary genres, each requiring an appropriate reading strategy. In this sense, all the references from the book of Job[18] belong to the wisdom poems stated in the form of anamnesis, dialogue and rhetorical questions (Job 3:1–42:6).[19] Further, the references from Proverbs and Qoheleth[20] are proverb poems, riddles and sayings (maxims), while Sirach provides us with hymnal material praising wisdom and delighting in creation. The book of Wisdom of Solomon provides us with materials of literary diptychs using the comparing and contrasting elements of poetic *syncrisis*.[21]

Practically, our literary reading strategies consist of exposing the ways that the genres of wisdom poems or sayings (maxims) are presented with parallelisms or word-pairs and chiasms before uncovering the ecological significance of water and water-related phenomena in a given text. That is, the procedural task consists of acknowledging and surpassing the historical insights while focusing on how the individual wisdom poems (proverbs) or metaphors give several meaning possibilities. The analysis will not only focus on standard formulas utilised by poets of the wisdom traditions, but will also explore how each poet casts traditional forms and uses 'water metaphors' in his or her unique style in response to a given context. This is the case for the ironical references in the book of Qoheleth.

In order to avoid anachronism or imposing the current realities on biblical texts' focus, the insights of Gadamer about the three worlds of a text (the worlds *behind, in,* and *in front of*) will be seriously valued. For Gadamer,[22] the world *behind* the text refers to its historical setting, the

---

17. Carol R. Fontaine, 'Proverb Performance in the Hebrew Bible', in *Wise Words: Essays on the Proverbs*, ed. Wolf Mieder (New York: Garland, 1994), 395.

18. Only Job 1:1–2:13 and 42:7-17 (respectively the prologue and epilogue of the book) are written in prosaic form.

19. Carol A. Newsom, 'The Book of Job', *NIB* 4:320.

20. Qoheleth is the transliteration of the Hebrew name for the book of Ecclesiastes.

21. Michael Kolarcik, 'The Book of Wisdom', *NIB* 5:443.

22. Gadamer, *Truth and Method*, 254–64.

world *of the text* refers to the text itself and the world *in front of* the text alludes to the new world of meaning made possible by interpretation – which is, in our case, the eco-theological interpretative possibility of the text.

1.6.3. *Elements of Metaphor Theory*

In the introduction of his essay on metaphor, Grünfeld stated: 'Metaphor provides us with a way of learning something new about the world and about how the world may be perceived and understood'.[23] It is normally said that people use metaphor when the resources of literal language are not enough to articulate significant insights about what is expected to be conveyed. In this sense, Ben Zvi[24] concluded that it is because of its puzzling nature that water turned into a central metaphor in which Israel could express, formulate, reformulate and communicate in comprehensible ways concepts that would have been difficult for them to say in other language.

A metaphor has three elements: the vehicle, the referent and the tenor.[25] The tenor links the vehicle and the referent. In Prov. 5:15-20, for instance, the element of nature serves as the vehicle. The tenor concerns elements of the vehicle (water or water-related phenomenon) that invite particular understandings of the referent (erotic love). Erotic love is the referent, which is linked to the vehicle through the tenor. In Sir. 24:23-34, for example, the tenor concerns features of the vehicle (abundance, fertility and sustenance of the six ancient Near Eastern rivers) that convey specific considerations of the relevance of the referent (wisdom/Torah).

Therefore, the main focus is on which assumptions about water are reflected in the authors' use of water imagery in an attempt to address certain matters. Each water-related metaphorical word is 'studied as an instance of restructuring or redescription of some sphere of human experience'[26] before retrieving its ecological wisdom.

---

23. Joseph Grünfeld, 'Étude Critique: Kittay's Theory of Metaphor', *Science et Esprit* 44, no. 1 (1992): 83.

24. Ehud Ben Zvi, 'Thinking of Water in Late Persian/Early Hellenistic Judah: An Exploration', in Ben Zvi and Levin, eds., *Thinking of Water in the Early Second Temple Period*, 27.

25. See R. Boer, *Keeping It Literal: The Economy of the Song of Songs*, Available online from: www.jhsonline.org/Articles/article_67.pdf (accessed 17 July 2019).

26. Göran Eidevall, *Grapes in the Desert: Metaphors, Models, and Themes in Hosea 4–14* (Stockholm: Almqvist & Wiksell, 1996), 47.

1.7. Delimitation and Selection of Biblical Texts

1.7.1. Delimitation and Scope of the Study

This study is neither a treatise of meteorology nor hydrology, although it uses insights of these subjects to understand the ecological wisdom of water and water-related phenomena in the selected wisdom texts. Given that no single study can deal with all passages in the wisdom books containing waters, this book limits its scope to a sample of references about water in the wisdom books.[27]

1.7.2. References to Water in the Wisdom Books

The selection of wisdom texts on water and water-related phenomena has been made possible by the use of the electronic Bible-Works version 7, the NRSV concordance of Köhlenberger III (1991) and the NRSV Exhaustive Concordance of Metzger (1991). Two appendices that list references to water in the wisdom books can be found at the end of this book.

The first, Appendix A, is a list of more than 600 references to water in the Old Testament wisdom books. The second, Appendix B, has a narrow focus, since it contains a list of texts that give voice to the life-giving or life-threatening potential of water and water-related phenomena, plus minor instances regarding other aspects of water, such as water use and water management.

Appendix B, therefore, reflects the focus and scope of this study, while Appendix A provides the bigger picture. In other words, Appendix A serves as support material for our attempt to show that references to water and water-related phenomena abound in the Old Testament wisdom literature. This appendix mainly concerns the first of the two reductionist tendencies previously stated: favouring certain texts and therefore keeping others out of view.

Appendix B serves as an overview of some texts that are discussed in depth in this study. This appendix mainly concerns the second of the two reductionist tendencies: offering an overly romantic view of nature/water. It identifies more than one hundred instances of the life-giving and life-threatening potential of water and water-related phenomena in the Old Testament wisdom books.[28]

---

27. This book focuses on the wisdom books only. Other wisdom texts disseminated in the Bible are not concerned with the analysis of this book.

28. See the classification of texts in Appendix B.

For the purpose of efficiency, I limited my eco-theological analyses to a number of texts. In the book of Job, this study involves the analysis of Job 14:7-12; 36:26–37:13 and Job 38:22-38. In the book of Proverbs, attention is given to the use of water as a metaphor (Prov. 5:15-20; 9:13-18 and 25:23-26) and wisdom poems where water appears as a physical entity, namely 3:19-20 and 8:22-31.

In Qoheleth, I explore the ecological insights of waters in Qoh. 1:4-11; 2:4-6 and 11:1-6. As to the Deutero-canonical wisdom books, the book explores Sir. 24:23-34 and 43:13-46 before concluding with Wis. 11:2-14 and 19:1-12. These texts are studied in depth, while occasional references are made to other biblical texts in which water appears. The reasons for this selection are given in the introductory sections of exegetical chapters of this book, namely the third, fourth, fifth and sixth chapters.

1.8. *Difficulties and Limitations of the Study*

The main difficulty in conducting this study was the rarity of publications about water in the Old Testament wisdom books. This study is mostly a kind of a reconstructive attempt of tiny and fragmentary information loosely spread elsewhere. This book is one step towards the great ecological insights that the wisdom books offer about water.

The limitations of this study were of both a hermeneutical and practical nature. As to the hermeneutical limitation, this study confronted the hiatus between our world and the ancient ones in which the Old Testament wisdom books were composed. Some of the information in these texts are indeed in line with contemporary issues. Job 14:7-12 regards water as intrinsically life-giving and its vanishing as a great loss, while in Job 38 water has the potential to cause life and death.

However, other information cannot apply to today's scientific world given the danger of being anachronistic. The hydrological process that is attributed to God in Elihu's speech (Job 36:26-28), for instance, is viewed today as a natural fact. In addition, although I use the modern term 'natural laws' for the acting of the water-related phenomena in Wis. 11:2-14, I know that this term is absent in the ancient world. Still, the text seems to denote the autonomous movements of nature.

It is important to stress that I am not arguing for the literal application of all the ideas about water in the Old Testament wisdom books. Rather, it is argued that the Old Testament wisdom literature's insights about water can provide both inspiration and concrete resources for re-imagining new models regarding our relationships with nature, especially water and water-related phenomena.

Concerning the practical limitation, this study could not undertake the analysis of the eco-theological insights about water in all the texts of the Old Testament wisdom books where water and water-related phenomena occur. This study was based on a selection of specific texts on water in the Old Testament wisdom books. As such, this study invites biblical scholars to turn to wisdom books for the study of water for additional ecological wisdom about water in those books.

1.9. *Division of Chapters*

This book contains seven chapters. The first one is devoted to giving a general introduction, while the second reviews biblical studies on water and water-related phenomena in the Old Testament. In Chapters 3–6 I examine texts on water in the five wisdom books and their relevance for an ecological interpretation. The final chapter offers ecological implications on how insights about water in Old Testament wisdom can inspire contemporary concerns to address water crises. It also proposes insights for further investigations in the future.

Chapter 2

Previous Studies on Water and Water-Related Phenomena in the Old Testament

2.1. *Introduction*

The structure of this chapter covers four main sections: general studies about water and water-related phenomena in the Old Testament; eco-theological studies on water and water-related phenomena; studies on the Old Testament wisdom texts containing water and water-related phenomena; and a brief synthesis of the literature review by way of conclusion. At the end of this chapter, I will argue the relevance of the present study and its expected original contribution in Old Testament scholarship.

2.2. *Old Testament Studies on Water and Water-related Phenomena*

2.2.1. *Introduction*

A great number of publications deal with the issue of water in the Old Testament. This part of the literature review focuses on a representative selection of works, ones that claim either to be about water in the Old Testament as a whole[1] or have explicitly limited their scope to bodies of text with the Old Testament. This section does not deal with the way these works have interpreted the subject of water or water-related phenomena, but investigates to what extent they made use of the Old Testament wisdom books, and with that, how they dealt with the texts they enlisted. The section encompasses a number of dictionaries and encyclopaedias due to their claim of being comprehensive, as well as general books and articles about water or water-related phenomena in the Old Testament.

---

1. This implies that the three main parts of the Hebrew Bible (Pentateuch, Prophets and Writings) would have been given equal value and attention in those studies.

2.2.2. *Studies on Water in Biblical Dictionaries and Encyclopaedias*

Most Bible dictionaries and encyclopaedias typically contain no explicit entries or references to wisdom books as primary loci for the study of water and water-related phenomena; when such are given, they are only afforded a secondary status. A few dictionaries I consulted completely ignored the Old Testament wisdom books; others have made scant use of these biblical texts.

2.2.2.1. *On ignoring the Old Testament Wisdom books.* The dictionary entitled *A Theological Wordbook of the Bible* features among the early dictionaries of theological scholarship. Water is carefully explored in various parts of the Bible, notably excluding the wisdom books.[2] The same trend is visible in more recent dictionaries, namely the *Eerdmans Dictionary of the Bible* and *The New Interpreter's Dictionary of the Bible*. The essays contained in these volumes focus on issues related to the physical and theological significance of water-related phenomena, such as fountains, floods or rivers, or else simply ignore the Old Testament wisdom books.[3]

With regard to encyclopaedias, the situation is even worse. The *Zondervan Pictorial Encyclopaedia of the Bible* and the *Baker Encyclopaedia of the Bible* are notable reference volumes that simply ignored the wisdom books in their entries on water in the Bible.[4] This leads us to question why this decision was taken, given that water and its various functions clearly feature in those biblical works.

While it has to be admitted that the Old Testament wisdom books do not have many references related to the ritual use of water, the dictionaries and encyclopaedias cannot be excused for neglecting the other roles water plays within the wisdom books – water brings destruction, delivers fruitfulness and refreshment; there are abundant metaphorical uses of water.

2.2.2.2. *On the scant references to the Old Testament Wisdom books.* Published in 1962, *The Interpreter's Dictionary of the Bible* boasted that it provided the scholarly world and the general public with an up-to-date and comprehensive treatment of all significant biblical subjects in the canonical and deuterocanonical books. Its article dealing with

---

2. C. Walls, 'Wash, Water & Unclean: Water, Drink, Fountain, Sea & Wash', in *A Theological Word Book*, ed. Alan Richardson (London: SCM, 1957), 279–81.

3. See Timothy P. Jenney, 'Water', in *Eerdmans Dictionary of the Bible*, ed. David N. Freedman (Grand Rapids, MI/Cambridge, UK: Eerdmans, 2000), 1367–9.

4. See D. R. Bowes, 'Water', in *The Zondervan Pictorial Encyclopaedia of the Bible*, ed. Merrill C. Tenny (Grand Rapids, MI: Zondervan, 1975), 902–6.

water carefully makes use of many texts from the Pentateuch, Prophets, Psalms and New Testament, but does not pay enough attention to the Old Testament wisdom books in this regard.[5] Ritual matters, curses, cleansing, baptism, floods and human sustenance are the main issues reflected within its selected references. Scant references to Prov. 8:22-31; 27:29; Job 26:10-13, 38:8-11 are used in a secondary position to other bodies of the Bible, seemingly serving as additional loci for the studied subjects, but not as primary sources.

The *Theological Wordbook of the Old Testament* continues the same tendency. Its article on water and its related phenomena – such as water for ritual (washing and purification), metaphorical use of water (God as living water, much water as distress) and eschatological use of water (water freshness as restoration) – evaluates from the perspective of other bodies of the Old Testament.[6] There are passing references to Prov. 5:15; 9:17 and Job 36:27, but no proper analysis is offered.

The *Theological Dictionary of the Old Testament* followed the same trend. The dictionary has practically nothing about the Hebrew word מַיִם (water) in the Old Testament wisdom books, aside from brief mentions of the book of Job.[7] Likewise, the *New International Dictionary of Old Testament Theology and Exegesis* is not free of the habit of favouring certain texts in the study of water. Its treatment of the Hebrew word for water, מַיִם, and its related concepts follows the same pattern.[8]

In my view, these dictionaries and encyclopaedias have impacted many later publications, principally regarding the selection of references related to water in the Old Testament.

2.2.3. *Specific Publications on Water and Water-related Phenomena in the Old Testament*

It should be noted here that most books and articles on water in the Old Testament explicitly confine the scope of their research to passages of the Pentateuch, Prophets and Psalms. A few studies have claimed to undertake a comprehensive exploration of water in the Old Testament as a whole. In my review of the scholarly literature I have sought to determine whether the given book/article explicitly defines the focus of analysis. What follows is a critical analysis of a given work according to its scope of study.

---

5. See Bernhard W. Anderson, 'Water', in *The Interpreter's Dictionary of the Bible*, vol 4, ed. George A. Buttrick (New York/Nashville: Abingdon, 1962), 806–10.
6. See Walter C. Kaiser, 'מָטָר (rain), מַיִם (water)', *TWOT* 1:500–503.
7. See Heinz-Josef Fabry, 'מַיִם (Mayim)', *TDOT* 8:265–88.
8. Michael A. Grisanti, 'מַיִם (mayim)', *NIDOTTE* 2:929–34.

2.2.3.1. *Books on water in the Old Testament.* In 1958, Reymond wrote about water and its meaning in the Old Testament. While this book purported to undertake a comprehensive exploration of water and/or water-related phenomena in the Old Testament, it made scarcely any use of the wisdom books.[9] From the 1980s, various works with scopes explicitly limited to the Pentateuch, Prophets and Psalms began to appear. In his 1987 book *Water in the Wilderness*, which seeks to offer a careful analysis of water in the Old Testament, Propp barely mentions Job 28:9-11.[10] In his *The Earth and the Waters in Genesis 1 and 2*, Tsumura does make reference to Job 36:27,[11] though only in support of this thesis about 'אֵד-waters' in Gen. 2:6.[12]

In an effort to establish a link between his archaeological findings about water resources in ancient Palestine and Bible texts, Issar[13] thoroughly selected texts from the Bible – with the exception of the wisdom books. To be fair to Issar, this author, whose primary concern was interpretation of archaeological remains, is not to be criticised too harshly, since his study is not about a *theological* analysis of biblical texts. As a scholar working outside of the field of biblical studies, he referred to the biblical texts that are most often treated by those working with this literature. Thus, his selection reflects the tendency towards favouring certain texts that has characterised theological and biblical studies on water in the Bible.

Alongside those works that display a tendency for favouring certain texts and ignoring the wisdom books, many studies display a clear inclination towards the romantic understanding of water. This is the case for Hembrom's 2007 article,[14] which enlists five notions of the significance of water in the Old Testament: the essentiality of water for survival, water as a cleansing agent, the ritual use of water, water and food making and some metaphorical uses of water to mean fertility. The same trend is visible in

---

9. Philippe Reymond, *L'eau, sa Vie et sa Signification dans l'Ancien Testament* (Leiden: Brill, 1958).

10. W. H. Propp, *Water in the Wilderness: A Biblical Motif and its Mythological Background* (Atlanta, GA: Scholars Press, 1987), 37.

11. David Toshio Tsumura, *The Earth and the Waters in Genesis 1 and 2: A Linguistic Investigation* (Sheffield: JSOT, 1989), 99–105.

12. These matters will be discussed further in Chapter 3, in the text-critical analysis of the Hebrew text of Job 36:26–37:13.

13. A. S. Issar, *Water Shall Flow from the Rock: Hydrogeology and Climate in the Land of the Bible* (Berlin: Springer-Verlag, 1990).

14. Timotheas Hembrom, 'Significance of Water in the Old Testament', in *Water Struggle*, ed. V. J. John (Kolkata: Bishop's College, 2007), 49–56.

Ross's 'Water for Life, Water of Life and Water as Life'. Not only does Ross omit a discussion of the wisdom books, but he also radically affirms that water has always meant life in the Bible.[15] For him, even when water was used as a destructive agent against enemies, it was for the higher purpose of saving God's people.

Likewise, Caleb's essay, 'The Use of Water as a Metaphor and Symbol in Biblical Theology',[16] not only ignores the wisdom books but also points to texts in which water and water-related phenomena appear with romantic potential: water as a symbol for life and strength, water as a symbol for purity and humility and water as a metaphor for God's justice. What is striking is that, despite the purported emphasis on metaphor in the title of his study, Caleb omitted the Old Testament wisdom books – the very portion of the biblical canon that displays the most metaphorical uses of water! (Cf. Appendix A.)

The favouring of texts outside the wisdom collection can further be seen in Stéphanie Anthonioz's 2009 book, *L'eau, Enjeux Politiques et Théologiques, de Sumer à la Bible*.[17] This work sees the deliberate exclusion of what are considered to be 'pragmatic texts' – the wisdom books.

More recently, an outstanding collection of essays has been published under the title *Thinking of Water in the Early Second Temple Period*.[18] In this volume a number of distinguished biblical scholars engage with the ideological and linguistic symbol of water and water-related phenomena in the literature of the early Second Temple period. Yet, while Proverbs, Qoheleth, Sirach and Wisdom of Solomon belong to this time period, the views on water within these works are simply overlooked in favour of Pentateuchal and prophetic texts. Having said that, there is 'a brief overview' on the images of water in the book of Job. Furthermore, unlike many previous publications, the book is at least aware of the life-giving and life-threatening function of water in biblical texts.

While the above review is admittedly very short, it should have become clear that the publications discussed, and more besides, have inherited the habit of favouring certain texts that are traditionally and intuitively held as the primary loci for the study of water and water-related phenomena.

---

15. M. M. Ross, 'Water for Life, Water of Life and Water as Life: Meaning and Symbol in Theology', in John, ed., *Water Struggle*, 88.

16. Sunil M. Caleb, 'The Use of Water as a Metaphor and Symbol in Biblical Theology: An Exploration', in John, ed., *Water Struggle*, 69–79.

17. Stéphanie Anthonioz, *L'eau, Enjeux Politiques et Théologiques, de Sumer à la Bible* (Leiden: Brill, 2009).

18. Ben Zvi and Levin, eds., *Thinking of Water in the Early Second Temple Period*.

2.2.3.2. *Articles on water in the Old Testament.* In an article explicitly oriented towards aspects of creation in Psalms and the Prophets, Klopper[19] demonstrates that springs and wells occur in three different contexts: in historical texts of the wilderness; in creation texts with a mythological background (primarily in the Psalms); and in prophetic texts dealing with postexilic recreation. Within this framework Klopper deliberately explored texts from the Psalms and the prophetic books. Strikingly, this neatly formulated set of contexts does not take into account the several mentions of springs and wells within the wisdom books that cannot be classified in any of the three evoked contexts.[20] In this Klopper is not alone – many earlier and subsequent studies about springs engage in repetitive analyses of certain favoured references from the Pentateuchal and prophetic books.

Since Gunkel's book *Schöpfung und Chaos in Urzeit und Endzeit* (1895),[21] several articles have sought to study the watery chaos motif in the book of Psalms. An early example is the 1955 article by May,[22] which focuses on the cosmic connotations of 'many waters' (מים רבים). Here again, the author mainly makes use of references from the prophetic books and Psalms.

Recent publications include articles by Prinsloo[23] and Sylva,[24] which explore the waters of chaos in specific psalms. We should also note the article of Rudman,[25] focusing on the metaphorical use of water to mean Sheol in many texts of the Old Testament. In the course of his study Rudman engages with some of the water references within the book of Job, as these are among the rare instances in the Old Testament where the word Sheol appears in connection with water imagery.

---

19. Frances Klopper, 'Aspects of Creation: The Water in the Wilderness Motif in the Psalms and the Prophets', *OTE* 18, no. 2 (2005): 253.

20. For references, see Appendices A and B.

21. Hermann Gunkel, *Creation and Chaos in the Primeval Era and the Eschaton: A Religion-Historical Study of Genesis 1 and Revelation 12*, trans. K. W. Whitney (Grand Rapids, MI: Eerdmans, 2006).

22. Herbert G. May, 'Some Cosmic Connotations of Mayim Rabbîm, Many Waters', *JBL* 74 (1955): 9–21.

23. Gert M. Prinsloo, 'Historical Reality and Mythological Metaphor in Psalm 124', *OTE* 18, no. 3 (2003): 790–810.

24. Dennis Sylva, 'The Rising נהרות of Psalm 93: The Chaotic Order', *JSOT* 36 (2012): 471–82.

25. Dominic Rudman, 'The Use of Water Imagery in Descriptions of Sheol', *ZAW* 113 (2001): 241.

From the above, it should be clear that the Old Testament wisdom books have not yet received significant attention from scholars engaging in the study of water and water-related phenomena. As far as I know, no single study has been devoted to the investigation of water in the wisdom books. Major studies that purported to be comprehensive have, sadly, focused on references from the books of the Pentateuch, the Prophets and the Psalms, with wisdom texts appearing only as supplementary sources. Furthermore, many publications have explicitly fixed their gaze on other sections of the biblical canon, presumably because these parts of the Bible are considered to be the primary loci.

Finally, it should be stated clearly that not only have previous publications dealing with water largely ignored the wisdom books, but also almost all of them display a clear inclination towards the 'romantic' aspects of water. With this in mind, let us now turn to eco-theological studies of the wisdom texts and the references to water contained in them.

2.3. *Eco-theological Studies about Water and Water-related Phenomena*

To the best of my knowledge no scholarly eco-theological investigation of water and water-related phenomena in the Old Testament wisdom books has been attempted. This section reviews several eco-theological studies that have explored the topic in relation to the Bible in general, or the Old Testament in particular. Several essays bearing the near-standard title 'Water in the Old Testament' will also be included in the debate.

Of the essays appearing in the second volume of the Earth Bible Project, only one study deals with water and water-related phenomena. Written by Hobgood-Oster,[26] this essay selects not only texts from the book of Genesis, but also chooses texts reflecting the positive potential of water found at springs and wells.[27] A few references to water and water-related phenomena as life-threatening entities feature, with an apparent supplementary status, in analyses of the *voice of Earth* in the flood stories of Genesis 6 and 9.[28]

---

26. See L. Hobgood-Oster, 'For Out of that Well the Flocks Were Watered: Stories of Wells in Genesis', in *The Earth Story in Genesis*, ed. N. C. Habel and S. Wurst (Sheffield: Sheffield Academic; Cleveland: Pilgrim, 2000), 187–99.

27. The biblical references to wells and springs include Gen. 21:17-20 (Hagar, Ishmael and the well); 21:25-34; and 26:17-22 (Abraham, Isaac and Abimelech on conflict over water supply).

28. Anne Gardner, 'Ecojustice: A Study of Genesis 6:11-13', 117–30; Wali Fejo, 'The Voice of the Earth: An Indigenous Reading of Genesis 9', 140–6, both in Habel and Wurst, eds., *The Earth Story in Genesis*.

Similarly, in her magnificent thesis on the religious function of springs and wells in the Hebrew Bible, Klopper claims to re-evaluate nature in the Hebrew Bible and view humans as not standing over, but as part of nature. While illustrating her argument, Klopper carefully shows that groundwater sources were not only life-giving agents in the arid setting of Israel, but also functioned as cultic centres where theophanies took place, kings were crowned, lawsuits were conducted and marriage promises were made. Her biblical texts are drawn from the Pentateuch, Prophets and Psalms, along with a few isolated verses in the book of Proverbs.[29]

Acknowledgment should be made of an essay by Tsumura that devotes specific attention to references to water and water-related phenomena in Job 36–37. In addition to broad analyses of several texts about water and water-related phenomena (dew, snow, rain, etc.), this scholar enlisted Job 36:27 and 37:6-7, texts which he sees as offering 'the most extensive theology of rain and weather in the entire Bible'.[30] This would suggest that anybody undertaking a study of the theme of rain in the Old Testament would at least quote Job 36:26 and 37:6-13 among other basic references.

Finally, the 2011 volume of the journal *Interface* entitled *Water: A Matter of Life and Death* is one of the most noteworthy biblical and eco-theological studies on water and water-related phenomena in the Bible. This volume provides a series of essays by theologians, biblical scholars and scientists who seriously engage with the concept of water 'as a spiritual well and also as a physical resource for all living beings on earth'.[31] However, even in this volume, which is explicitly entitled to be about the life-preserving and life-extinguishing aspects of water, most essays focus on the positive value of water. None of the essays deal with texts from the Old Testament wisdom books.[32]

---

29. Klopper, 'Aspects of Creation', 254.

30. David T. Tsumura, 'A Biblical Theology of Water: Plenty, Food and Drought in the Created Order', in *Keeping God's Earth: The Global Environment in Biblical Perspective*, ed. Noah J. Toly and Daniel I. Block (Downers Grove: InterVarsity; Nottingham: Apollos, 2010), 174.

31. Habel and Trudinger, eds., *Water*, 4–5.

32. See Norman C. Habel, 'Introduction: Water: A Matter of Life and Death', in Habel and Trudinger, eds., *Water*, 1–8.

Regarding the few eco-theological studies that have been made of the wisdom books, one can notice that not only is there no study concerning water and water-related phenomena in these biblical texts, but also there is a decided inclination towards treating the romantic potential of water. The next section turns to look at studies that have been made on the wisdom texts containing references to water and water-related phenomena, and explores the ways scholars have dealt with the subject.

2.4. *Studies on Wisdom Texts Containing Water and Water-related Phenomena*

2.4.1. *Introduction*

As far as I know, no major essay, monograph or edited volume has solely focused on water and water-related phenomena in the Old Testament wisdom books. This is perhaps due to three factors. Firstly, 'not too long ago wisdom literature was somewhat of an orphan, even eliminated from the concern of Old Testament theology'.[33] It is only recently that they have gained the attention of scholars. Secondly, Protestant scholars simply ignore the Deutero-canonical wisdom books since these works are outside of their canonical sphere of interest. Finally, eco-theology is a very young discipline, and much needs to be done to cover all the books of the Bible.

It is accurate to say that there are very few – and mostly incidental – references to water and water-related phenomena in general publications, such as Bible commentaries, articles or books, and that these works are typically devoted to discussing other matters from the Old Testament wisdom books in which water references feature.

Given the great number of texts in the Old Testament wisdom books containing water and water-related phenomena, this review is limited to a number of representative passages. These are: Job 14:7-12; 36:26–37:13 and 38:22-38; Prov. 3:19-20; 5:15-20; 8:22-31; 9:13-18 and 25:23-26; Qoh. 1:4-11; 2:4-6 and 11:1-6; Wis. 11:2-14 and 19:1-12, as well as Sir. 24:23-34 and 43:13-26.

The following two factors seem to guide the scholarly selection of texts for study. Firstly, most Bible commentaries and monographs acknowledged the significance of water metaphors in some of these texts. Secondly, they have all been objects of exploration for various matters in many publications.

---

33. Roland E. Murphy, 'The Interpretation of Old Testament Wisdom Literature', *Interpretation* 23 (1969): 289.

2.4.2. *Studies on Texts Containing Water and Water-related Phenomena in Job*

In her comments on Job 36:26–37:13, Newsom[34] gave no attention to water-related phenomena (hail, clouds, snow, rainstorms) as subjects, but developed them in the background of the analysis of the wonders of God. Clines's commentary[35] on Job 14 is more specific: *anthropopathically* speaking, the tree can be said to have hope, a rare commodity in Job's life. Those human-centric readings are interested in the human condition or the significance of human suffering as reflected in the text; they overlook or silence the intrinsic worth of the water clearly expressed in the text. Nature images are thus auxiliary to human interest in the analysis.

In her 1981 article entitled 'God's Answer to Job', Brenner recognises that the text of Job 38 contains various references to water and water-related phenomena. She thinks that it is probably not an accident that most of Job 38 involves God's domination, conquest, subduing and control of water in its various forms/mutations. However, she mainly reads the text's water-related phenomena merely as supplementary, to show how humans are limited.[36] Has von Rad's[37] salvation-historical theology influenced the interpretation of this scholar here and many others later? To be sure, for von Rad[38] nature should not be viewed as having its own value; rather, it performs the secondary role of stimulating human faith in God. This anthropocentric view seems to be dominant in many interpretations or commentaries about Job 38.

In his 'Divine Creative Power and the Decentring of Creation', Patrick[39] argues that God's rhetorical speech in Job 38:22-27 invites us to recognise our limits and admire the cosmos from the creator's perspective. It is all about inviting humans to embrace a kind of cosmic humility within the created order, not to explain the ecological implication of water-related phenomena in Job 38.

---

34. See Newsom, *NIB*, 328.
35. David J. A. Clines, *Job 1–20* (Dallas, TX: Word, 1989), 328.
36. Athalya Brenner, 'God's Answer to Job', *VT* 31 (1981): 132.
37. Gerhard von Rad, 'The Theological Problem of the Old Testament Doctrine of Creation', in *The Problem of the Hexateuch and Other Essays* (London: SCM, 1984), 132.
38. Ibid., 138–9.
39. D. Patrick, 'Divine Creative Power and the Decentring of Creation: The Subtext of the Lord's Addresses to Job', in Habel and Wurst, eds., *The Earth Story in Wisdom Traditions*, 115.

In this sense, the destructive rainstorms, hail, snow and wind of Job 38 are interpreted in relation to their frequent occurrences in the context of theophanic glory and judgment of the wicked or salvation of God's people (humans).[40] In this way, Luc[41] comments that in Job 38:22-24, God reserves and commands the meteorological forces to sustain his purposes of sentence and battle. Job should then change and view his case in light of the total cosmic design of the created order because only God has power over the hail, snow and rain.

In her book on the voice from the whirlwind, Schifferdecker[42] argues that Job 38 reacts to Job 12:15, which conveys God's tyrannical work in the natural world. The water-related phenomena in 12:15 are, therefore, presented in terms of the unjust nature of God causing drought and flood on earth at will, the way God made Job lose everything with no clear justifications. In her 'Job 12: The Cosmic Devastation and Social Turmoil', Sinnott[43] argues that this text portrays God as promoting destruction in the cosmos rather than peace, order and stability. The focus is not on water, but on Job's existential struggle to reconcile his own experience while in the midst of crushing isolation, poverty and emotional pain.

Brenner has observed that the numerous water-related phenomena featuring in Job 38 indirectly depict God's nature as dual:

> It [i.e. water] may be a blessing, indeed is indispensable; but, at the same time, if it appears in the form of a flood (v. 25) it is immensely dangerous and potentially destructive. Water can transform a desert into a garden (vv. 26-27), but as snow and hail (v. 23) it can cause great damage…[44]

For this author, water serves as an appropriate basis for dealing with the paradox of the two-sided Godhead – the creator and the supreme destroyer. Brenner is among the few scholars who have paid attention to both aspects of water, though her primary focus was on the magnificence of God's handiwork as controller of the created order. It is for this reason that Brenner immediately shifted to Job 38:8-11, showing God wrapping up the sea like a baby.

---

40. Claus Westermann, *The Structure of the Book of Job* (Philadelphia: Fortress, 1981), 202.

41. Alex Luc, 'Storm and the Message of Job', *JSOT* 87 (2000): 120.

42. Kathryn Schifferdecker, *Out of the Whirlwind: Creation Theology in the Book of Job* (Cambridge, MA: Harvard University Press, 2008), 43.

43. Alice M. Sinnott, 'Job 12: Cosmic Devastation and Social Turmoil', in Habel and Wurst, eds., *The Earth Story in Wisdom Traditions*, 78.

44. Brenner, 'God's Answer', 132.

Likewise, in her reassessment of the chaos motif in the Hebrew Bible, Watson[45] maintains that the water images in Job indicate that God comforts and cares for his own creation as a mother would. Here, the water-related phenomena serve as a background for explaining the scholar's interest in God's answer to Job (and all humans) and the mystery of the created order.

The ecological relevance of water and water-related phenomena themselves, as they are depicted in several passages of Job, has not yet gained the attention of scholars. In short, scholarly readers are primarily interested in the topic of God responding to Job by pointing to elements of creation that are beyond his means, and then inviting his humility.

Special credit must be given to Nõmmik, who wrote an overview entitled 'Thinking of Water in the Book of Job'. Nõmmik points out that water occurs with ambivalent and multivalent portrayals in the book of Job.[46] However, not only is the essay a 'brief overview', but it is also more concerned with the ideology of water than its ecological exploration. The overview offered by Nõmmik features amongst the rare studies on water in the book of Job and calls for in-depth exploration.

In summary, no substantial work has yet been published on the theme of water in Job, especially from an ecological perspective – we find only incidental notes on water and water-related phenomena in isolated paragraphs of general works written on the book of Job in commentaries. Thus, no scholar has investigated the subject of water in the book of Job for the aim of explaining its ecological significance.

2.4.3. *Studies on Texts Containing Water and Water-related Phenomena in Proverbs*

2.4.3.1. *Studies on Proverbs 5:15-20.* Proverbs 5:15-20 is regularly interpreted in terms of two main readings: the feminist approach and the erotic interpretation.

2.4.3.1.1. *Feminist approaches to Proverbs 5:15-20.* In her essay, 'Visual Metaphors and Proverbs 5:15-20', Fontaine states that 'the cistern and well remind us of the male effort in stabilising the waters by providing a useful container'.[47] It is argued that Prov. 5:15-20 is a clear

---

45. Rebecca Watson, *Chaos Uncreated: A Reassessment of the Theme* (Berlin: de Gruyter, 2005), 278.

46. Urmas Nõmmik, 'Thinking of Water in the Book of Job: A Fluvial Introduction to the Job Literature', in Ben Zvi and Levin, eds., *Thinking of Water in the Early Second Temple Period*, 297.

47. See Carol R. Fontaine, 'Visual Metaphors and Proverbs 5:15-20: Some Archaeological Reflections on Gendered Iconography', in *Seeking the Wisdom of the*

echo of patriarchy in which female images are 'stationary' (cistern/well) contrary to male 'movable' water-related images (spring, fountain or streams).

The metaphor is thus seen as using stereotypical male language picturing the woman as an object of the man. It echoes a kind of patriarchal structure in which the male gender is the owner of the female. The gendered image of the female body as a vessel (cistern or well) is loaded with patriarchal fantasies of control. Briefly, for the feminists, the female element in Prov. 5:15-20 is reduced to an instrument in the service of the master of the waters, namely the husband.

2.4.3.1.2. *Erotic readings of Proverbs 5:15-20.* In her commentary on Proverbs, Davis[48] argues that this text sets forth a sharp contrast between a healthy eroticism, protected by the fresh-flowing waters of the wife of one's youth (v. 18), and a perverse attraction to the strange woman (v. 20). Fox[49] explains that the text commands continued sexual fidelity to one's wife, while the images of a cistern/well suggest 'cool, limpid refreshment for hot [sexual] desires, which are satisfied by "drinking", that is, lovemaking'. This view is shared by the commentaries of Perdue[50] and Waltke,[51] who views the whole passage as advising 'faithful sexual intimacy in marriage'.

Indeed, the text is about marriage. However, since the sage used the image of water to address the issue of sexuality in marriage, it could be asked why the author found the cistern/well metaphor appropriate to talk about this matter. What assumptions about or attitudes towards water are reflected in the writer's use of water management metaphors in an attempt to promote faithfulness in marriage? As far as I know, no specific study has asked such questions about Prov. 5:15-20.

Scholars do recognise that the metaphor reflects the 'significance of water in its real, materialist sense in an arid region where cisterns were

---

Ancient: Essays Offered to Honour Michael V. Fox on the Occasion of his Sixty-Fifth Birthday, ed. Roland L. Troxel, Kelvin G. Friebel and Dennis R. Magary (Winona Lake, IN: Eisenbrauns, 2005), 205.

48. Ellen F. Davis, *Proverbs, Ecclesiastes, and the Song of Songs* (Louisville: John Knox, 2000), 51.

49. Michael V. Fox, *Proverbs 1–9* (New York: Doubleday, 2000), 199.

50. Leo G. Perdue, *Proverbs*, Interpretation: A Bible Commentary for Teaching and Preaching (Louisville: John Knox, 2000), 121.

51. See Bruce K. Waltke, *The Book of Proverbs: Chapters 1–15* (Grand Rapids, MI: Eerdmans, 2004), 316.

built to store water for irrigation and survival'.[52] However, no attention has been paid to the significance of the water image itself; instead, the focus has fallen chiefly on what specifically the cistern/well metaphors designate within marriage.

The present study argues that the 'root metaphor' of 'water management' used in Prov. 5:15-20 advising the son to drink water from his own cistern/well and warning against the useless spilling of spring/fountain streams on public areas provides us with a means of understanding its valuable ecological wisdom. In this sense, this work will point to the transformative power of Prov. 5:15-20 that assumes the value of water and the necessity of its proper management in a land where water was scarce.

2.4.3.2. *Studies on Proverbs 9:13-18 and 25:23-26.* As is the case for Prov. 5:15-20, the references to water in Prov. 9:13-18 and 25:23-26 are taken metaphorically, often interpreted in terms of the target domains, the subject conveyed by the metaphor. Proverbs 9:13-18, for instance, is taken to be about adultery and secret liaisons with the prostitute.[53] Some have even read the text as a metaphor dealing with religious ideas, comparing the victim of the prostitute with people who give way to apostasy and then prove themselves to be false disciples and worthy of death (1 Cor. 15:2; Col. 1:22-23; 2 Tim. 2:12).[54] The reference to water in Prov. 9:13-18 typically goes unmentioned in such discussions.

However, heightened ecological sensitivity would lead scholars to ask why the sage found it suitable to link adulterous behaviour with the stolen waters that lead to the depths of Sheol. What does this water metaphor teach us about this aspect/function of water? As far as I know, no study has investigated the ecological potential of this metaphor.

Similarly, the water-related phenomena in Prov. 25:23-26 have not yet interested eco-theological readings. In fact, 25:23-26 consists of two proverb pairs (vv. 23-24 and vv. 25-26), using water and water-related images respectively pertaining to unexpected conflict due to hostile speech and contrasting restoration with ruin.

Typically, however, scholars are more interested in contrasting the slanderous wife of Prov. 25:23-24 with the sexually satisfying wife of Prov. 5:15-20. In 25:23-24, the husband would rather live in a corner of the roof, unprotected from the rain, than live in the same house as his

---

52. See Raymond C. Van Leeuwen, *NIB* 5:68. See also Milton P. Horne, *Smyth & Helwys Bible Commentary: Proverbs–Ecclesiastes* (Macon, GA: Smyth & Helwys, 2003), 96; and Tremper Longman III, *Proverbs* (Grand Rapids: Baker, 2006), 161.

53. Fox, *Proverbs 1–9*, 302; and Horne, *Proverbs–Ecclesiastes*, 137.

54. Waltke, *Proverbs 1–15*, 445.

spouse.⁵⁵ As for 25:25-26, debate focuses either on the exhausted person's thirst rather than on the cold water itself, or on the wavering righteous person rather than the muddied spring itself.⁵⁶ In these texts, both the texts and modern readers show an anthropocentric bias which prevents the retrieval of ecological wisdom of water and water-related phenomena occurring in these texts.

2.4.3.3. *Studies on Proverbs 3:19-20 and Proverbs 8:22-31.* Proverbs 3:19-20 and 8:22-31 are generally understood to be the main texts treating creation in a cosmic sense within the longer context of the Woman Wisdom section (Prov. 1–9). Notably, studies on these texts mainly focus on the role of Wisdom in creation rather than on the elements of creation, including water and water-related phenomena that are the main features of the poem.⁵⁷

2.4.4. *Studies on Texts Containing Water and Water-related Phenomena in Qoheleth*

There are not many references to water and water-related phenomena in the book of Qoheleth. Significantly, the few references to water in this book, such as Qoh. 1:4-11; 11:1-6 and 2:4-6, are often muted in favour of anthropocentric debates. The metaphor of water continuously flowing to the sea in Qoh. 1:7 is often understood in terms of a comparison with the routine and futile nature of human work.⁵⁸ The text is said to explain the futility of human life by the use of natural phenomena: the courses of the sun, the wind and the rivers.

Similarly, scholars naturally link the riddle of Qoh. 11:1-6 – 'send out your bread upon the water' (v. 1) – with trade matters. In his article

---

55. Meir L. Malbim, *The Commentary of Rabbi Meir Leibush Malbim on the Book of Proverbs* (Jerusalem: Feldeim, 1973), 262; and Richard J. Clifford, *Proverbs: A Commentary* (Louisville: John Knox, 1999), 226.

56. Van Leeuwen, 'The Book of Proverbs', 220; Horne, *Proverbs–Ecclesiastes*, 309; Longman III, *Proverbs*, 459.

57. See Richard J. Clifford, 'The Theology of Creation in Proverbs 8:22-31', in *Creation in the Biblical Traditions,* ed. Richards J. Clifford and John J. Collins (Washington, DC: CBAA, 1992), 85–96; Waltke, *Proverbs 1–15*, 408–22.

58. See Roger N. Whybray, 'Ecclesiastes 1:5-7 and the Wonders of Nature', *JSOT* 41 (1988): 105–12; James L. Crenshaw, 'Nothing New Under the Sun: Ecclesiastes 1:4-11', in *Reflecting with Solomon: Selected Studies on the Book of Ecclesiastes,* ed. Roy B. Zuck (Grand Rapids, MI: Baker, 1994), 241–48; and Perdue, *Wisdom Literature*, 49–58.

entitled 'Principles of Financial investment: Ecclesiastes 11:1-8', Hubbard[59] declares that 'bread upon the waters to be found later' is Qoheleth's way of depicting investment in prevailing mercantile enterprises.

By contrast, the commentary of Perry[60] attempts to link the riddle with sexual issues since, in his view, the Hebrew verb שלח ('send') means sexual intercourse in Qoh. 3:5, while לחם ('bread') relates to sex in Prov. 9:17 and 20:17.

Most publications are focused on understanding the meaning of the riddle in terms of charity and business. Indeed, these interpretations of charity or investment are in line with many parallels in the ancient Near East. Attention is often given, for instance, to the Egyptian proverb, 'Do a good deed and throw it in the water, and when it dries you will find it', and an Arabic saying, 'Do good, throw your bread on the waters, and one day you will find it'.[61] However, if one reads Qoh. 11:1-6 as a whole unit, the text may also possibly be connected with the Egyptian hymn to the god Hapi, the personified River Nile whose annual inundations water the land.

Given its ecological awareness, the present study will investigate whether the metaphor of Qoh. 11:1, the expression 'send out your bread upon the waters (על־פני המים)', makes any allusion to Gen. 1:2b, which is related to the primeval deep prior to the fertility of the land before the separation process of the cosmos. This assumption draws on the thought that Qoh. 11:1 alludes to both the Hapi hymn and the Egyptian practice of crop sowing by casting the seed from the boats during the Nile inundation so that when the waters retreat the grains germinate in the alluvial soil (Isa. 32:20). Does Qoh. 11:1 have make an ecological assumptions about water and the fertility of the land since vv. 2-4 directly relate to an agricultural context?[62]

Concerning Qoh. 2:4-6, it is notable that commentators have not given much attention to references to 'making pools to water the forest' and the 'irrigation system of the garden and parks'. Instead, they have been dismissed as terms belonging to Solomon's fabulous 'measures of a life of

---

59. David A. Hubbard, 'Principles of Financial Investment: Ecclesiastes 11:1-8', in Zuck, ed., *Reflecting with Solomon*, 342; See also Choon-Leong Seow, *Ecclesiastes: A New Translation with Introduction and Commentary* (New Haven/London: Yale University Press, 1997), 343.

60. Theodore A. Perry, *Dialogue with Kohelet: The Book of Ecclesiastes, Translation and Commentary* (University Park: Penn State University Press, 1993), 161.

61. Miriam Lichtheim, *Ancient Egyptian Literature*, vol. 3 (Berkeley: University of California Press, 1980), 174.

62. Sowing during the Nile inundation is also an act of risk similar to the metaphor of scattering bread upon the sea in Qoh. 11:1.

luxury'.[63] And yet, rather than simply understanding these projects simply as measures of pleasure (שִׂמְחָה), one might justifiably ask what they mean when the text is read from an ecological perspective?

Specifically, did the building projects of ancient kings – making pools and creating garden irrigation systems – presume the ecological relevance of water given the aridness of Palestine? Does the text of Qoh. 2:4-6 relate ecologically to other texts highlighting the significance of water in the garden motif? Can ancient Near Eastern inscriptions about parks, cisterns and reservoirs for water supply and crop watering shed light on the significance of water in Qoh. 2:4-6? Finally, can Qoheleth's boasts about building water canals (sanitation) not for his people but only for himself (לִי) aid us to challenge or criticise the modern unbalanced distribution of water supply? This self-centred boasting is only found in the book of Qoheleth as an ironic jibe against the king's failure to provide water and sanitation for his people.

2.4.5. *Studies on Texts Containing Water and Water-related Phenomena in the Deutero-canonical Wisdom Books*

2.4.5.1. *Introduction.* While there are few references to the Old Testament wisdom texts in studies on water and water-related phenomena, the situation is even worse for the Deutero-canonical wisdom books. To some extent this situation may be the result of issues related to canonical status – for Protestants, the books are apocryphal, while for Roman Catholics they are Deutero-canonical books. Be that as it may, I found that these books provide some fascinating references to water and water-related phenomena.

2.4.5.2. *Studies on texts containing water and water-related phenomena in the Wisdom of Solomon.* Wisdom 11:2-14 contains many ecological insights about water and water-related phenomena. It establishes a contrast between life-giving water in the wilderness and the deadly waters of the Nile (Wis. 11:4-7). God benefited the Israelites through the same natural element of creation (water) by which he punished the Egyptians in the first plague. However, commentaries on this text focus mainly on anthropocentric issues relating to the blessing of the righteous and punishment of sinners.[64]

---

63. Yee-Von Koh, *Royal Autobiography in the Book of Qoheleth* (Berlin/New York: de Gruyter, 2006), 30.

64. See, for instance, Roland E. Murphy, *The Tree of Life: An Exploration of Biblical Wisdom Literature*, 3rd ed. (Grand Rapids, MI: Eerdmans, 1990), 90.

In Wis. 19:1-12,[65] the rhetoric draws a contrast between the destruction of the Egyptians in the Red Sea and the salvation of the Israelites and their march through same expanse of water. However, as usual, the debate turns on the positive function of the cosmos to highlight the final moment of salvation of God's people. The eschatological water phenomena (hail, water, storms, rivers etc.) of Wis. 5:22-23 are subsumed into the generic term 'creation'.[66]

2.4.5.3. Studies on texts containing water and water-related phenomena in Jesus Son of Sirach. The book of Jesus Son of Sirach (hereafter Sirach) contains significant ecological insights about water and water-related phenomena. The poem of Sir. 24:23-34 is about the praise of Wisdom equated with the Torah and further likened to the six rivers.[67] In many commentaries on Sir. 24:23-34, the rivers Pishon and Gihon are observed only in relation to the prehistory of Israel (Gen. 1–11), while the other four rivers (Tigris, Euphrates, Nile and Jordan) are simply linked with the real history of Israel.[68]

These statements are noteworthy, but still the focus is on the praise of wisdom rather than on water itself. Further comments bring the readers to appreciate the significance not of water, but of the wisdom, accessible via the Torah, that will be sent forth even to the Jewish diaspora and to future generations, to shine like the dawn (Sir. 24:32-34). For Sheppard,[69] here Sirach praises wisdom in terms of 'her presence in the Edenic garden of intellectual, material, and religious delights'. The ecological awareness of researchers will lead them to consider why the sage takes the life-sustaining water of these rivers to be an appropriate way of portraying wisdom. What valuable ecological insights associated with water and water-related phenomena can be drawn from Sir. 43:13-26?

2.5. *Conclusion*

It is clear that the Old Testament wisdom books have not only been ignored in the Old Testament publications on water and water-related phenomena, but also have been viewed through a romantic lens. No major

---

65. See also Wis. 10:18-19.
66. See Kolarcik, 'The Book of Wisdom', 486.
67. See Patrick W. Skehan and Alexander A. Di Lella, *The Wisdom of Ben Sira* (New Haven/London: Yale University Press, 1987), 336.
68. Perdue, *Wisdom Literature*, 247.
69. Gerald T. Sheppard, *Wisdom as a Hermeneutical Construct: A Study in the Sapientializing of the Old Testament* (Berlin/New York: de Gruyter, 1980), 69.

monograph on water and water-related phenomena in the Old Testament wisdom books has been attempted.

Indeed, even when studies have focussed on wisdom passages containing water and water-related phenomena, the subject of water is usually bypassed. This might best be understood as a symptom of the anthropocentric bias exhibited by both the ancient texts themselves and their contemporary readers.

Habel[70] rightly drew attention to the anthropocentric nature of the Old Testament, while maintaining that he believed ecological retrieval remains possible – though not without a radical reorientation towards the text. My task takes up Habel's challenge and will thus consist of the identification and retrieval of ecological insights into water and water-related phenomena, which the anthropocentric traditions of the Bible and interpreters have either muted or hitherto ignored. This task will be observable in the subsequent chapters, in which my ecological awareness is deployed in the analysis of the text.

---

70. Norman C. Habel, 'Introducing Ecological Hermeneutics', in *Exploring Ecological Hermeneutics*, ed. Norman C. Habel and Peter Trudinger (Atlanta: SBL, 2008), 1–2.

Chapter 3

WATER AND WATER-RELATED PHENOMENA IN THE BOOK OF JOB

3.1. *Introduction*

This chapter attempts an ecological reading of certain Joban passages on the potential of water and water-related phenomena as life-giving or life-threatening entities. I will explore one text from Job's speeches (Job 14:7-12), one from other characters (Job 36:26–37:13) and one text from God's speeches (Job 38:22-38) to discern whether one can retrieve ecological wisdom from these passages.

3.2. *Introduction to the Book of Job*

3.2.1. *The Date and Context of the Book of Job*

The date of the book of Job is not the main concern of this endeavour. Still, an outline of the diachronic issues of the book deserves some attention in order to understand better why the author of the book finds it appropriate to use elements of creation, mostly cast in terms of water and water-related phenomena, in many parts of the book of Job to address various human matters. Thus, I am not trying to replace scholarly publications about the book of Job, but drawing on their various insights in order to address the theme of this book.

There is no conclusive answer on dating the book of Job. A number of modern scholars place the final form of the book to the postexilic era, while recognising that some parts might have been written during the pre-exilic or even the exilic times.[1] This inconclusiveness on the dating of the book results from a lack of clear historical clues, notably references

---

1. Avi Hurvitz, 'The Date of the Prose-Tale of Job Linguistically Recognised', *HTR* 67 (1974): 33.

to specific kings or time periods. The Hebrew of the poetic part of the book (Job 3:1–42:6) contains many *hapax legomena*, words which appear nowhere else in the Bible. The only connection between Job and other biblical texts is found not in the book of Job, but in places where the prophet Ezekiel presents Job alongside Noah and Daniel as models of righteousness.[2]

Despite the uncertainty, I would say that the composition of the book is unlikely to have taken place earlier than the Babylonian exile, with the great possibility that the final product came about in early postexilic times.[3] Whether the issues addressed were those of the Babylonian exile or events arising soon thereafter cannot be known fully. Surely, the writing of Job occurred after that of Proverbs; as such, it must be read against the traditional wisdom in the book of Proverbs.

Like Proverbs, the book of Job responds to human suffering, not by pointing to elements of the doctrine of salvation, but rather to elements of the created order in all their complexity. That is why water and water-related phenomena overflow in the book – they serve as an appropriate vehicle for talking about the puzzling nature of human life.

3.2.2. *Literary Structure and Genres of the Book*

The frame of the book consists of a prose prologue (1:1–2:13) and epilogue (42:7-17), using a blend of speech and action to tell the story of a righteous person who patiently suffers terrible disaster 'for no reason' (2:3), and who at the end is fully rewarded for his fidelity. The centre of the book comprises a long series of dialogues between Job and his friends (chs. 3–31), and between Job and God (38:1–42:6).

The long series of dialogues is written in poetry and is filled with the speech (but not actions) of the characters. Through literary genres of disputation and lament, these speeches display various profiles for the friends, Job and God. Job's friends, who are compassionate and silent in the prologue (1:1–2:13), gradually become vociferous interlocutors in Job 3–37; their aim is clearly not to comfort Job but to convict him. While the prologue/epilogue basically confirms that God can be trusted to make prosper the righteous and punish the wicked, the dialogues between Job and his friends contest this statement.[4]

---

2. The wealth of their flocks (Gen. 26:13-14 and Job 1:3; Gen. 30:29-30 and Job 1:10) and death (Job 42:17 and Gen. 25:8; 35:29). The currency in Job is the same as at the time of Jacob (Job 42:11 and Gen. 33:19).
   3. Hurvitz, 'The Date of the Prose-Tale', 30.
   4. Schifferdecker, *Out of the Whirlwind*, 32.

Through irony in Job 38–41, God confuses Job with the intricate details of the created order. Whether God's objective is to minimise Job's contribution to God's hopes and expectations for the world remains a matter for debate. However, there can be little question that the voice from the whirlwind (Job 38) is a dramatic exchange between the Creator and creation in which elements of the created order, including water and water-related phenomena, are considered either for themselves or as acting forces of destruction and blessing.

3.2.3. *The Created Order and Waters in the Book of Job*

Unlike the Pentateuch or the Prophets (notably Hosea), the book of Job does not point at the Sinai ברית (covenant) as a source of teaching; instead, Wisdom is exhorted through the perspective of elements of the created order. Significantly, the book does not present a single vision of the created order. Creation is presented in the book via three different visions: Job's speeches, friends' speeches and God's speeches.

Job's speeches are predominantly questioning God's violent attack towards creation, maintaining that God's power is arbitrarily used at the cost of innocent people like him (12:1-6; 13:1-2). By contrast, his friends' speeches are dominated by the theology of retribution in reaction to Job's claims (32–37). God's speeches (chs. 38–41) go beyond the retribution theology in friends' speeches. In all three speeches, the ecological insights of water and water-related phenomena are frequently expressed.

In God's speeches, the created order, and especially water-related phenomena, such as the rainstorms (38:22-27), are presented as having their own way (דרך). For Habel, the terms מקום (place) and דרך (way) throughout the book indicate the belief that the Earth (i.e. created order) is 'not governed by direct divine intervention, but rather by internally regulated systems within which each component of Earth has its locus and function in the system'.[5] Creation in the book is presented in such a way that there is no other entity out of the created order that is responsible for evil or good.

It is possibly for this reason that the book deals with a number of water and water-related phenomena, notably the *places* and *ways* they affect the created order for good or evil. Water is presented as an indispensable blessing, while when it appears in the form of a flood (Job 12:15) it is

---

5. Norman C. Habel, 'Earth First: Inverse Cosmology in Job', in Habel and Wurst, eds., *The Earth Story in Wisdom Traditions*, 75.

dangerous and potentially destructive. Water restores life to a dead plant (Job 14:7-9) and it may transform a desert into a fruitful land (38:26-27); yet, as hail (38:22-23), water can cause great damage. In the form of rain (36:27-28), water provides humans with abundant food; as a rainstorm, water causes beasts to hide (37:6-8).

It is therefore not an accident that most references in the book examine the reining in, the conquest and the subsequent functions of water in its various forms and mutations.[6] Most water-related phenomena such as rain or hail are unpredictable and volatile and may also affect other elements of the created order, including humans and animals, for better or for worse (37:6-13). Water is perhaps the basic natural element that lends itself best to the depiction of the dual potential of elements of creation to respond to intricate questions of God's justice during the exilic or post-exilic contexts.

3.3. Water and Water-related Phenomena in Job 14:7-12

3.3.1. Translation of Job 14:7-12

> [7] For a tree, there is hope that if cut down,
>   it will sprout again, that its shoots will continue to grow.
> [8] Though its roots grow old in the earth
>   and its stump dies in the ground,
> [9] yet at the scent of water it will bud
>   and put forth branches like a young plant.
> [10] But mortals die and dwindle away;
>   humans expire and are no more.
> [11] Water disappears from the sea,
>   and rivers dry up and wither away.
> [12] so people lie down and do not arise;
>   until the heavens are no more, they do not awake,
>   they are not roused from their sleep.

3.3.2. Exegetical Remarks

3.3.2.1. *Delimitation of the text.*
Job 14 as a whole belongs to Job's third speech (Job 12–14). Habel discerns two major units in Job 14: vv. 1-6, focussing on the brevity of human life, and vv. 7-22, exploring the issue of hope.[7] This second unit (vv. 7-22) has three sub-units, namely vv.

---

6. Brenner, 'God's Answer', 133.
7. Norman C. Habel, *Job: A Commentary* (London: SCM 1985), 239.

7-12, 13-17 and 18-22. Job 14 as a whole deals with Job's claims that human life is short and full of troubles.[8] In his pessimism about traditional wisdom, Job 14 contrasts bold images of nature and traditional axioms about mortals.

The force of the three sub-units (14:7-12, 13-17 and 18-22) is to show that there is no hope that Job will live and be vindicated after death.[9] Humans are unlike the tree that can revive (vv. 7-9); instead, they are like a river that can disappear forever (vv. 10-12). The tree has hope because it can have new life even after death by means of a mere 'scent of water'; humans, by contrast, disappear at death just as 'water dries up'. The worst thing is that, according to Job, it is God who is responsible for all of this.

This tension fits well with Job's protests to God, and arises when faith in a certain tradition clashes with the reality of one's experience.[10] That is where the use of water imagery became relevant. Ben Zvi concluded that it is because of its puzzling nature that water became a dominant metaphor in which Israel could express the complexity of life.[11]

Water plays a central role in this text. For the tree water is life-giving (v. 9), but for humans, who are like water that dries up (drought) (v. 11), the absence of water (life-threatening potential) is a symbol of God's destruction of human hope at death. Both aspects of water are used in the text to highlight the contrast between the hope of new life for a tree and the destruction of such hope for humankind. This can be discerned in the following structure.

3.3.2.2. *Literary structure.*

A		there is hope for a dead tree (vv. 7-8)
B		by a scent of *water* it will revive (v. 9)
A'		but mortals die forever lifeless (v. 10)
B'		they are like inland *waters* that vanish (vv. 11-12)

Table 1. *The Structure of Job 14:7-12*

This parallelism is literarily framed within the third of Job's speeches (Job 12–14), reflecting an interesting progression of nature images

---

8. Lindsay Wilson, *Job* (Grand Rapids: Eerdmans, 2015), 86.
9. Suzanne Boorer, 'Job's Hope: A Reading of the Book of Job from the Perspective of Hope', *Colloquium* 30, no. 2 (1998): 110.
10. Wilson, *Job*, 86.
11. Ben Zvi, 'Thinking of Water', 27.

juxtaposed with traditional axioms about human death.¹² The framework consists of two major units (14:1-6 and 7-22), both conveying traditional beliefs about mortals and bold images from nature. In our poem (14:7-12), the poetry makes an exciting analogy between water imageries and human fate. The issue is why the author found it suitable to use water and water-related metaphors while contrasting the renewal of a dead tree with the ephemerality of mortals who are like inland waters that vanish forever.

In order to respond to this exegetical question, one has to understand how the poetry functions and the relevance of water images that are the pivotal motifs of the poem.

3.3.2.3. *Linguistic and semiotic analysis of Job 14:7-12.* This poem is made in what is called 'an alternating parallelism', represented in the form ABA′B′.¹³ The stichs A (vv. 7-8) and A′ (v. 10) depict the compared/parallel subjects (tree and humans), while B (v. 9) and B′ (vv. 11-12) contain aspects of the vehicle used for the comparison. The verb מות (to die) occurs in both A and A′, conveying the basic principle of similarity of natural fate (death) for both plants and humans. However, only plants experience the rebirth power by water, while human death is compared to the drying up (drought) of a river that disappears forever. Drought points to the life-threatening potential of water.

Thus, the contrast of hope between the tree and humans is presented by two aspects of water in BB′. First, there is water reviving a dead plant (B), whose disappearance is likened to humans, who remain forever lifeless in death (B′). The word חלש (v. 10) entails human loss of power after death, which is contrasted with the tree's renewal by the merest scent of water after it is cut down (vv. 7-9). The alternating pattern of the poetry contrasts the life-giving power of water reviving a dead tree (vv. 7-9) with its destructive potential pictured in terms of drought (drying up of water), which is a symbol of human death (vv. 10-12). As a result of this, scholars have argued that Job 14:7-12 recalls Isa. 19:5-10, which is also about drought. This is further developed later in the eco-theological retrieval of the text.

---

12. Habel, *Job*, 235.
13. John T. Willis, 'Alternating (ABA'B') Parallelism in the Old Testament', in *Directions in Biblical Hebrew Poetry*, ed. Elaine R. Follis (Sheffield: JSOT, 1987), 50.

In addition, Job 14:7-12 links up with imagery found in the wider context of Job 4–27, where water and water-related phenomena provide metaphors for attitudes and actions of Job and his friends. Job likens his friends to a wadi that dries up in summer (6:15-17); Bildad replies by likening the wicked (Job) to a reed that withers because of lack of water (8:11-13); Eliphaz advises Job that once he repents, he will come out of his grave just as grain sprouts in its season (5:26). All those statements relate to certain aspects of water.

3.3.3. *Eco-theological Retrieval of the Text*

3.3.3.1. *Water and the flora kingdom (vv. 7-9)*. Job 14:7-9 highly praises the life-giving potential of water, which allows a dead plant to sprout again. The Qal imperfect לא תחדל (literally: will not cease or will sprout again) in v. 7 recalls that of v. 6 implying that Job (i.e. humans) will cease to be (v. 6a), but a tree with its branches will flourish.[14] The section clearly contrasts the hope of new life of a tree with the lack of such hope for humans. For Job, plants and humans both die (מות), but plants can recover life while humans expire forever (v. 10).

Modern-day ecologists maintain that unless humans refrain from their current anthropogenic deforestation, the flora of the Earth has no hope. However, according to Job, the main problem is not deforestation – plants can be cut down (v. 7) – but rather the scarcity of water, since a mere 'scent of water' can revive a tree (v. 9). In other words, as long as the earth is watered, there is hope for forest and waning trees.

Like a good plant that is able to 'look within stones' (8:17), presumably to find water, the generic plant of Job 14 is able to detect the 'scent of water'.[15] The expression מריח מים (at the scent of water) in v. 9 amplifies the life-giving potential of water. It ecologically implies 'the slightest contact with the source of life' (water) similar to the expression בהריחו אש (when it touches/smells fire) in Judg. 16:9.

A tree may appear to be lifeless, but can sprout again when it encounters a mere scent of water. The idea is not that the tree will be replaced by another one, but that it will regain the power to grow and live again. When we consider real-world agricultural practices, the image

---

14. Walter L. Michel, *Job: In Light of Northwest Semitic* (Rome: Biblical Institute, 1987), 322.
15. Choon-Leong Seow, 'Hope in Two Keys: Musical Impact and the Poetics of Job 14', in *Congress Volume: Ljubljana, 2007*, ed. André Lemaire (Leiden: Brill, 2010), 501.

of water reviving a tree may assume the practice, widespread in the Transjordanian region, of cutting back old fig trees, pomegranates and vines close to the ground, so that in the next rainy season new shoots may sprout forth freely.[16]

The tree is a symbol of the gift of immortality in ancient Near Eastern myths. Some death myths state that humans can die and be rejuvenated either by shedding their skins, like snakes, or by sprouting, like plants.[17] Job's complaint questions why the power of rejuvenation possessed by a tree is not available to humans.

Healthy trees typically occur around streams of water. That is why the restored Jerusalem in Ezek. 47:1-12 is depicted with a fresh stream of water flowing eastwards towards the Dead Sea and bringing abundant fertility to the arid land of Israel. This fertility is marked by evergreen trees growing on the banks of the stream, which are a constant source of fresh fruit that provides food and healing (cf. Ps. 1:3 and Job 14:8-9). The beloved woman of Song 4:12-15 is also depicted as a locked garden with flowing springs sourced from Lebanon.

3.3.3.2. *Humans as dried up sea/river (vv 10-12).* Humans are ironically depicted as גבר (hero) figures, which would emphasise their strength and virility in contrast to the fragility of אדם in Job 14:1. However, despite their force, they disappear forever – similar to the drying up of a sea or a river.

It should be noted here that Job 14:10-12 does not point to seasonal drying up of these bodies of water that may replenish (renew) at the next rainfall, but drought similar to the drying up of the Nile in Isa. 19:5-10. Job's simile is more challenging since the disappearance is related to mythological bodies of water that were viewed as pre-existing and perennial water supplies (ים, sea/ocean, and נהר, river) contrary to words like נהל (water-place) or נחל (wadi) used for seasonal water courses.

Possibly, Job uses the term river rather than wadi because the latter often dries up and then, with rain or melting snow, comes to replenish itself. In an absurd thought, Job 14:10-12 compares an irretrievable situation of the drying up of perennial water supplies (sea/river) with the death of human beings. The simile is appropriate to ancient Israel, which was:

---

16. Samuel E. Balentine, *Smyth & Helwys Bible Commentary: Job* (Macon: Smyth & Helwys, 2006), 218.

17. Habel, *Job*, 238.

> Un pays où la présence – et l'absence – d'eau se font sentir davantage qu'ailleurs. S'il y a beaucoup d'eau, le pays devient un « pays de délice » (אֶרֶץ חֵפֶץ, Ml 3:12). Mais d'ordinaire il n'y en a pas trop et le danger de la sécheresse est toujours présent.[18]

In pointing to drought (withering of the sea/river) as a symbol of human death, the text highlights how the absence of water is destructive. The effect of the disappearance of such bodies of water would have horrible effects on the ecosystems (humans, plants and animals and the land). The language used in Isa. 19:5-10 recalls the tradition of the drying up of the Nile River, an example of a perennial water supply totally vanishing.

Isaiah 19:5-10 is placed in an Egyptian context where the Nile was the source of life, whose yearly inundation provided fertility for agriculture.[19] That is why, in hymns to the god Hapi, Egyptians sang about the Nile River bringing food and life to the country. It was well known in most regions of the ancient Near East, including Judah, that Egypt was dependent on the periodic inundation of the Nile. It is for this reason that ancient Egypt has no flood narratives, since the flooding of the Nile was viewed not as a threat, but as a generous event providing blessing and life-giving water to the country and the Nile valley.[20]

The wide range of water-related phenomena in Isa. 19:5-6 (ים, נהרות, יאור) and the expressions ונשתו־מים מהים (and the water shall fail from the sea) and ויבש (and will be parched) portray a total collapse of Egypt's ecosystem due to the dryness of the Nile. Distinctive water plants such as papyrus and reed, inseparably related to the Egyptian landscape, as well as the hieroglyphic symbols of Lower and Upper Egypt, will wither.[21] The fields where agricultural plants would grow (מזרע) will also dry up once the desired Nile flooding stays away (vv. 5-7).

The dryness of the Nile will also impact its fauna. There will be no fish in the rivers, and consequently no work and food for Egypt's anglers and those relying on their products (v. 8). Water is also essential for the flax that is used in Egyptian textile industries. Once the Nile is dried up, Egypt's textile workers will become jobless (vv. 9-10). Briefly, the drying up of the Nile would affect vast swathes of Egyptian society from the most prominent (שתות), to low rank wageworkers (עשי־שכר). The whole passage of Isa. 19:5-10 may be summarised as:

18. Reymond, *L'eau*, 1–2.
19. Csaba Balogh, *The Stele of YHWH in Egypt: The Prophecies of Isaiah 18–20 Concerning Egypt and Kush* (Leiden: Brill, 2011), 242.
20. Caleb, 'The Use of Water', 70.
21. Balogh, *The Stele of YHWH*, 304.

> The progression of events from the drying of the watercourses, through the destruction of reed beds and farmland, to the devastation of the fishing and weaving industries based around the Nile...when the mighty Nile ceases to flow, the whole of society grinds to a halt.[22]

For Isa. 19, drought and its ruinous effects on the social and cosmic order are results of the judgment of YHWH (Isa. 19:1-4, 11-14). It is possible that Job 14:11-12, which was written after Proto-Isaiah, was informed by traditions of the desiccation of bodies of water that were considered eternal blessing and sources of life. By using drought as an image for human death, the text affirms the life-threatening potential of water: if water vanishes, life is in danger.

Thus, the drying up of the Nile (drought) in Isa. 19:5-10, which has disastrous effects on plants, humans, fish and the cosmic order (*ma'at*[23] in Egypt), is echoed in the thoughts of Job 14:10-12 as a metaphor for human death. Humans, like dried up waters, will remain extinct until the heavens are no more (v. 12). In other words, if there was to be an undoing of the reality of death, it could only occur in the hopelessly remote prospect of the end of the universe. We have here an affirmation of a life-threatening, irreversible situation.

The same idea is also found in Job 7:9, which states: 'As the cloud fades and vanishes, so those who go down to Sheol do not come up'. That is why Habel thinks that the Hebrew verb שכב in Job 14:12a might also mean 'laid to rest' in Sheol, a reading suggested for Job 14:13 and other verses in the book of Job (3:3; 7:21; 20:11; 21:26).[24]

Wisdom 2:1 depicts the supreme power of Sheol/death, making clear that no one has come back from Hades. Job 12:12c expresses a similar sentiment, saying that the skies would cease to exist before humans would wake up from death. Jonah 2:2-6 is even more explicit about the terror that תהום and Sheol inflict on the world of mortals – God is ultimately more powerful, able to extricate faithful people from the depths.

3.3.3.3. *Eco-theological synthesis.* The insight behind Job 14:7-12 presumes awareness of the life-giving potential of water stated either in its connectedness with the realm of flora (vv. 7-9) or in Job's comparison of human death with the irretrievable vanishing of this natural blessing

---

22. Hilary Marlow, 'The Lament over the River Nile – Isaiah xix:5-10 in its Wider Context', *VT* 57 (2007): 232.

23. The *ma'at* is the Egyptian concept for the principle of moral and cosmic order upon which depends the stability of the created order.

24. Habel, *Job*, 241.

(vv. 10-12). An eco-justice reading assumes that the author of the text would possess a perception of the intrinsic value of water, whose drying up would be apocalyptic, as depicted in Isa. 19:5-10: the entire ecosystem will suffer.

Humans are portrayed as *unlike* the tree that rejuvenates upon contact with water and *like* water that disappears forever.[25] The dual potential of water served as an appropriate vehicle for talking about the intricate fate of humans. For the tree water is life-giving (v. 9), but humans are like water that dries up (v. 11): the absence of water (drought) is a symbol of death.

The detailed depiction of drought in Isa. 19:5-10 and its echo in the metaphorical words of Job 14:11 reveal valuable ecological insights. In current sub-Saharan Africa, where water shortage is one of the main problems threatening the life of so many people, it is worth noticing that Job 14:10-12 was aware of the relevance of a reliable water supply and of the effect of drought on the social order. The simile of Job 14:10-12 implies the ecological insight that:

> L'eau est donc considérée en Palestine avant tout comme quelque chose de bon, d'utile, mais aussi comme quelque chose dont on risque facilement de manquer.[26]

Yet, the current problems related to the scarcity of water may largely be attributed to human activity rather than to divine fiat. Be that as it may, as a wisdom text, Job 14:11 encompasses Israel's view of water. It virtually calls on people to become aware of the fact that a water supply can dry up irreversibly and forever. Isaiah 19:5-10 shows how this kind of situation can undermine the order of a society. Drought is symbol of human death. There is no substitute for water just as there is none for human death.

3.4. *Water and Water-related Phenomena in Job 36:26–37:13*

This literary unit touches on more than simply the life-giving potential of water and water-related phenomena. The following translation draws on that of the NRSV, with some *italicised changes resulting from my ecological understanding of the Hebrew text*.

---

25. John J. Bimson, 'Has the Rain a Father? A Biblical Theology of Water', *EMJ* 42 (2012): 5.
26. Reymond, *L'eau*, 2.

3.4.1. *Translation of Job 36:26–37:13*

³⁶:²⁶ Surely God is great, and we do not know him;
    the number of his years is unsearchable.
²⁷ When he draws up drops from the sea,
    they distil as rain from his raincloud,
²⁸ which the skies pour down
    and drop upon mortals abundantly.
²⁹ Can anyone understand the spreading of the clouds,
    the thundering of his pavilion?
³⁰ Behold, the Most High spreads his lightning
    and covers the depths of the sea.
³¹ For by these he feeds peoples;
    he gives food in abundance.
³² He covers his hands with the lightning,
    and commands it to strike the mark.
³³ *The thunderclap announces the coming storm,
    and apprises the cattle of the storm's approach.*[27]
³⁷:¹ At this also my heart trembles,
    and leaps out of its place.
² Listen, listen to the thunder of his voice
    and the rumbling that comes from his mouth.
³ Under the whole heaven he lets it loose,
    and his lightnings to the corners of the earth.
⁴ After it his voice roars; he thunders with his majestic voice
    and he does not restrain the lightning when his voice is heard.
⁵ God thunders wondrously with his voice;
    he does great things that we cannot comprehend.
⁶ For to the snow he says, 'Fall on the earth';
    and the shower of rain, his heavy shower of rain,
⁷ serves as a sign on everyone's hand,
    so that all whom he has made may know it.
⁸ Then the animals go into their lairs
    and remain in their dens.
⁹ From its chamber comes the whirlwind,
    and cold (water) from the scattering winds.
¹⁰ By the breath of God ice is given,
    and the broad waters are frozen fast.
¹¹ He loads the thick cloud with moisture;
    the clouds scatter his lightning.

---

27. The translation of TOB is adopted here: 'Son tonnerre annonce sa venue, les troupeaux même pressentent son approche'.

¹² They turn round and round by his guidance,
   to accomplish all that he commands them
   on the face of the habitable *earth*.
¹³ Whether for a curse – even on his own earth –
   Or for a blessing, he causes it to happen.

3.4.2. *The Literary Observations*

3.4.2.1. *Delimitation of the text*. This literary sequence of Job 36:26–37:13 is part of the six chapters (32–37) attributed to Elihu, the fourth person appearing from nowhere, after the three supposed friends of Job (Elphaz, Bildad and Zophar) failed to make Job retract his allegations. Job 32–37 covers five separate speeches,[28] presenting a unique perspective on the dilemma and suffering of Job.[29] This text belongs to the final admonitions of Elihu (36:1–37:13) and consists of two parts: the first describes God's dealings with humans (36:1-21); the second is the splendid creation hymn that celebrates God's power and majesty (36:22–37:24).

The whole speech contains a great number of creation images, principally in the last unit, which is best understood as a 'sapiential hymn'[30] offering an arrayed depiction of creation combining the aspects of a hymn of praise and a sapiential teaching to address Job's allegations (see also Sir. 42:15–43:33). The argument of Elihu in Job 36:1–37:13 is basically the same as that of the previous three friends, namely that Job must admit that God is always right and that Job as a mere human being is wrong. However, in contrast to the former three friends, Elihu based his assumption on elements of the creation, mostly water-related phenomena.

Job 36:26–37:13 lists a number of water and water-related phenomena, namely rainclouds, lightning, thunder, storm, snow, cold wind, frost, hail, all acting under the divine command, whether for curse or for blessing (37:13). For Elihu, one cannot fully understand God's power unless one pays attention to elements of creation. This can be discerned in the structure that follows.

---

28. Job 32:6-22; 33:1-33; 34:2-37; 35:2-16; 36:1–37:24.

29. Larry J. Waters, 'The Authenticity of the Elihu Speeches in Job 32–37', *BSac* 156 (1999): 29.

30. Carol A. Newsom, *The Book of Job: A Contest of Moral Imaginations* (Oxford: Oxford University Press, 2003), 228.

3.4.2.2. *Literary structure.* The literary structure of Job 36:26–37:13 can be presented as follows:[31]

A	The mystery of rainclouds	36:26-29
B	The purpose of thunder and lightning	36:30-33
B′	The mystery of thunder and lightning	37:1-4
C	The purpose of winter storms	37:5-7
C′	The mystery of winter storms	37:8-10
A′	The purpose of rainclouds	37:11-13

Table 2. *The Literary Structure of Job 36:26–37:13*

The speech is articulated on two modes of meteorological operations. The first mode which is descriptive and emotive highlights the mystery of the process and evokes a response of wonder (A, B, C). The second mode relates to the 'purpose' of God's atmospheric operations in his overall governance of earth (B′, C′, A′). As one can see, Elihu focuses on the natural phenomenon of rainstorms combined with the hydrological cycle as mysterious elements of nature that God uses in ruling over the earth for curse or blessing.

The rhetoric of Elihu's speech in Job 36:26–37:13 includes:

> A balanced interplay between mystery and meaning, between amazement in the face of the incomprehensible and comprehending its purpose, between hymnic description and wisdom interpretation of the same phenomenon.[32]

The gathering of water from the sea that is poured on earth as rain is, for instance, one of the mysteries that none can understand (36:27-29). The thunder and lightning are other meteorological phenomena accompanying the rainclouds whose functions on earth provoke awe (37:1). In addition, the purpose of the rainclouds, thunder and lightning is to judge and feed people on earth (36:31). The function of the rain or rainstorm is to serve as a sign of God's works either for curse or blessing (37:5-13).

3.4.3. *Eco-theological Observations*

3.4.3.1. *Ecological significance of the rain (Job 36:26-28).* In Job 36:26, Elihu says that God is beyond human understanding, and in vv. 27-28 God is portrayed as the rain-maker. God does it by gathering drops of waters from the sea (נטפי־מים) before distilling them as rain from the

---

31. Habel, *Job*, 504.
32. Ibid., 505.

raincloud (לְאֵדוֹ). The word אֵד is found again in Gen. 2:6, where it refers to the subterranean river watering the garden. Tsumura argued that אֵד means underground water in both instances,[33] while the NRSV translates it as a *mist*, following the LXX rendition of אֵד as νεφελην (vapour) in Job 36:26, in contrast to אֵד as πηγη (spring/fountain) in Gen. 2:6.

It seems that אֵד refers here to a celestial reservoir of water or rainclouds, given the idea of the rain-making in vv. 27-28. Both the sea (יָם) and אֵד-water (raincloud) are not viewed in Job 36:27-28 as created by God, but as pre-existing spheres that play a great role in the rain-making process. The Targum comments that God 'holds back the drops of water [which] would drop as rain into His clouds', implying that the clouds receive the rain already as liquid.[34] For modern people, this idea of the clouds receiving water from the sea calls to mind the process of evaporation.

Syntactically, the Hebrew word לְאֵדוֹ probably refers to the source from which comes מָטָר (rain) in Job 36:28. In connection with the Semitic word *i-du*, אֵד refers here to something like 'raincloud', the celestial source of heavy rain (*ga-šúm*, in Eblaite) or rain (מטר, in Hebrew) that soaks the land during the months of November–December, the period of heavy rain mentioned in the old Eblaite calendar *Itu ga-šúm*.[35] While these rains were often dangerously heavy, they also resulted in the fertility of the land, and thus food in abundance (Job 36:28). Joel 2:23 refers to them as the 'first (or early) rains' (גשם בראשון). Although they were dramatic in form (cf. Job 37:6-7), the 'early rains' were vital for the success of agricultural activity to the point that their arrival was longed for and celebrated (Ps. 65:9-13). Ancient Israel also experienced a season of heavy rains corresponding to April–May that is referred to in Joel 2:23. These 'latter rains' (גשם ומלקוש) were expected to persist through to the grain harvest; without them the summer drought would be ruinous for crops and animals.[36]

---

33. Tsumura, *The Earth and the Waters*, 105.
34. Edmund F. Sutcliffe, 'The Clouds as Water-Carriers in Hebrew Thought', *VT* 3 (1953): 100.
35. The Old Eblaite calendar was agricultural in character in the sense that the names of the months reflected the main activity of a given month. The new calendar introduced by king Ibbis-Sipis is more theological, in that the months are named after the deities responsible for the execution or success of the specific activities of the month dedicated to them. For instance, while July–August was called *itu ṣa-'à-tum* or *ṣa-'à-na-at* (the month of flocks), in the new calendar it is called *itu-aštar* (the month of Ashtar), the divinity responsible for the fertility of the flocks. See Mitchell J. Dahood, 'Eblaite Ì-du and Hebrew *'ēd*, Rain Cloud', *CBQ* 43 (1981): 535.
36. Bimson, 'Has the Rain a Father?' 1.

It seems that Job 36:27-28 is referring to the latter rains, given the notion of rain and harvest (food) – though the early rains might also be implied. The early rains are clearly expressed in Job 37:6-7. Both rainy seasons are seen as gifts from above. That is why Deut. 11:13-15 formulates God's promise in terms of the continuous provision of both early and later rains.

Elihu shares the cosmological views typical in most regions of the ancient Near East, where it was believed that a cosmic reservoir existed above the earth, with the waters being held in check by a dome (Gen. 1:6). Sometimes this dome was obscured by clouds, but sometimes the windows were opened to allow water to flow earthward.[37] We find echoes of this in the hydrological cycle of Job 36:27-28, where we have the gathering up of water from the sea (water below) to the raincloud (water above), before it falls to earth as rain, resulting in the fertility of the land.[38]

The words יגרט נטפי־מים (he draws drops of water, 36:27) reinforce the intrinsic value of water. The sea (ים) is not said to be created by God but implied in Job 36:26-28 as a pre-existent entity upon which God draws when he collects drops of water that are further distilled from the raincloud (לאדו) to produce rain (מטר), causing abundant food on earth. Water is here a precious and pre-existent commodity that functions for the good of human beings.

The text is decidedly anthropocentric since the rain is said to be poured only on human beings in v. 28. It is stated that God sends abundant rain on אדם (humans) rather than on אדמה (ground/land), as is the case in Gen. 2:5. Dahood suggests that אדם may be the equivalent of אדמה, as in Gen. 16:12, Jer. 32:30, Zech. 13:5 and Prov. 30:14.[39] While his argument is possible for other texts, it is unlikely in Job 36:28, since Elihu's focus is not on the land, but on humans (Job), who must experience God's mystery. In Job 38:26, God corrects the anthropocentrism of Elihu by stating that rain may fall on a land empty of human life, a desert.

---

37. James L. Crenshaw, *Reading Job: A Literary and Theological Commentary* (Macon: Smyth & Helwys, 2011), 145.

38. Rain was a guarantee for the fertility of the land. Sufficient rain resulted in the sprouting of grass (Ps. 72:6; 2 Sam. 23:4), the growing of flowers (Song 2:12) and cereals (Isa. 32:20; Hos. 2:24) and even the trees may put forth fruit (Ezek. 34:27; Ps. 1:3).

39. Mitchell J. Dahood, 'Zacharia 9:1, 'Ên 'Ādām', *CBQ* 25 (1963): 124.

3.4.3.2. *Ecological significance of the rainstorm (36:29–37:5)*. God is depicted as the producer of clouds and thunder. God is presented as a storm-God who not only manages the dispensation of moisture, but sends the thundering (תשאות) from his pavilion. The meteorological word תואשת requires listening (יבין) to the voice of God (Job 36:29), since in Job 37:2, Elihu, who is terrified of the natural phenomenon, asks Job to listen carefully to the thunder (ברגז) of his voice (קלו). The Hebrew syntax consisting of an infinitive absolute preceded or followed by a verbal form of the same verb, such as שמעו שמוע in Job 37:2, is called *paronomasia*, denoting the intensity of the order.⁴⁰ The infinitive absolute שמוע emphasises not only the meaning denoted by the verb's stem שמע but also the force of the verb in context, in the sense that שמעו שמוע literally means 'listen very carefully'.

Thus, Elihu challenges Job to listen carefully to the mighty roaring of the rainstorm sent by God, and to temper the allegations he makes against God. For Elihu, the rainstorm, which is mainly made by water, is mastered by God, but terrifies humans. Earlier, Elihu argued that no one can understand (יבין) the spreading of the clouds and God's sending of rain, lightning and thunder (36:29), since it is by these natural phenomena that God nourishes mortals, governs people and shows forth his anger and/or judgment (36:31-33).

In other words, Job is not challenged to listen to the word of God, but to the rainstorm (whose main ingredient is water), which is the voice of God. This water-related phenomenon is depicted as having a voice, and thus of being a subject. The word קל (voice, or rather thunder in this text) occurs five times in Job 37:2-5. Ironically, the constant rumbling of a rainstorm has the same effect on earth as Job's sickness, bringing רגז (quaking; cf. Job 3:26). Elihu compares the roaring of the rainstorm with that of a lion (ישאג־קול) or the rumbling of an earthquake (Job 37:4).

Storm imagery is often linked with Baal or YHWH, but in Elihu's speech they are connected with El.⁴¹ The word pavilion (סכתו) is the celestial tent made for the storm-God, from which he will appear in glory with his meteorological agents.⁴² In Job 36:30, the deity rides the clouds and scatters lightning that covers the roots of the sea above. The images of

---

40. Bruce K. Waltke and Michael P. O'Connor, *An Introduction to Biblical Hebrew Syntax* (Winona Lake: Eisenbrauns, 1990), 585.

41. YHWH is the national God for Israel. Baal is the storm god of Canaan. El is at the top god of the Canaanite Pantheon. Later, during the Babylonian exile, YHWH came to be known as El or Elohim.

42. Habel, *Job*, 511.

storm-God connected with water are also found in Ps. 29:3-11, in which the thunder of God roars over the waters, and God sits over the flood and strengthens and blesses his people. The image is similar here: lightning covers the surface of the sea and from the rainstorm God governs and feeds people abundantly (v. 31) – the latter detail thus highlighting the anthropocentric focus of the text (Job 36:30).

The image of the rainstorm is ambiguous: it is both positive and negative. Luc has shown that the storm imagery in the whole book of Job basically points in two directions: 'in various forms the storm provides a negative image for Job's suffering but a positive portrayal of God's design and control'.[43] What is implied in Elihu's speech is that the rainstorm does not have only a romantic potential, but is both fascinating and terrifying. For water, one of the fundamental elements of a rainstorm is the unity of beneficial and destructive features of life and death. Elihu witnesses the dual potential of storms as demonstrations of God's judicial role (vv. 31-32).

The idea is that the purpose of the storm-God in causing rain (vv. 27-28) and revealing his majesty to the depths of the sea (vv. 29-30) involves both sustenance and control (v. 31). Not only does the rainstorm bring rain that causes abundant harvest, but it also sets into motion the lightning bolts that strike their targets with absolute accuracy.[44] Providing food (נתן אכלה) in due time is part of God's caring activity in Ps. 104:27, as is the giving of rain (Ps. 104:13). God's responsibility for the provision of water is precisely seized upon by Job's mocking words to God in Job 24:8. Elihu reacts that the rainfall is unpredictable and volatile for humans (36:29), and thus Job, who does not possess the ability to comprehend, should refrain from criticising God for sending rainfall on the poorly dressed people.

3.4.3.3. *Ecological insights of the snow, wind and shower rain (37:6-12).* God is depicted as commanding/directing the snow and wind earthward. Elihu focuses on their effect on humans and animals. The beasts (חיה) retreat into their lairs to escape the tempest. The violent summer storms and extreme ice and snow can immobilise even the great creatures. In the book of Job, the חיה belong to the fauna that inspire strength and power; they live independently from the human domain.[45] However, here in Job 37:8 they are said to also be fragile to the power of heavy rain, which

---

43. Luc, 'Storm', 122.
44. Crenshaw, *Reading Job*, 144.
45. See Job 38:39–39:30.

operates on the direct command of God, since they go into their lairs to escape the rainstorm.

The heavy rain (37:6), which is here read גשם מטר, can be linked with the Eblaite noun *ga-šúm* (torrential rain) in the sense of destructive rain that occurred in November–December. Job 37:6 may refer to the instances of heavy rainfall over the hills that can become flash floods, provoking land erosion and sometimes sweeping people away. Hence, the greatest challenge of cultivating sloping ground was controlling the erosive power of rain and promoting water absorption rather than surface runoff.[46] There could be no sustainable agriculture in the highlands of Canaan if the problem went unsolved.

The meaning of the verb הוא in Job 37:6 is likely related to the Arabic word *hayâ* or the Hebrew word הוי found in Zech. 2:10. Here God calls or invites his attendants, including the snow and rain, just as one calls a horse for a battle.[47] Job 37:6 says that God commands the snow, as a partner or subject, to fall earthward, just as God demanded the waters in Gen. 1:6 to retreat so that the dry land may appear. It is implied here that natural phenomena can respond as subjects.

For this reason, Job 37:6-7 highlights the positive response of the snow and heavy rain, which falls earthward as a sign for humans. Job 37:8 says that the beasts seek protection from the deluge and go into their lairs until the storms pass. It is from these lairs (חדר) that the סופה (storm or whirlwind) comes (v. 9). The word אצרות relates to the storehouse of water-related phenomena. In Job 26:8, God is stated to be the one who 'binds up the waters in his thick cloud' (צרר־מים בעביו), while in Prov. 30:4 God is the one 'who has bound (צרר) the waters in his garment'. Jeremiah 18:14 implies that God binds the snow in a store when he asks: 'Will the snow of Lebanon leave the storehouse of Shaddai?'

Storehouse imagery appears elsewhere, in 2 Kgs 19:24, where the Assyrian king Sennacherib boasts to the people of Judah that he had dug and drunk the זרים (foreign) waters and that he had dried up all the rivers of God's storehouse (מצור) in the cosmic reservoir. Sennacherib claims to have besieged the storing places (מצור)[48] where fresh water is kept, mocking Hezekiah for having trusted in his God. In the ancient Near East, a common military strategy was to besiege a water supply in order to

---

46. Daniel Hillel, *The Natural History of the Bible: An Environmental Exploration of the Hebrew Scriptures* (New York: Columbian University Press, 2006), 34.

47. Naftali H. Tur-Sinai, *The Book of Job* (Jerusalem: Kiriath Sepher, 1967), 508.

48. The מָצוֹר as a place from where cold waters come is also mentioned in Isa. 37:25 and Jer. 18:14.

force enemies to surrender (see 2 Chr. 32:4). In Job 37:9-11, מזרים refers to God's precious water store, while rain (מטר), snow (שלג) and ice are squeezed out of the clouds.

God freezes the abundant waters of the celestial sea behind a solid (מוצק) dome. This dome (רקיע in Job 37:18) is clearly very strong, as it can permanently hold the mass of primeval waters above. The dome can sometimes be opened for destruction (as flood in Gen. 6–9) or for blessing (as rain in Gen. 2:5-6). Job 37:10 thus alludes to the idea that God restrains the waters above by means of a solid firmament. This idea of fixing the limits of the waters is further highlighted in God's speech in Job 38:8-11.

3.4.3.4. *Eco-theological synthesis.* The above analysis shows that the text highlights the intrinsic value of water, which exists separately from the human realm but which is closely associated with God, who can use it for a particular reason. Job 37:13 concludes that God uses weather, water and water-related phenomena for curse or for blessing. They thus reflect deeper ordering and wisdom beyond human understanding.

Job 37:2, for instance, tries to demonstrate how the voice of God is identical to the rainstorm of God, which is portrayed as a subject with voice. How many times have we listened to the voice of nature when it reacts against our anthropocentric use of its resources? For Elihu, Job does not need an encounter with God's word, but with his voice expressed through the water-related phenomena. In other words, elements of the created order may raise their voice to humans as God's agents.

God, as a cosmic pilot, guides the rainstorms like ships or chariots on their appointed courses across the sky. In addition, he controls their moisture content and lightning in order to bring about curse (לשבט) or mercy/blessing (חסד). The antithesis אם־לשבט (for curse) and אם־לחסד (for mercy/blessing) testifies to the dual potential of rainstorms – whose main ingredient, of course, is water (Job 37:13). This is reflected in the falling of the heavy rains, which are both dangerous (37:6-7) and beneficial for the land's fertility (36:27-28).

The water-related phenomena are clearly seen in Job 36:26–37:13 to have life-giving and life-threatening potential. The message is for Job to restrain his allegations based on a one-sided view of nature. This is explained by the fact that all the water-related phenomena in 36:27-28 (sea, rainstorm and rain) are anthropocentrically depicted as God's partners, ones involved in the nourishment of human beings and the enacting of divine judgments on them (36:31).

A close analysis of the text shows that natural forces are all used in accordance with some purpose. Job 37:6-7 depicts God as directly bringing the rain (מטר) and snow (שלג) on earth to serve as a sign for humans. Even the icy water and clouds exist to accomplish God's will (37:10-12), not the people's.

3.5. Water and Water-related Phenomena in Job 38:22-38

3.5.1. Introduction

Job 38–41 is filled with many sequences containing water-related phenomena. The most important ones are: Job 38:8-11, about the limits of the sea and earth; 38:22-38, containing various references to water and water-related phenomena; and chs. 40–41, involving two beasts (Leviathan and Behemoth) that live in watery abodes. I will here focus on Job 38:22-30, since it offers a comprehensive example dealing with major aspects of water.

3.5.2. Translation of Job 38:22-38

> [22] Have you entered the storehouses of the snow,
>   or have you seen the storehouses of the hail,
> [23] which I have reserved for the time of *scarcity*,
>   for the day of battle and war?
> [24] *Where is the way where the lightning (heat) is distributed,*
>   or where the east wind is scattered upon the earth?
> [25] Who *cuts* a channel for the torrents of rain,
>   and a way for the thunderbolt *(rainstorms)*,
> [26] to bring rain on a land where no one lives,
>   on the desert, which is empty of human life,
> [27] *to irrigate (water) the waste and desolate land,*
>   and to make the grass spring up from the dry ground?
> [28] Has the rain a father,
>   or who has begotten the drops of dew?
> [29] From whose womb did the ice come forth,
>   and who has given birth to the hoarfrost of *skies*?
> [30] The waters become hard like stone,
>   and the face of the deep is frozen.
> [31] Can you bind the chains of the Pleiades,
>   or loose the cords of Orion?
> [32] Can you lead forth the Mazzaroth in their season,
>   or can you guide Aldebaran with its Hyades (trains)?

³³ Do you know the ordinances of the *skies*?
    Can you establish their rule on the earth?
³⁴ Can you lift up your voice to the clouds,
    And make the torrents of waters (rains) answer you?
³⁵ Can you send forth lightnings,
    so that they may go and say to you,
    'Here we are'?
³⁶ Who has put wisdom in the Ibis?
    Or who gave understanding to the Cock?
³⁷ Who has the wisdom to number the clouds?
    Or who can tilt the waterskins of the *skies*
³⁸ when the dust runs into a mass
    and the clods cling together?

3.5.3. *Literary Position of Job 38:22-38*

Job 38:22-38 belongs to the wider section of God's speeches in Job 38–41, describing the wonders of the created order that are beyond human wisdom. God is pointing to natural phenomena not just to show Job's limitations, but also to draw attention to something that human beings can clearly see if they only broaden their perspective: God's wisdom and power reflected in the deeper ordering and rules of the created order.

God's speeches in chs. 38–41 are divided into two main sections (38:1–40:2 and 40:6–41:26), which are separated by a brief answer from Job (40:3-5). The first speech, 38:1–40:2, comprises a series of God's rhetorical questions to Job about the vast expanse of the created order: the founding of the world and the origin of the sea, as well as about meteorological forces, the constellations and wild beasts. The second speech (40:6–41:26) depicts two mythic animals: Behemoth and Leviathan. Both speeches 'are majestic poems, rich in lyric artistry, literary ambiguity, and theological profundity'.[49]

Our text, Job 38:22-38, belongs to God's first speech related to the founding of creation (38:1–40:2). A careful analysis of the speech shows that 38:22-38 occupies the central position. Its opening report (38:1-21) depicts the establishment of creation or the created order in general, while 38:39–40:2 concerns the wild animals. The centre, 38:22-38, contains the comprehensive life-giving and life-threatening potential of water and water-related phenomena in the created order as one of God's responses to Job's claims. It should be precisely stated that the whole section of 38:22-38 deals with the rain and other water-related phenomena such as the

---

49. Habel, *Job*, 526.

upper-water (sea-above), clouds as water-carriers, lightning as acolytes of rain as well as other forms of moisture (ice, dew, hail, snow) and the rule of the stars over rainy seasons.

3.5.4. *Retrieval of Ecological Wisdom in the Text*

3.5.4.1. *Ecological significance of the storehouses (Job 38:22-24)*. The Hebrew word אוצר can refer either to a treasure-house (Neh. 10:39), a treasury or the valuable store/supply of food or drink (2 Chr. 11:11) or wealth (Prov. 8:21; 15:16), or an arsenal of weapons (Jer. 50:25). In Ps. 135:7 it is referred to as the store of the cloud, while in Qoh. 43:14 it is the supply of the celestial sea or the upper-waters. The word is used in reference to a store of rain in Deut. 28:12 or of wind in Jer. 10:13 and 51:16, as well as a store of waters (תהומות) in Ps. 33:7.

In Job 38:22, the plural אצרות is used for the storehouses of God for snow and hail. In the Bible, hail (ברד) appears with threatening connotations, mostly functioning as a divine weapon used to punish the wicked (Isa. 28:17; Ezek. 13:11) and Israel's enemies (Josh. 10:1; Isa. 30:30), or to destroy crops (Exod. 9:22-26; Hag. 2:17). The effects of hail on agriculture include the destruction (הרג) of vines (Ps. 78:47), the smashing (שבר) of trees (Exod. 9:25) as well as the death of humans and animals (Exod. 9:19; Ps. 78:48). Here in Job 38:22, hail is reserved for the time of battle as a life-threatening weapon.

Job 38:23 is slightly ambiguous. It seems to be referring to a storehouse and its contents, which are being kept for a time of scarcity (לעת־צר) and battle (ומלחמה). Although the two parts of v. 23 present a parallelism of scarcity and war – in the sense that the time of war is a time of scarcity/distress – it seems that שלג relates to scarcity (v. 23a) while ברד is directly linked to battle (v. 23b).

Snow (שלג) is not presented as a damaging weapon, but rather as a source of water whose refreshing qualities can be called upon during the times of scarcity associated with war. In Jer. 18:4, the prophet exclaims regarding the water-stores: 'Will the snow of Lebanon leave the storing-place of Shaddai?' In a time of scarcity, the snow is welcome as an auxiliary source of water for the crops. In ancient Israel, snow, alongside rain, was seen as a moistening and fertilising agent of the land. Isaiah 55:10-11 reads:

> [10] For just as rain and snow fall from the sky and do not return there, but water the earth, causing it to bud and produce, giving seed to the sower and bread to the eater; [11] so is my word that goes out from my mouth – it will not return to me unfulfilled; but it will accomplish what I intend, and cause to succeed what I sent it to do. (CJB)

The coolness of the snow in time of harvest is metaphorically linked to its refreshing function in Prov. 25:13: 'Like the cold of snow in the time of harvest are faithful messengers to those who send them; they refresh the spirit of their masters' (NRSV). Snow is also a sign of cleanness (Lam. 4:7). Job 38:22-23, therefore, uses two water-related phenomena – snow and hail – that have two different functions during times of trouble. Hail is a life-threatening weapon, while snow is a friendly, life-giving water-related phenomenon. Hail should, perhaps, be seen as stock imagery related to the divine military arsenal.[50]

What is striking is that these water-related phenomena are not only stored up in treasuries (i.e. specific locations), but are also designed to be used during specific 'times' (i.e. of scarcity and battle). As such, the text testifies to an awareness of the intrinsic worth of these water-related phenomena (snow and hail), which are valuable commodities to be drawn upon 'when' needed. These water-related phenomena, which are at God's disposal for both seasonal and retributive functions, are called to celebrate their Lord in Ps. 148:8.[51]

The word אוּר – translated elsewhere as a reference to heat – in Job 38:24 must be understood to mean the storehouse of heat scattered across the earth through the east wind. The latter, also identified as sirocco (קדים), is a naturally hot and violent wind from the desert which has earlier been referred to by Job (15:2) as a hot and dangerous force.[52] The words wind, water and light/heat in Job 38:22-24 are not random, but common motifs in the ancient Near Eastern texts related to creation.[53] The word דרך (way) in 38:24 implies that the wind that scatters heat across the earth acts in accordance with a fixed course governing its movements within the design of the cosmos and in relation to the water-related phenomenon they are connected to, namely the rain.

The repetition of the word דרך in Job 38:24-25 implies that the meteorological forces related to water (wind and lightning) respect a fixed course (דרך) that results in deep order in the cosmos. In this sense, in texts where the storehouses of water are subjects, it is stated that their windows automatically open/close in due course. This is the case in Gen. 7:11 and

---

50. David J. Clines, *Job 38–42* (Nashville: Thomas Nelson, 2011), 1049.
51. Habel, *Job*, 542.
52. Clines, *Job 38–42*, 1109.
53. The 1934 discovery of the epigraphic from Tell Balāṭa (biblical Shechem) offers proof that wind, water and light/heat are common in many cosmogonies. See Julian Obermann, 'Wind, Water, and Light in an Archaic Inscription from Shechem', *JBL* 57, no. 3 (1938): 249.

Isa. 24:18, where the windows burst forth (פתח, in Niphal), while in Gen. 8:2 the windows close themselves (סכר, in Niphal) on God's order. In other cases, God may decide to open the storehouses in order to bless his people (Mal. 3:10; Ps. 78:23).

3.5.4.2. *The ecological potential of the rain in Job 38:25-27.* Job 38:25-27 has a different perspective from that found in Elihu's statement in 36:27-28 about the rain. Job 38:25-27 is a strophe describing the delivery of rain on earth in torrents, even on land that is apparently useless for humans (vv. 25-27). In contrast to Elihu's speech depicting God as a rainmaker, here the focus is on the regular cycle of nature.

The word תעלה is used as stream/channel for פלג לשטף (cutting out for the flood). The course (תעלה) that the rain takes links the sky (שמים) and the earth. This is similar to the Genesis flood account, where the waters-above fall down via a great gate (ארבת) of the sky (Gen. 7:11). The word תעלה (course, Job 38:25) would be a surprising term here, since rain normally falls in drops rather than as an unending stream. In 2 Kgs 18:17 and Isa. 7:3, the plural form of תעלה is used to refer to the constant conduit linked to a pool.

However, the focus in Job 38:25 is on שטף (flood of water-above), which was believed to be held/limited in the sky (שמים) and which sometimes might fall earthward as rain by following a fixed conduit (תעלה). This airy aqueduct was viewed as a means of both ensuring and regulating the supply of upper-waters on Earth:

> Given that these upper-waters are supported by the solid vault of the heavens [sky] and yet descend upon the earth, it was believed that there must be apertures [holes/channels] in the sky capable of being opened and shut as occasion requires. If these were opened and the water allowed to descend on the earth without the intermediary of clouds, the effect was devastating and destructive (Gen. 7:11; 8:2; Isa. 24:18).[54]

In this sense, the rainstorm (חזיז) also has a fixed way (דרך) to follow in its distribution of lightning and moisture on earth. It should be noted that rains in ancient Israel were often accompanied by violent lightning. As such, Ps. 135:7 declares that YHWH made the lightning for the rain. Indeed, the terms תעלה (course) and דרך (way), and the notion of 'time', emphasise the principle of the cosmic order. As Reymond declares, accidental rain could result in disastrous effects:

---

54. Sutcliffe, 'The Clouds as Waters', 99.

Une pluie accidentelle venant au milieu de l'été ne serait guère utile si ce n'est pour rafraîchir l'atmosphère et donner un supplément d'eau potable; mais souvent elle risque d'être nuisible en détruisant les récoltes par sa violence.[55]

In the ancient Near East a solid dome (רקיע), blue in colour (Ezek. 1:26), formed the sky (שמים). This dome was assumed to be holding back the upper waters, so that they may fall down at specific times. The word שמים is etymologically defined as 'what relates to water'. Sachs[56] argues that the Hebrew letter ש prefixed to the three-letter root מים extends the underlying idea of שמים (sha-mayim) as the superlative of מים (water), suggesting that there is water above the sky.

This idea is present in some African cultures. For the *Nandes*, an ethnic group in the east of D.R. Congo, the name for the sky was traditionally spelled out as *OLUBHULA* referring to a water-jar above that pours out water earthwards as rain (*MBULA*). This conception has been altered into a spiritualistic concept, *ELUBULA* (heaven), following the influence of the Christian eschatology. Just as for ancient Israel, this agrarian African people believes that there is a water-reserve above the sky.

Therefore, 'as water falls, in the form of rain, from on high, the only conclusion possible seemed to be that there exists above a great reservoir and the only position that could be assigned for this was above the vault of heaven'.[57] The idea in Job 38:25 is not about the ordinary rain (מטר or מחר), but the torrential rainfall (פלג לשטף) that follows a given course (תעלה) to reach the earth and overwhelm it with life-giving or life-threatening waters.

However, the significance of the torrential rains and thunderstorms is not restricted solely to the channels by which they are delivered, but is to be found also – perhaps primarily – in their life-giving benefits of the supply of water, through rain, even on land where no one lives (Job 38:26). While Job alleged that God withholds and releases celestial waters (12:15) as well as the storm (9:17) for destructive rather than salutary purposes, 38:26-27 provides the antithesis. God sends the rain to irrigate the waste and desolate land (שאה ומשאה) and to cause the dry ground and desolate (שאה) land to put forth fresh grass (38:27).

The word שאה (*shoah*) implies total desolation and it is contemporarily utilised for the crime of the Jewish holocaust. In the Bible, the expression שאה ומשאה occurs in Job 30:3 and Zeph. 1:15 with reference to terrible

---

55. Reymond, *L'eau*, 5.
56. Gerardo Sachs, 'Why Shamayim as Sky', *JBQ* 34, no. 2 (2006): 130.
57. Sutcliffe, 'The Clouds as Waters', 99.

affliction. In Job 30:3, the words are used for people who are counted among the dogs and who gnaw at the desolate ground. Job 38:27 implies that God sends life-giving rain even to those places usually despised by Job (i.e. humans). In other words, 'God satisfies even such a desolate place, providing rain so that it sprouts grass, bringing forth life in a land that humanity has rejected as worthless'.[58]

The sprouting grass (דשא מצא) in Job 38:27 might be read as echoing the sprouting of vegetation in Gen. 1:11-12 (דשא הארץ צאותו), implying the present fertility of the land that was previously barren. In Genesis, the desolation is described in terms of תהו ובהו (formless wasteland), while in Job the land is in a situation of שאה ומשאה (total desolation). In both texts, the land was in a state of desolation brought about by the actions of water. In Genesis, the fertility of the land is made possible by the further separation of waters, which created the dry land. It was this dry land that later put forth grass. In Job, the fertility of the land is made possible by the beneficial distribution of life-giving rain to desolate areas. In both texts, water is the basis of the productivity/barrenness of the land.

Finally, water-related phenomena are not presented in terms of their usefulness for humans in Job 48. Instead, they have their own value. The target of the rain in this text is not just the productive land worked to satisfy human hunger, as in Job 36:27-28, but also the wilderness which is transformed into fertile land. Although animals are not referred to explicitly, they are implied as the beneficiaries of the rains, which results in dry ground putting forth their foodstuff (Job 38:27).

3.5.4.3. The potential of other forms of moisture (Job 38:28-30). The focus in theses verses shifts from the majestic torrential rainfalls – the source of life-giving waters – to the softer forms of moisture: the rain (מָטָר, v. 28a), dew (אֲגְלֵי־טַל, v. 28b), ice (קרח, v. 29a) and hoar-frost (כפר, v. 29b). In Job 38:28-29, the duo of unfrozen water sources – rain and dew drops (אגלים) – stands in interlinear parallelism with the pair of frozen forms – ice and hoar-frost. The question 'Does the rain have a father?' is a rhetorical question expecting a 'No' answer. All the questions in Job 38:28-30 about the origin of rain, dew, ice and hoar-frost should be answered as follows: no one begot the rain and the dew drops; the ice came from no one's womb and no one gave birth to the hoar-frost.

The book of Job implies that God is the one who brings rain. Here we see a contrast with the mythology of the Canaanites, where the entourage of the storm god Baal comprised Pirdya, daughter of mist, and

---

58. Schifferdecker, *Out of the Whirlwind*, 71.

Taliya (Dew), daughter of showers.[59] Schökel and Díaz have argued that Job 38:28-29 is an obvious vestige of mythology that had the male sky fertilise the female earth through the 'semen' of rain and dew.[60]

However, the fertilising role of rain and dew is not in view in our text. Instead, the focus is on their birth. Job 38:28 serves, in part, to refute the notion that Baal is responsible for the rain and dew. This is something we also find in the polemical words of Jer. 14:22. Earlier, Job's friend Eliphaz stated that God is 'the one who gives rain on the earth and sends waters on the fields' (Job 5:10, NRSV). It is implied that their mysterious origin would testify to the extraordinary roles they can play on earth.

The author and the implied reader of Job 38:28 are surely aware of the relevance of rain and dew in the arid land of Israel. Ancient Palestine was a land whose fertility depended exclusively on the fall of the yearly rain (Deut. 10:11-17). Due to its ecological relevance for the land of Israel, rain was even the subject of prayer (1 Sam. 12:17). That is why the aim of the Sukkot festival during the days of the Temple's reconstruction was to assure the fall of rain.[61]

During the dry season, dew was a very significant source of water. It is for this reason that rain and dew occur together so many times in many parts of the Bible (e.g. Deut. 32:2). The issue is that, apart from human efforts at water-storage and irrigation, crops that grow during summer (olives, figs and grapes) depend on dew, especially in the central coastal plain where dew contributes up to 55mm of water per year.[62] Indeed, dew cover is so plentiful that Gideon could wake up early in the morning and wring a bowlful of water from his fleece (Judg. 6:38). In this arid zone, the amount of collected dew can exceed that of rainfall, and at times can even be the *only* source of liquid water for plants and survival.[63]

In Gen. 27:28, dew is part of the blessings that Isaac entrusted to his son Jacob. The withdrawal of dew was regarded as a curse from God (2 Sam. 1:21). In 2 Sam. 17:12 and Ps. 110:31, dew is viewed as a symbol

---

59. Habel, *Job*, 542.

60. L. A. Schökel and J. L. Díaz, *Job: Commentario Teológico Y Literario* (Madrid: Cristiandad, 1983), 560.

61. Raphael Patai, 'The Control of Rain in Ancient Palestine: A Study in Comparative Religion', *HUCA* 14 (1939): 253.

62. See M. Gilead and N. Rosenan, 'Ten Years of Dew Observation in Israel', *IEJ* 4, no. 2 (1954): 120–3.

63. Ninari Agam and Pedro R. Berliner, 'Dew Formation and Water Vapor Absorption in Semi-arid Environments: A Review', *Journal of Arid Environments* 65 (2006): 572.

of wealth, and as an emblem of fraternal love and harmony in Ps. 133:3. Rain and dew are therefore seen not only as two important sources of water from the sky, but also as falling and acting without human effort. As Mic. 5:7 declares:

> Then the remnant of Jacob, surrounded by many peoples, shall be like dew from the LORD, like showers on the grass, which do not depend upon people or wait for any mortal. (NRSV)

It is, thus, implicit in Job 38:28 that the falling of rain and dew is not an accidental event, even though Job does not understand it, but a proof of the deeper order in nature. Rain and dew are so relevant in ancient Israel that the simile in Hos. 6:3 can say that YHWH will come to Israel like the spring rains that water the earth. Hosea 14:6 takes this further, saying that God will be like the refreshing dew of Lebanon for Israel. Isaiah 26:19 expresses the idea that certain dead people could receive unction of the vivifying dew to bring them back to life. This refreshing power of dew will make the dust bring back the dead.

Other forms of moisture include frost and ice (Job 38:29-30). Psalm 78:47 depicts frost as a life-threatening water-related phenomenon that can destroy a sycamore tree, while Zech. 14:6 views the day of the Lord as lacking threats of cold and frost. Ice is often depicted as something that cannot last, something temporary that disappears with a rise in temperature (Job 6:16-17). And yet, in Job 38:29-30 ice plays a significant role of hiding the face of the Deep (תהום), together with its chaotic terrors, from created order. In Job 38:16-17, Job is rhetorically exposed to massive unruly secrets that keep the תהום:

> [16] Have you gone to the springs that fill the sea, or walked about in the recesses of the deep? [17] Have the gates of death been revealed to you, or have you seen the gates of deep darkness? (NRSV)

Briefly, the whole strophe of Job 38:28-29 focuses the reader's attention on the diverse and amazing life-giving functions that the enlisted water-related phenomena play in nature. The rain and dew have no father, but play a major role in creation, to which humans are witness. Though the water of the sea is notoriously unruly (Job 38:16-17) and impossible to collect once it is spilled on the ground (2 Sam. 14:14; Ps. 22:15), God is able to gather the water up into small, delicate drops of dew, distributing it over the surface of the earth. This God-given water source plays a significant role in agriculture and involves no human effort. The slim rocks of frost and huge chunks of ice hide the terror of the Deep. The water-related phenomena are viewed in their own right, in relation to their 'way' (דרך) in the created order, and not for how they can be useful for humans.

3.5.4.4. The role of constellations related to water (Job 38:31-33). The four constellations in this strophe are all connected with the coming of rains. The identity of Pleiades and Orion is widely accepted, while Mazzaroth and Aldebaran still give rise to debate.[64] The presence of these four constellations here is perhaps due to their importance for their rain-predicting function. Job's ability to establish or influence these stars is then challenged. In other words, if Job was responsible for the governing of the universe as he earlier alleged, he would at least need to manage the rain-bringing stars, whose function is vital for life on earth. It should be noted that stars were generally believed to exert influence on the seasons and weather on Earth (see Gen. 1:14-16).

The expression 'bind (קשר) the Pleiades and loose (פתח) the cords of Orion' (v. 31) presumes the ability to establish these stars in their places, which are respectively the portent of spring and herald of winter.[65] In other words, the phrase to 'bind' the Pleiades would mean, functionally, to check the spring rains that they release, while 'loosing' Orion's belt would be to disable the autumn rains.[66]

As we can see, the issue here is not about the creation of these stars, but rather the controlling of their role as omens of spring or autumn rains. In fact, ancient people believed that the stars were suspended from the sky by a cord, which could also be used to move them from side to side and thus control the seasons. The context suggests the question whether Job, like God, can control their supposed seasonal influences.

The phrase 'bring out (יצא) Mazzaroth and guide (נחה) Aldebaran with its Hyades' in Job 38:32 refers to the same rhetorical questions posed to Job. The verb יצא also occurs in Isa. 40:26 in relation to the idea of God 'calling out' the stars one by one by their names, while in Neh. 4:15 it refers to the 'coming out' of the stars. Job is asked whether he can bring out the star known as Mazzaroth into the night sky. The action of guiding (נחה) the star called Aldebaran with its train (Hyades) would also relate to the same challenge. What is important here is that all four stars are related to the coming of rain. Like Gen. 1:14-18, the Joban text is not

---

64. See Godfrey R. Driver, 'Two Astronomical Passages in the Old Testament', *JTS* 7 (1956): 1–11.
65. Clines, *Job 38–42*, 1113.
66. Driver, 'Two Astrological Passages', 7.

concerned with the identity of the stars, but with their role as signs for time/seasons.

Importantly, in 38:33, Job is challenged about the laws of the sky on earth. Not only were the stars believed to influence seasons and events on earth, but also the שמים (sky) itself impacts life on earth. The word שמים is closely related to water in ancient cosmogonies. As stated above, the words denoting sky in the Semitic languages are all spelled by prefixing ש to words meaning water.[67] The word שמים in Hebrew and Aramaic, as well as *shamu* in Akkadian, could therefore be seen as terms combining 'of/one of which' (ש) and 'waters' (מים), thereby indicating the assumption that the sky is 'one of the waters/of the waters'.[68] This would explain why the role of שמים (sky) in Gen. 1:6 is *only* to separate the מים above from the מים below.

Given the rain context of the text, it seems that the governance of the upper-waters (water above, שמים) falling earthward is one of the laws/ordinances referred to in Job 38:33. The related text in Job 28:26 affirms that the rain does not happen accidentally, but follows a rule (חוק) set for it. We are not dealing here with the rules that govern the movements of the stars (as in Isa. 47:13), but with the connection of a given star with the spring or autumn rainy seasons.

The book of Job provides a comprehensive rebuttal of Job's allegations. God's response in Job 38:33 points to the cosmic order in which earth and sky are united by 'laws' written in the sky that exercise their rule over the earth, especially in relation to rain provision on earth.

3.5.4.5. *The clouds as water-carriers (Job 38:34-38)*. Job 38:34-38 describes the falling of rain from the clouds as a response to the voice of God. The whole strophe is about the majestic control of God over the rains (vv. 34-35), animals' prediction of the arrival of rain (cock and ibis, v. 36), and a famous image of the sending down of the rains and their effects on earth (vv. 37-38).

In contrast to Elihu's speech in Job 36:26–37:13, where the clouds with their water and lightning are couched as life-giving or life-threatening, these water-related phenomena are primarily presented as manifestations of God's involvement in his universe and his skill in its maintenance.

---

67. Ellen van Wolde, 'Facing the Earth: Primeval History in a New Perspective', in *The World of Genesis: Persons, Places*, ed. Philip R. Davies and David J. A. Clines (Sheffield: Sheffield Academic, 1998), 24.

68. Min Suc Kee, 'A Study on the Dual Form of Mayim, Water', *JBQ* 40, no. 3 (2012): 187.

By the question 'can you lift up your voice…?' (v. 34) Job is challenged about whether the abundant waters-above will obey his command and fall down the way they respond to God's order. With an ironic tone, it is implied that even were Job to shout as loudly as possible, his voice would not even reach the clouds, the carriers of waters-above (Job 36:29) that fall earthward as rain (v. 35).

The ideal is to reinforce the intrinsic worth of nature and human limits in controlling nature, especially the upper-waters, clouds or the lightning. What is interesting is that the text presents water-related phenomena as 'subjects that can hear the voice', ones able to answer 'here we are' (הננו). The word הננו presents the lightning as servants acting as full subjects to accomplish a particular mission, the way Samuel (1 Sam. 3:8) or Isaiah (Isa. 6:8) replied to God's voice.

Ecologically speaking, the clouds, the torrents of waters/rains and their accompanying lightning have intrinsic worth and voice, and they purposely act in relation to the created order. God is apparently challenging Job (i.e. human beings) to reconsider his (their) claim that nature testifies to the tyranny of God, and instead discover the voice and intrinsic value of the earth teaching God's wisdom in nature.

The idea of the wisdom of God in nature continues in v. 36, which is a problematic text for scholars. Any rendering of the verse as being about the wisdom of the clouds would be in line with the meteorological context of the text. It must, however, be admitted that it sounds strange to attribute wisdom to the clouds. There are good reasons for seeing this verse as being about the wisdom and understanding of the ibis and the cock, since both birds are often seen in the ancient Near East as foretellers of the arrival of rain from the clouds.[69]

The ibis (טחות) was famously respected for its ability to foretell the rising of the Nile in Egypt, while the cock (שכוי) was valued for its capacity to forecast the rain from the clouds.[70] Job 12:7-8 supports the idea that certain animals and birds have wisdom:

> [7] But ask the animals, and they will teach you; the birds of the air, and they will tell you; [8] ask the plants of the earth, and they will teach you; and the fish of the sea will declare to you. (NRSV)

---

69. John J. Peters, 'The Cock in the Old Testament', *JBL* 33, no. 2 (1994): 152–56.

70. Antonin Jaussen, 'Le coq et la pluie dans la tradition palestinienne', *RB* 33 (1924): 574–82.

The rising of the Nile and the coming of rains from the sky are two phenomena that fit with the main theme of the text. Therefore, Today's English Version (TEV) simply rendered Job 38:36 as:

> Who tells the Ibis that the Nile will flood? Or who tells the Rooster that the rain will fall?

The response is obviously God. The text implies that these birds have wisdom (חכמה) and understanding (בינה) greater than normal, inserted in them by God. By contrast, Job/humans lack(s) this skill of foretelling the rains in addition to his/their inability to command the cloudburst and the lightning. These birds are only a testimony to the actions of the clouds, which are like water-skins pouring down rain earthward.

In this sense, Job 38:37 depicts how, in order to bring rain on earth, God first counts (ספר) the clouds before tilting (שכב) or literally 'to cause to lie down' these 'water jars' or water-skins so that their contents spill out and fall on earth. Rain therefore reaches the earth directly from the clouds, since:

> As the celestial reservoir contains the water already in liquid form and ready to come down as rain, the most obvious hypothesis would seem to be that the water passed through the firmament into the clouds to be carried by them to that part of the earth which was to receive the rain.[71]

Therefore, the verb ספר in Job 38:37 about the sky denotes the right assessment of the clouds' water as their contents must only be poured out with deliberate purpose. The effect of rain from the clouds is the accumulation of the dust into a compact mass (v. 38). Job 38:38 probably implies the early rains of October–November that fall down after the summer heat and soak the soil. Hillel views this natural phenomenon as a sign of the fertility because:

> The effectiveness of rain in sustaining crops depends on the presence of a receptive and retentive soil. To be productive, the soil must be able to absorb the rainwater rather than shed it; it must store the moisture in the rooting zone of the crops to be grown.[72]

---

71. Sutcliffe, 'The Clouds as Waters', 100.
72. Hillel, *The Natural History*, 146.

This clue testifies to the text's consciousness of the preciousness and intrinsic value of water contained in the clouds, which is to be poured out for the purpose of enabling agricultural fertility. Humans do not control this phenomenon.

3.5.4.6. Eco-theological synthesis. The above analysis shows that all the water-related phenomena depicted are viewed for their intrinsic value and purpose. The purpose and intrinsic worth of hail and snow are shown in the fact that these water-related phenomena are not only kept in treasuries (places), but are also designed to be used during specific times (of scarcity and war) (Job 38:22-23). The occurrence of the word דרך in 38:24-25 implies that the meteorological forces accompanying rain (wind and lightning) respect a fixed course in accordance with a deep order in the cosmos.

In addition, Job 38:25-27 turns to the significance of the פלג לשטף (torrential rains) and thunderstorm (חזיז), which not only follow fixed routes and ways (תעלה and דרך), but also supply life-giving water to the land where no one lives (v. 26). In contrast to Elihu's speech, rain is not viewed for its usefulness for humans, but for its own value – its ability to create life in a desolate land. The target of the rain here is not just the fruitful land worked to feed people as in Job 36:27-28, but the wilderness, a home for other creatures.

Later, Job 38:31-33 turns to the four stars related to the coming of rain. Like Gen. 1:14-18, the main issue is not the identification of these stars, but rather their role as signs for time and seasons. In this sense, the principle of purpose is highlighted in v. 33 that the earth and the sky are connected by 'laws' written in the sky that exercise their rule over the earth, especially in relation to rain provision on earth.

Finally, Job 38:34-38 presents the clouds as water-carriers. What is interesting is that the text presents the rainstorm/thunderstorm as subjects that can hear the voice and answer 'here we are'. The Hebrew, הננו, presents the rainstorm/lightning as servants acting as subjects to accomplish a specific mission the way people responded to God's call. This is ecologically insightful, indicating that nature can express itself and raise its voice. The text also refers to birds that can sense the coming of rain, a skill that humans lack.

3.6. Comparative Conclusion

In addition to offering a general introduction on the book of Job and an overview on water in the book, this chapter involved the analysis of three different texts from three main characters of the book: Job, Job's friends and God. I have tried to discern the voice and the intrinsic value of water and water-related phenomena and how they are presented as acting purposefully according to certain rules within the created order.

Job 14:7-12 exclusively views water as having inherent value and a life-giving function. This ecological awareness is stated in its power to revive a dead tree (vv. 7-9) and in comparing human death with the vanishing perennial bodies of water. However, the absence of water (drought) as a metaphor for death is life-threatening in view of the effects of the drying up of the Nile River in Isa. 19:5-10.

Unlike Job's speech in Job 14:7-12, Elihu's speech in Job 36:26–37:13 is explicit about the potential of water as a source of both life and death. Job 37:13 concludes that God uses water and water-related phenomena for curse or for blessing. However, the text is highly anthropocentric since humans are the sole beneficiaries of the rain (36:27-28).

In contrast to Elihu's speech, God's words in Job 38:22-38 depict water-related phenomena for their own worth regardless of the interest of humans. In contrast to Elihu, rain is not viewed for its usefulness for humans, but for its own value, raining on places empty of human life. The target of the rain here is not just the fertile land worked to feed people, as in Job 36:27-28, but the desert and desolate land. The water-related phenomena are also presented in interconnectedness with other nature images (stars, sky, cock and ibis) for a specific purpose.

This is proof that the Old Testament wisdom books contain ecological insights on water that scholars have missed for years. The fact that water-related phenomena respond as subjects is specific to the book of Job. A number of the words used in the analysed verses are *hapax legomena*, a feature that serves to emphasise the book of Job's distinctive perspective. The text refers to the 'storehouses' of snow and hail, the unending course of rain to the land empty of human life, and the theme of punishing and blessing by the same water-related phenomenon (Job 37:13), which explicitly appears again only in Wis. 11:2-14 and 19:1-9.[73]

The next chapter focuses on retrieving ecological insights of water and water-related phenomena in the book of Proverbs.

---

73. It will be shown later that these texts of the book of Wisdom of Solomon explicitly interpret the traditions of Exodus not from a human (i.e. Israel's) perspective, but see elements of creation, especially water-related phenomena, as fashioned afresh to be an instrument of life and death.

Chapter 4

WATER AND WATER-RELATED PHENOMENA IN THE BOOK OF PROVERBS

4.1. Introduction

This chapter attempts an eco-theological reading of certain texts of the book of Proverbs containing references related to water. Notably, these are presented either as a metaphor for human matters (Prov. 5:15-20, 9:13-18 and 25:23-26), or as real, physical entities (Prov. 3:19-20 and 8:22-31).

4.2. References to Water in the Metaphorical Texts of Proverbs

The selected metaphorical texts in this study are Prov. 5:15-20; 9:13-18 and 25:23-26. The three texts will be examined in turn.

4.2.1. Water and Water-related Phenomena in Proverbs 5:15-20

4.2.1.1. *Major textual variant in Proverbs 5:16.* The jussive form, יפוצו, in v. 16 of the MT reads 'Let your springs flow into the streets'. This reading is adopted by many modern translations, including the CJB and JPS. The MT reading would, however, contradict the claim of v. 15, confining sexual activity within a marriage framework. The LXX, for example, realised the problem, and translated the verse as 'lest your springs overflow like a stream in the open street', adopting the Greek negative preposition μή (lest) of the Codex Vaticanus in the sense of preventing infidelity by one's wife.

Chisholm thinks that Prov. 5:16 implies that one's wife may satisfy or attract many men just like a prostitute.[1] The verse is understood in

---

1. Robert B. Chisholm Jr, 'Drink Water from Your Own Cistern: A Literary Study of Proverbs 5:15-23', *BSac* 157 (2000): 400.

the sense that the husband's unfaithfulness can lead his wife to adultery. This interpretation, which is adopted by BFC translation, is unlikely, given that it is not even certain whether the particle μή belonged to the Greek original text as it is absent in important manuscripts, such as the Alexandrinus and Sinaiticus.

Given the problem, others have rendered the verse in such a way that it indicates the result: 'and so your springs will flow'. The translation understands 'springs' and 'streams' as offspring in the sense that if someone restricts his sexual activity to his wife, he will have many legitimate children in the community (see JPS). Yet, this translation is also dubious because, as far as I can determine, nowhere in the Bible do springs/streams of water refer to descendants.

Another option has been to resolve the matter by suggesting that the text is about 'private' versus 'common' property: one's cistern (wife) as against springs of water (harlots) in the open squares – the water that belongs to you alone contrary to waters which are available in public areas.[2] The weakness of this reading resides in its failure to explain how the expression יהיו־לך לבדך (let them [springs/fountains] be yours alone) in v. 17 could refer to prostitutes (harlots).

The possible sense of Prov. 5:16 seems to be that this verse is a rhetorical question expecting a 'No' answer, in the sense that springs and streams of water refer to the husband's sexuality which must be used only within the framework of marriage. Skehan[3] explains that v. 16 might have been introduced by איך (how should, see v. 12), which was probably left out due to an error of haplography since the preceding word is בארך (your well, v. 15b).

4.2.1.2. *Translation.* The present translation draws on the NRSV, except at v. 16, which is the fruit of our textual discussion above.

> [15] Drink water from your own cistern,
> flowing water from your own well.
> [16] *How should your springs be scattered abroad,*
> streams of water in the streets?
> [17] Let them be for yourself alone,
> and not for sharing with strangers.
> [18] Let your fountain be blessed,
> and rejoice in the wife of your youth,

2. Paul A. Kruger, 'Promiscuity or Marriage Fidelity? A Note on Proverbs 5:15-18', *JNSL* 13 (1987): 67–8.
3. Patrick W. Skehan, 'Proverbs 5:15-19 and 6:20-24', *CBQ* 8 (1946): 295.

¹⁹ A lovely deer, a graceful doe.
May her breasts satisfy you at all times;
May you be intoxicated always by her love.
²⁰ Why should you be intoxicated, my son, by another woman
and embrace the bosom of an adulteress?

4.2.1.3. Proverbs 5:15-20 in its literary structure. It is widely agreed that the book of Proverbs is by nature a collection of sayings from anonymous sages over a number of generations, at least from Solomon's reign (tenth century BCE) to somewhere during the exile or the postexilic (Persian and Hellenistic) eras, but before Ben Sira (second century BCE).[4] It is also agreed that Solomon is not its author in the modern sense of the term. Instead, authorship was assigned to him in an honorary or pseudepigraphic sense, as was the common custom in the ancient Near Eastern literature. The book is therefore not a single composition, but an anthology of different works consisting of various poems, instructions, speeches and a few sayings dispersed in several collections.

Proverbs 1–9, which is the original literary context of Prov. 5:15-20, constitutes the first section of the book. This section, which consists of twelve wisdom poems,[5] may have formerly stood as an independent book prior to the editorial composition. It is thought to be the latest redaction[6] due to its precise pedagogic form, its philosophical conceptions, its strict view against certain sins (adultery and robbery), as well as its status as a kind of introductory framework within which to read the rest of the book.[7] Its discourses do not display a logical flow of thought from one instruction to another; rather, they address the issue of seduction from different angles and through distinct rhetorical strategies.[8]

The intention is to prepare young people to face the problems and dangers of the adult world, so that they may become wise and responsible. This can be seen most clearly in those wisdom poems that take the form of being instructions from parent to child (or teacher to pupil), explaining how to make right choices and find the way of wisdom and life rather

---

4. Katharine J. Dell, *The Book of Proverbs in Social and Theological Context* (New York: Cambridge University Press, 2006), 19.

5. Eleven lectures of the father to his son: 1:8-19; 2:1-22; 3:1-12, 13-35; 4:1-9, 10-19, 20-27; 5:1-23; 6:1-19, 20-35; 7:1-27) and two interludes, extended addresses of the Woman Wisdom (1:20-33; 8:1-36).

6. Dell, *The Book of Proverbs*, 18.

7. Fox, *Proverbs 1–9*, 7.

8. Christopher B. Ansberry, *Be Wise, My Son, and Make My Heart Glad: An Exploration of the Courtly Nature of the Book of Proverbs* (Berlin: de Gruyter, 2011), 44.

than the way to folly and death. It seems significant that Prov. 3:1–4:27 and Prov. 5:1–6:35 – teaching about and warning against adulterous sex – occupy the central position of Prov. 1–9.[9]

Several scholars have argued convincingly that Prov. 5:1-20, comprising teachings from father/teacher to son/pupil about the avoidance of extra-marital sexual relationships is a distinct literary unit, one which is linked to 6:1-19 by an editorial addition, namely 5:21-23.[10] It is understood that apart from the introduction (5:1) and the editorial concluding remarks (5:21-23), 5:1-20 contains two opposite speeches: one commanding avoidance of liaisons with harlots whose way leads to Sheol (5:2-14), and another (5:15-20) advising faithfulness in marriage.

Through the effective use of water-related metaphors, the son's wife in Prov. 5:15-20 is described as an appropriate receptacle (cistern and well) of trustworthy water fit for consumption, while the male semen is cast as springs, streams of water and fountains that should not be spilled or wasted on public areas with harlots (vv. 15-18). In both cases, water and water-related phenomena serve as vehicles for human sexuality. Wells and cisterns are a private property intended for one's own water usage. These images contrast with the common property of streets and squares, locations where the loose women roam.

As mentioned earlier in Chapter 2, a great number of studies have shown that Prov. 5:15-20 is about a father/teacher instructing his son/pupil that sexual happiness is found within the framework of marriage. While I would agree with erotic readings of Prov. 5:15-20, my aim here is the possible retrieval of ecological wisdom suggested by water and water-related metaphors that are found in the text. The question is: What assumptions about or attitudes towards water are reflected in the author's use of water-related management metaphors in an attempt to promote faithfulness in marriage?

4.2.1.4. *The structure of Proverbs 5:15-20.* The text offers an exciting structure as follows:

    A   Drink water from your own cistern/well (v. 15)
    B   Should your springs/fountains be scattered abroad? (v. 16)
    B'   Let them be for you alone, and let them be blessed (vv. 17-18a)
    A'   Be intoxicated by (or rejoice in) your wife (vv. 18b-20)

Table 3. *The Rhetorical Structure of Proverbs 5:15-20*

---

9. Waltke, *Proverbs 1–15*, 12.
10. See Fox, *Proverbs 1–9*, 204.

This structure is a kind of alternating parallelism (ring composition).[11] AA' are employed in such a way that the metaphors of cistern/well in A point to the idea of being intoxicated by one's own wife in A'. The imperative 'drink water (שתה־מים) from your own cistern/well' (v. 15) is used as a synonym for being intoxicated (תשגה, v. 19) by your own wife, in the literal sense of becoming drunk on your wife's water. That is why the Piel (i.e. intensive) form, ירוך (from the root רוה), literarily refers to the plenitude of water in one's wife, which will quench thirst 'all the time' (בכל־עת) and 'always' (תמיד) (v. 19). I will return to the possible ecological significance of this statement later.

Furthermore, the water-related metaphors of springs and streams of water in B point to the idea of responsible water management reflected in B'. Despite the fact that springs and fountain streams are natural ones, it is assumed that they may not last forever. In this sense, B is a rhetorical question that assumes a 'No' answer. This is further commented upon in B', which makes clear that water should not be used for the wrong purposes, and should be consumed within specific limits.

While AA' relate to a wife pictured as a cistern/well of water, BB' refer to male sexuality (semen) as natural water that must be managed properly. The wife's 'water' constitutes the frame of the passage (vv. 15, 18b, 19-20), while the husband's water fills its poetic body (vv. 16-18a). The unit contrasts the dangers from 'outside' (streets) and the security from 'inside' in the sense that one's wife is a shield against such dangers and safeguards a man's wealth or health.[12]

4.2.1.5. *Retrieving the ecological wisdom of Proverbs 5:15-20.* This section is devoted to the retrieval of ecological implication of the expressions wells and cisterns (v. 15ab), as well as springs and fountains (vv. 16-18). Attention will first be given to the relevance of these water-related phenomena in the Old Testament. Following this, an attempt will be made at retrieving the ecological wisdom of Prov. 5:15-20, a text in which water and associated phenomena are used as vehicles for discussing sexuality and fidelity in marriage.

4.2.1.5.1. *Cisterns and wells in the Old Testament (v. 15ab).* Prior to the Late Bronze period, people in Canaan settled only in the Jordan Valley, where life was made possible by the presence of water for agriculture and

---

11. Willis, 'Alternating', 49.
12. William P. Brown, *The Ethos of the Cosmos: The Genesis of Moral Imagination in the Bible* (Grand Rapids: Eerdmans, 1999), 293; and Dell, *The Book of Proverbs*, 41.

livestock.[13] The construction of cisterns and wells eventually facilitated settlement in other areas, namely the highlands of Canaan. The Hebrew expression באר מים חיים (a well of living water), which appears in many parts of the Bible, implies a well with a good water supply, one assured even in times of drought. It was therefore the responsibility of the king (2 Chr. 32:2-5)[14] to dig and manage the well or cistern for a city (Num. 21:18). In this sense:

> Such wells required communal action to dig, maintain, and regulate, and they provided a reliable, long-term supply of water for an entire village or town. Indeed, the well of each town became the center of communal life, an important meeting place but occasionally also a focus of rivalry.[15]

That is why the main concern of the builders of city wells and water tunnels was to secure a reliable water supply that could be protected during a siege. However, given that wells could not be drilled everywhere, the establishment of an abundant and reliable cistern was a considerable boon that boosted human settlement, especially in places where perennial streams and other water sources were not numerous, reliable or voluminous.[16] Modern data from the Palestinian territories show that, due to unreliable water supplies, contemporary Palestinian houses sometimes make use of several water cisterns.[17]

It should be said here that apart from their limited use for garden irrigation, cisterns more likely stored water for human consumption or for watering livestock kept within the settlement. They were used either as a private water supplement during the summer (when wells and springs dried up), or functioned as wells – that is, they were for public use – in places where it was difficult to dig a well.[18] The advantage of a cistern over a well is that cisterns can be constructed anywhere (in gardens, fields, deserts, at home), and in any number of dimensions, since the question of depth is not applicable.

---

13. Reymond, *L'eau*, 123.

14. Philip King and Lawrence E. Stager, *Life in Biblical Israel* (Louisville: John Knox, 2001), 210–23.

15. Hillel, *The Natural History*, 316.

16. R. W. Hamilton, 'Waterworks', *IBD* 4:812.

17. Amnesty International, *Troubled Waters: Palestinians Denied Fair Access to Water: Israel-Occupied Palestinian Territories* (London: Amnesty International, 2009), 15.

18. David C. Hopkins, *The Highlands of Canaan: An Agricultural Life in the Early Iron Age* (Sheffield: Almond, 1985), 95; Reymond, *L'eau*, 134.

The construction of cisterns and wells required hard work, as indicated by several Hebrew verbs used: חפר, to drill, in Gen. 21:30 (חפרתי את־הבאר, I dug the well); נקר, to dig in Isa. 51:1; ברה, to excavate, in Gen. 26:25. Archaeological findings reveal that cisterns were cut directly into bedrock.[19] Given the amount of effort required to make a cistern, one can easily understand why the authors of Deut. 6:11 considered it a privilege for Israel to take over land in which a number of cisterns were already available.

Cisterns and wells also required thorough maintenance checks in order to keep them in good condition. Without maintenance, the cistern would soon become useless. That is why, without mentioning the cause of the fractures, Jer. 2:13 shows how broken cisterns (ברות נשברות) are useless: they cannot hold or maintain water. The reference to a woman covering the well's mouth in 2 Sam. 17:19, as well as the use of the adjective צרה (narrow) for a well in Prov. 18:27, suggest that the makers of cisterns and wells purposefully made the openings as small as possible, most likely in order to prevent evaporation and keep water fresh (Jer. 6:7). In this sense, cistern and well images in Prov. 5:15 imply strong ecological insights about water management.

4.2.1.5.2. *The significance of well/cistern metaphors (v. 15)*. In Prov. 15:15 the relationship between husband and wife is expressed through images of water, a powerful metaphor in an arid land in which sustenance and fertility were important issues of life.[20] One's wife is not *like* but *is* fresh flowing water (נוזלים), as in Song 4:15, where the beloved is 'a garden spring, a well of living water, and flowing water (נוזלים) from Lebanon'. Just as the deeps that fertilise the earth in Prov. 3:20, so the wife is depicted as the source of sexual sustenance – the well and cistern of reliable water.

The instruction to שתה־מים מבורך (drink water from your own cistern) from your own well (מבורך) reflects the context of the eighth century BCE,[21] where private cisterns in homes prevailed over the city reservoirs.[22] The wife's 'water', which frames the passage (vv. 15 and 18b-20), implies the life-giving power attached to the well-managed water in private containers: domestic/home life depended on them. In ancient

---

19. Fontaine, 'Visual Metaphors', 198.
20. Brown, *The Ethos*, 293.
21. It is said in 2 Kgs 18:31 that people will drink water from their own cistern.
22. Fontaine, 'Visual Metaphors', 200.

Israel, where natural rivers were so scarce, it was the life-giving rainwater collected in cisterns, and fresh water caught in wells hewn into bedrock by hard labour, that ensured the continued survival of humans, their crops and their animals.

The text depicts the wife both as a cistern (בור), a purposefully constructed reservoir used to catch rainfall, and as a well (באר), which is a source of fresh water supplied by an underground spring. This distinction is not merely a poetic wordplay, but a deliberate contrast between human-made and natural sources of water. The text assumes that one's wife plays the role of both a 'basic' and a 'supplementary' source of water (the well and the cistern, respectively). Ecologically speaking, the text assumes that there will be no water shortage no matter the season/time, on condition that water is maintained in reliable infrastructures.

The Hebrew word נזלים (v. 15b) elsewhere refers to streams bubbling from a rock in the desert (Ps. 78:16), the streams of Egypt (Ps. 78:44), streams produced by rainfall (Isa. 44:3) and the waves of the Red Sea (Exod. 15:8). In both Song 4:15 and Prov. 5:15, the expression means living water. The restriction מארך מתוך (from your own well) thus implies that public wells and cisterns – ones not managed by you – are not to be trusted. In this sense, a prostitute (a public well/cistern) is equated to a deep pit (שוחה) and a narrow well (Prov. 23:27), a source of danger. That is why cisterns and wells were from time to time used as prisons, since escape was not possible without the help of others (Gen. 37:20; Isa. 24:22; Zech. 9:11).

The metaphor of a wife as cistern/well reinforces the intrinsic value of water, which should be contained and restrained in reliable private receptacles, in contrast to public vessels accessible for everyone. It is only this kind of container that can reliably hold water. The breasts (דדיה) of a wife must intoxicate (ירוך) the husband at all times (בכל־עת) and for always (תמי) (v. 19).

The sage continues by equating male sexuality with springs and fountains, which are also two vital water-related phenomena in Israel (vv. 16-18).

4.2.1.5.3. *Springs and fountains in the Old Testament (vv. 16-18)*. In Gen. 1:6-10, the created order resulted from the separation of the primal waters. This was achieved by means of a dome (רקיע), and resulted in the waters-above and the lower-waters, including the seas and underground waters. The lower-waters were referred to as תהום, which constantly threatened to break out and turn into chaos the created order. Despite being part of תהום, springs and fountains represent positive aspects, since they provide the earth's surface with life-giving and controlled water.[23]

Springs and fountains are formed by natural outflows of underground water to the surface of the earth at places where the underground water-resistant rock level meets the ground surface. As natural features, they stand in contrast to humanmade wells and cisterns. The porous state of limestone in the area occupied by ancient Israel favoured the formation of springs and fountains. Good use of such springs resulted in the building of terrace systems below the springs/fountains for irrigation purposes. Springs often determined the location of human settlements. This is underlined by the frequency of the root עין (spring) in place names: עין־דר (Josh. 17:11); עין־גדי and עין עגלים (Ezek. 47:10); עין־גנים (Josh. 15:34); עין גדי (Josh. 15:62); עין־חדה (Josh. 19:21); עין־הקורא (Judg. 15:19); עין רמון (Neh. 11:29), and so on.

Topographically, Canaan has a limited number of effective fountain streams which flow for a few hours after each rain shower in the Negev,[24] for a few days in the Judean uplands and for a few weeks in the north.[25] Most streams were ephemeral, meagre and subject to fluctuations, as they are affected by the rainfall of the previous winter. Even the perennial streams that are nurtured by upflowing groundwater renewed by seasonal precipitation are reduced to a mere trickle during the summer season.[26]

Feliks asserts that 'there is no evidence that in ancient times there were more than the hundreds of small springs and the few moderate and large fountains which now exist'.[27] The metaphorical language of Prov. 5:16 about avoiding scattering the springs (water spill) on the streets is possibly informed by the ecological awareness of the scarcity of this natural resource. Proverbs 25:25 serves to highlight the significance of a scarce source of water becoming polluted. I will come back to the ecological significance of these texts later.

Furthermore, in Canaan, with its soft limestone geology, most springs carve themselves into deep channels, meaning that they tend to flow through deeply incised valleys with limited floodplains. As a result of this naturally occurring phenomenon, the extent of areas potentially irrigable by fountains and streams remains quite limited. Indeed, this factor reduces

23. Frances Klopper, 'The Rhetoric of Conflicting Metaphors: A Fountain Desired in the Song of Songs but Abhorred in Leviticus', *OTE* 15, no. 3 (2002): 676.
24. The Hebrew word for Negev literally means 'dried up'.
25. Hopkins, *The Highlands*, 95.
26. Efraim Orni and Elisha Efrat, *Geography of Israel* (Philadelphia: Jewish Publication Society, 1973), 441–2.
27. Yehuda Feliks, 'Agriculture in the Land of Israel', *EncJud* 2:388.

agricultural activities in other areas where water could be intercepted, distributed and stored during the seasonal flow of the streams.[28]

It should come as no surprise that springs and fountains were considered to be a manifestation of God's care in the arid land. That is why God's special concern/care for the poor and needy is pictured in terms of providing fountains and springs in Isa. 41:17-18. Against this backdrop, let us now assess whether these water-related phenomena offer ecological wisdom in Prov. 5:16-18, where they are equated with male sexuality in a marriage.

4.2.1.5.3. Ecological insights of springs/fountain images (vv. 16-18). The rhetorical question in v. 16 – 'Should your springs flow into the streets?' – expects a 'No' answer. The husband must only engage in sexual activity with his wife. This is in accordance with Isa. 48:1, where fountains may mean 'sperm' in the expression וממי יהודה (from the fountains/springs of Judah). As such, the Proverbs text is obviously discouraging the husband's infidelity. The direct order of Prov. 5:16–17 would have been 'Don't look for sexual pleasure in the streets'.

The husband is also a source of water, whose streams are to flow to a limited area, his wife (vv. 16-17), just as springs in Canaan had sharply carved the limestone through which they flow 'all the time' and 'always'. The father/teacher warns that any departure from this instruction will result in the son's springs dissipating to the streets and strangers (vv. 16-17), something that would result in the failing of his life. Streets (חוצה) and squares (רחבות) were often viewed as unsafe places where harlots and bandits lurked (Prov. 1:20; 7:20). The idea behind the verb פוץ (to scatter) does not therefore imply the increase of the springs' water flow, but the waste of this natural resource.

The rhetorical insight behind the text is that adultery will lead, inter alia, to impotence. In more ecological terms, wrong attitudes towards water resources will lead, ultimately, to water depletion. That is why one of the principles of water management in modern Israeli water law states that 'Every person is entitled to use water, as long as that use does not cause the salination or depletion of the water resource'.[29] In a land in which water was scarce, where cisterns were built to store every drop of rainwater for

---

28. Hopkins, *The Highlands*, 95.
29. See Israeli Water Law and Water Authorities. 'Water Law 5719-1959'. Available online: http://www.sviva.gov.il/English/Legislation/Documents/Water%20Laws%20and%20Regulations/WaterLaw1959-Excerpts.pdf (accessed 16 September 2018).

the sake of irrigation and survival, the restriction of avoiding treating water in a haphazard manner reveals that water was considered as:

> Quelque chose de bon, d'utile, mais aussi comme quelque chose dont on risque facilement de manquer.[30]

Proverbs 5:16 is informed by the principle of the intrinsic worth of water, a resource that had to be used sustainably and up to a certain limit. It is not an accident that ancient civilisations flourished in river valleys and undertook extensive programs of spring-water irrigation and water management. In most of these civilisations, water management was part of the royal code of the empire, to the point that:

> To spurn or disrespect the waters was an insult, an act of defiance against a figure of authority with the power to punish.[31]

The needless spilling of water was seen as a disrespectful act towards water and testifies to the ignorance of the notion of sustainability. Just as adultery drains away the life of the self, so water stagnating on the streets is implicated in many diseases in Africa. Proverbs 5:9-10 supports this interpretation, mentioning that sexual liaison with the harlot drains away the man's vigour and wealth. The text is clearly rooted in the desolate Israelite-Arabian context of aridity. The desert issues related to water scarcity may have informed Prov. 5:16, which expresses the need for careful management of the available resources. A parallel Arabian metaphor states: 'Don't pour away your water on the strength of a mirage'.[32]

The spilling of water in the private cistern/well (v. 15) is to be viewed positively, interconnected with the man's life in terms of health and wealth. By contrast, springs spilled in the streets (v. 16) would attract illness and misfortune. Proverbs 5:9-13 mention the dangers of adultery:[33]

> Loss of reputation and health (verse 9), loss of wealth (verse 10), and hence finding oneself on the inevitable path to death and destruction bewailing one's lack of discipline (verses 11–13).[34]

---

30. Reymond, *L'eau*, 2.

31. Ruth A. Morgan and James L. Smith, 'Premodern Streams of Thought in Twenty-First-Century Water Management', *Radical History Review* 116 (2013): 109.

32. Martin H. Manser, *The Facts on File Dictionary of Proverbs: Meaning and Origins of More than 1,700 Popular Sayings* (New York: Facts on File, 2007), 11.

33. Adultery would culminate in auto-destruction and death. In fact, death is the prescribed punishment for adulterers and adulteresses in Lev. 20:10 and Deut. 22:22.

34. Dell, *The Book of Proverbs*, 42.

In this sense, vv. 17a and 18a form a synonymous parallel: the expression 'let them be for you alone' is the synonym of 'let your fountains be blessed'. The image of fountain streams is a significant metaphor for water that unites both the son/husband and the wife. Shared among these two sources (husband and wife), water is mutually given and received, providing life-giving enjoyment. As pointed out by some scholars, the text is not about making children, but sensual enjoyment. The basis for the text is Isa. 36:16, where 'drinking from one's cistern' is a sign of wealth. This joyful pleasure must not be shared with strangers. Brown clearly states:

> Reserved for them alone, the vehicle of life and erotic joy [fountain streams and springs] must not flow beyond their relationship [to the streets]. So also their passionate abandonment: only from the wife [water in private well and cisterns] must the husband become 'always intoxicated' and satisfied with her breasts (vv. 19-20).[35]

The wisdom poem assumes, then, an underlying view that water should not be wasted or used for the wrong purpose. As springs and fountains were scarce and meagre,[36] wasting the overflowing water from these sources could not be tolerated. Proverbs 5:16-18 assumes also that water is a life-giving entity if used in specific limits, the limitations suggested by Wisdom. As we shall see later, woman Folly encourages the breaking of limitations and the drinking of forbidden waters in Prov. 9:17.

So, water management is of paramount importance. Although springs and fountains bubble up by natural means, they call for judicious use, since they were neither numerous nor voluminous in ancient Israel. They were also not viewed as something that would last forever. In the preceding chapter, we saw how the Israelites were aware that even perennial and pre-existing streams could also vanish forever, just as humans are lifeless forever when they die (see Job 14:10-12). Proverbs 5:15-20 thus invites responsible water management.

---

35. Brown, *The Ethos*, 294.
36. Ancient Israel had tiny streams which barely sufficed for drinking water, alongside which the village women and girls sat and talked while waiting their turn to fill their jars, sometimes until late at night. See http://www.biblehistory.com/links.php?cat=39&sub=793&cat_name=Manners+%26+Customs&subcat_name=Springs+%26+Fountains (accessed 11 August 2014).

4.2.2. Water and Water-related Phenomena in Proverbs 9:13-18

4.2.2.1. Introduction. While the potential of water as source of life and death is mainly found in Prov. 9:17-18, I have decided to examine the wide passage, namely 9:13-18, since vv. 17-18 would not make sense if they were detached from their immediate literary context. Furthermore, the whole text is not about water, but uses water imagery to warn against adulterous attitudes.

4.2.2.2. Translation of Proverbs 9:13-18. Unlike Prov. 5:15-20, Prov. 9:13-18 does not present major textual problems, except that the LXX has added to v. 18 a fascinating statement urging the son to avoid foreign water (woman). The following translation draws on the NRSV that reads:

> [13] The foolish woman is loud;
>   she is ignorant and knows nothing.
> [14] She sits at the door of her house,
>   on a seat at the high places of the town,
> [15] calling to those who pass by,
>   who are going straight on their way,
> [16] 'You who are simple, turn in here!'
>   And to those without sense she says,
> [17] 'Stolen water is sweet,
>   and bread eaten in secret is pleasant'.
> [18] But they do not know that the dead are there,
>   that her guests are in the depths of Sheol.[37]

4.2.2.3. Social and literary contexts of Proverbs 9:13-18. This text is not about water, but in vv. 17-18 associates woman Folly with 'stolen sweet water', with her way leading to 'the depths of Sheol'. Proverbs 9:13-18 as a whole lies in the social context of refuting the strange or foreign woman, someone who is referred to as an adulterous woman threatening to undermine the order of the family and the society (Prov. 2:16-19; 5:1-23;

---

37. The LXX added a fascinating explanation here:
> [18a] Therefore, run away, do not delay in this place,
>   neither fix your eyes upon her,
> [18b] for thus will you go through foreign water
>   and pass through a foreign river.
> [18c] However, abstain from foreign water
>   and do not drink from a foreign fountain,
> [18d] that you may live for a long time
>   and years of life may be added to you.

6:20-35; 7:1-27). The portrayals of this strange woman have given rise to a variety of interpretations about the nature and function of the 'strange' or 'foreign' woman.[38]

Despite the existence of various descriptions of this woman, the father/teacher seems to present her as a single figure, the wife of another man or an adulterous woman. Several parental lectures portray the strange woman as a threat similar to the waters of Sheol (Prov. 2:18) or water in public areas (5:16-17). With her love understood as 'stolen sweet water' (9:17), she represents a loose woman violating her marriage (2:17) and seeking to seduce young men into an adulterous relationship (6:26; 7:10-21) that can last only for one night (7:18). She is thus not a foreigner from a distant land, but the woman next door, perhaps the neighbour's wife.[39]

The immediate literary context of 9:13-18 is the final interlude (vv. 1-18) of chs. 1–9, in which Woman Wisdom – embodying life (vv. 1-6) – stands in contrast to Woman Folly (a synonym of death, vv. 13-18). The two women (Prov. 9:1-6 and 9:13-18) are, structurally speaking, parallel, with both inviting those without sense to partake of their solid and liquid refreshment. However, while Woman Wisdom's banquet leads to life, the Woman Folly's leads to death.

Woman Folly is nothing more than the אשה זרה (loose woman) characterised by turbulence (7:11; 9:13), ignorance (5:6; 9:13), and whose path leads to the depths of Sheol (2:18; 5:5; 7:27; 9:18). While the text depicts Woman Wisdom as a noble host endowing life to her devotees (9:1-6), Woman Folly is depicted as a noisy hostess sitting (ישׁב) at the doorway of her house, and on a seat (כסא) at the heights of the city (9:13-14) trying to lure the naïve with her seductive words and 'stolen' meal.

Unlike Woman Wisdom, who builds (בנה) her house on seven pillars and invests energy and care in preparing her banquet before sending out her maidens and inviting guests (9:1-3),[40] Woman Folly is lazy and inept for she only 'sits' outside her house (לפתח ביתה). Woman Folly neither builds a house nor prepares a banquet; rather, she calls to passers-by from her chair 'outside' (streets/heights) offering 'stolen water' and 'hidden' food. Fox[41] indicates that the words 'sitting at the door of her house' relate to the way in which harlots presented themselves as available in ancient

---

38. For all leading interpretations, see Ansberry, *Be Wise*, 50–3.
39. Brown, *The Ethos*, 290.
40. This annotation suggests that unlike Woman Folly, Wisdom resides inside her house where the guests are supposed to find her (Prov. 9:4).
41. Fox, *Proverbs 1–9*, 301.

times. Therefore, the corresponding water-related metaphor of Woman Folly contrasts with that of the wife in Prov. 5:15, who is framed as a man's own well/cistern:

> Wells and cisterns tended to be private property for one's own water usage, images contrasted with the common property of streets and squares where the seductive woman roams.[42]

In this sense, Woman Folly is ambiguously portrayed in Prov. 9:17–18 as having 'sweet water' and 'leading to the depths of Sheol', since her water is drunk in secret or stolen. It should be stated that the ecological retrieval of the text will mainly concern these two verses. In the following section, I will investigate the ecological insights behind the sage's use of this metaphor linking adulterous behaviour with the 'stolen water', which leads to 'the depths of Sheol'.

4.2.2.4. *Ecological significance of Proverbs 9:17-18*

4.2.2.4.1. *Stolen water is sweet (v. 17)*. As noted above, the addressee in Prov. 1–9 is set in a liminal situation through a number of wisdom poems. This was shown, for instance, through the root metaphor of a wife depicted as a private well/cistern, implying human effort to hold water in a private container, as well as the command to avoid cheating behaviour consisting of spilling valuable water in public areas – implying the activity of harlots (Prov. 5:15-20). This idea is reflected here in Prov. 9:17, with the difference that it is not the father/teacher who speaks, but Woman Folly advertising that 'stolen water' is sweet.

The water of Woman Folly or an adulterous woman is depicted as stolen, sweet water. This woman, who is depicted in Prov. 23:27 as a deep pit, is cast here as having sweet water whose drinkers are thought to be many, as she advertises to passers-by. This is in contrast to Prov. 5:15, where a cistern/well is the property of one man in his home. Ecologically speaking, this implies that this kind of water is potentially dangerous. Her stolen water and secret bread (9:17) are chiastically paralleled to the bread and wine of Woman Wisdom (9:5).[43]

Indeed, in the biblical lands, where water was a precious commodity whose presence or shortage meant life or death, water theft was certainly committed. Therefore, people secretly emptied their neighbour's tanks and spared their own reserve for the time of drought. Theft and illegal

---

42. Dell, *The Book of Proverbs*, 42.
43. Gale A. Yee, '"I Have Perfumed My Bed with Myrrh": The Foreign Woman in Proverbs 1–9', *JSOT* 43 (1989): 65.

appropriation of water in an arid land has probably informed the use of the water metaphor in this erotic poem. The fact that the words 'stolen water is sweet' are put in the mouth of Wisdom Folly, implies that the sage is aware of water theft, a practice that would certainly undermine the wellbeing of the society.

The sage may have been informed by knowledge of conflicts arising from water theft. Especially in Gen. 26:18, we see the herders of Isaac and Gerar quarrelling over the ownership of a springing well/fountain water, implying that some are 'stealing water from others' wells'. It is possible that 'stolen waters are sweet' was a proverbial expression used to prohibit illicit gains. An ideal society is the one in which each member drinks from his or her own well (Prov. 5:15; 2 Kgs 18:31; Isa. 36:16), a reliable supply of living water.

Water is here presented with life-giving (sweet) potential. Yet such sweetness lasts only up to the morning (i.e. it is temporary), because it is stolen or drunk in secret (see Prov. 7:18). This proverb is particularly important in the modern world, where water shortages can arise through the theft of aqueduct materials or the illegal appropriation of water. 'Stolen' means that this water is illicitly gained. The LXX simply termed it as foreign water and foreign fountain (Prov. 9:18c).

In fact, both Prov. 5:15-20 and 9:17 reflect the time and context in which private wells/cisterns and their protection were important. It is implied in 9:17 that conflicts sometimes arose around private sources of water, which were often sealed and protected from the use of others.[44] People could either make their own wells/cisterns (5:15-20) or else simply steal water from neighbours' vessels (9:17). While the attitude of 5:15 was undoubtedly encouraged, the nefarious activity hinted at in 9:17, though prohibited, clearly offered the easiest solution to water shortage, given the hard work involved in the drilling of a well/cistern.

Woman Folly implies that legitimate pleasure (water) from one's wife (well/cistern) is deficient, and has to be supplemented by clandestine taste, stolen pleasure (water) that has a special flavours that delivers a feeling of surplus.[45] Woman Folly offers an insight that people might find her reasoning easy and attractive. The proverb 'stolen water is sweet' is a half-truth, for although it is pleasant for a while, in the end it is disgusting (Prov. 6:30). The Hebrew words מים־גנובים (stolen water) would indicate

---

44. Hillel (*The Natural History*, 57) comments that conflicts and disputes over territory, defiling rights and, especially, water resources were resolved through negotiation and compromise or violence (force).

45. Fox, *Proverbs 1–9*, 302.

that the sexual pleasure is being taken from a legitimate owner. Hidden food (ולחם סתרים) complements 'stolen water', for as a thief must steal from his victim, so the adulteress hides her theft. The sage continues that the way of Folly leads to Sheol (v. 18).

4.2.2.4.2. *Sheol and waters in the Old Testament.* שאול (sheol) is a unique Hebrew word designating the underworld. It indicates human fate in nearly two-thirds of the relevant texts (41/66 times) where it is used. Etymological study of the word שאול suggests a meaning along the lines of 'a pit of questionings'.[46] In the majority of its usages, Sheol is clearly or implicitly associated with the threatening images of water. Two scholarly explanations have been given to this association between Sheol and water. First, some have seen in such imagery the idea of shades of the dead crossing over water to reach Sheol.[47] Second, others have argued that such language serves as a metaphor for divine judgment, as in the flood stories.[48]

As for the identification of Sheol itself, some think Sheol is a physical location in the deepest recesses of earth, close to the primeval waters.[49] This interpretation perhaps draws on Job 36:5, where the inhabitants of the infernal world are thought to lie under the waters (מתחת מים). Pedersen[50] cautions against defining Sheol as the underworld since in other places Sheol occurs in relation to other threatening bodies, such as desert. It has also been proved that the Hebrew word ארץ means not only earth, but, as in the Ugaritic texts, everything under the sky including the underworld.[51]

Johnston argues that the term Sheol is especially used in contexts of judgment, and is to be construed metaphorically as it often occurs in poetic texts.[52] Therefore, rather than trying to locate Sheol in a recessed place under the earth, it would be wise to focus on the reasons why biblical texts characterised it with threatening aspects. In Isa. 14:11, Sheol relates to worms/maggots, grave in Gen. 37:5, darkness and being forgotten in Job 17:13 and Ps. 88:4-6 and death in Isa. 38:18.

---

46. William F. Albright, 'The Etymology of Šeʾôl', *AJSL* 34 (1918): 210.
47. May, 'Some Cosmic', 14.
48. Peter K. McCarter, 'The River Ordeal in Israelite Literature', *HTR* 66 (1973): 405.
49. Rudman, 'The Use of Water', 240–4.
50. Johannes Pedersen, *Israel, its Life and Culture (Parts I-II)* (London: Oxford University Press, 1940), 463.
51. Philip Johnston, 'The Underworld and the Dead in the Old Testament', *Tyndale Bulletin* 45, no. 2 (1994): 417.
52. Tsumura, *The Earth and the Waters*, 72.

In Jon. 2:2-3 Sheol relates to the depths or waters. It must be known that water 'has associations with Sheol since it is a force of chaos and destruction and is also located in the earth's depths'.[53] Jonah 2:2-3 states:

> ² I called to the LORD out of my distress, and he answered me; out of the belly of Sheol I cried, and you heard my voice. ³ You cast me into the deep, into the heart of the seas, and the flood surrounded me; all your waves and your billows passed over me.

The association of Sheol and waters (rivers) in Old Testament poetic texts relates to the conception of ים (sea), תחום or אד (cosmic ocean/river) or נחר (river) as a potential threat that is simply seen as death itself (Gen. 7:35; Job 7:9; Ps. 18:5). It is understood that it is from the flooding sea (Exod. 15:8; Ps. 69:3), its מים רבים (innumerable waters, 2 Sam. 22:17) and its depths (Ps. 88:7) that the dead fall down into and dwell.[54]

Therefore, what biblical texts speak about Sheol would not be a systematic description of 'a physical place' but the feeling of threat that תהום (deep waters, Job 38:16-17) reflected on humans. That is why Sheol is exclusively used in poetic texts, which naturally make use of figurative language.[55]

Psalm 69:1-3 metaphorically claims that the life of the psalmist is threatened by the rushing waters, those raging waters that threatened the created order in Gen. 6–9. The individual engulfed by chaos waters (depths) denotes the passing of that person from the realm of life to that of death (Sheol). Sheol appears along with the primeval chaos (sea/river and the deep) as a threatening entity inspiring death.[56] Waters are not death themselves, but they have life-threatening aspects that can lead to Sheol, death.

4.2.2.4.3. Ecological meaning of Sheol in Proverbs 9:18. In the book of Proverbs, the concept of Sheol is first found in Prov. 1:12 and is usually used to characterise dangers related to an adulterous woman. In Prov. 5:5, the loose woman is depicted as going herself down to Sheol, whereas 9:18 adds that those who enter her house will be brought to Sheol, a place of no return. Here, as in Prov. 7:26-27, the sage does not condemn the woman; instead his focus is on the foolish young men falling into her trap. The 'depths of Sheol/death' (9:18) await them.

---

53. Johnston, 'The Underworld', 416.
54. Reymond, *L'eau*, 213.
55. Robert L. Harris, 'The Meaning of the Word Sheol as Shown by Parallels in Poetic Text', *BETS* 4 no. 4 (1961): 133.
56. Bernard F. Batto, 'The Reed Sea: Requiescat in Pace', *JBL* 102 (1983): 23.

The words עמקי שאול (depths of Sheol) are the equivalent of the depths of an abyss, since in Isa. 51:10 the substantive מעמקי refers to the lowest part of the life-threatening waters of the sea (ים) and many waters bringing death to the created order.[57] It is thus not an accident that the word עמקים relates to the depths in Prov. 18:4 and 20:5.

The LXX's addition of 'foreign waters' as an explanation for Prov. 9:18 is thus significant. In v. 18b, the LXX reads: 'for thus will you go through foreign water and pass through a foreign river'. It seems that the LXX draws on Greek mythology, assuming that one has to cross the life-threatening river Styx on the way to Hades.[58] This assumption links up with the Canaanite myth that the cosmic waters were located at the entrance of the watery abode of Mot (Sheol).[59]

This would imply that ancient Israelites believed that Sheol was located near the deep. That is why death and watery chaos were often paralleled to the point that the expression מים רבים (many waters) simply means Sheol/death in Ps. 69:15-16 and Isa. 43:2. In the ancient Near East, it was believed that on a person's death, he/she would live in an infernal ocean, or must cross the infernal waters before reaching their final place.[60]

It is probable that Prov. 9:18 echoes this conception, mentioning the depths of Sheol as the destiny of those who follow the way of Folly. The same is attested in the epics of Gilgamesh, Aqhat and the Odyssey, where the woman's guests are invited to erotic encounters, but they end up in the underworld.[61] The Strange Woman in Proverbs is therefore linked or associated with the watery chaos that laps at the threshold of the self, threatening to submerge her victims. Proverbs 9:18 thus implies that:

> The chaos waters by their very nature are symbolic of the absence of order [life] and creation... For the writers of the OT [Prov. 9:18], who saw the formation of the individual as part of God's ongoing creative activity (Jer. 1:5; 49:5; Zech. 12:1), and who likewise saw death [Sheol] as a reversal of creation (Gen. 2:7; 3:19; Qoh. 12:7), the deep would be an appropriate image to denote the cessation of life.[62]

---

57. Johnston, 'The Underworld', 416.
58. Johann Cook, *The Septuagint of Proverbs Jewish and/or Hellenistic Proverbs: Concerning the Hellenistic Colouring of LXX Proverbs* (Leiden: Brill, 1997), 474.
59. McCarter, 'The River Ordeal', 405.
60. Reymond, *L'eau*, 212.
61. Clifford, *Proverbs*, 107.
62. Rudman, 'The Use of Water', 244.

Water is presented here with a life-threatening potential. The thieves of water or bread are destined not only for Sheol, but also to have to cross life-threatening waters at the gates of Sheol (see Prov. 18:18 in the LXX). On the basis of this, Haupt has argued that the word Sheol should be written שְׁאוֹל (with ṣerê, not šewa, in the first syllable) from the root Šûḥ (Šaḥt), denoting the idea of sinking into an 'uncomfortable' damp and wet pit.[63] It was thus believed that being in Sheol is like being in a real cistern of water (Ps. 30:2). Certain psalms, 30:2 and 40:3, compare a cistern with the peril of death while affirming that God delivered people by 'drawing (דלה) them from the hole'. Sheol was thus considered to be a great hole located not only under earth, but also under water in the cosmic sea. It seems the Israelites believed that the dead went in a real cistern.

Aware of this threat, the psalmist of Prov. 5:15 commands the son to drink water from his own container (his wife) since the path of public pots (harlots) leads to the depths of Sheol. At Prov. 9:18d, the LXX reads that avoiding the way of the whore will let the young man live for a long time. Water is thus seen to have life-threatening potential associated with death. Just as YHWH restrains and confines the watery chaos by Wisdom (Prov. 8:22-31), one can avoid the depths of Sheol through obedience to the decrees of wisdom. The depths of Sheol are life-threatening water-related phenomena representing the destiny of those who follow the way of Woman Folly.

4.2.3. *Water and Water-related Phenomena in Proverbs 25:23-26*

4.2.3.1. *Introduction.* This section is devoted to the ecological potential of water used as images in Prov. 25:23-26. The metaphor of 'north wind and rains' is used for unexpected conflicts due to a backbiting tongue (vv. 23-24), cold water for a weary person is a vehicle for good news from faraway, whereas a muddied spring or a polluted fountain is a metaphor for the righteous slipping before evil (vv. 25-26). My aim is to determine whether these water-related metaphors offer ecological wisdom.

4.2.3.2. *Translation.* There is considerable debate about whether v. 23 of the Hebrew text should be translated as 'north wind' or 'northwest wind'. My understating of v. 23 aligns with van der Ploeg,[64] who sees the word צפון (north, from the root צפן, hidden) as a paronomasia for hidden tongue in v. 23b. The word-play between רוח צפון (north/hidden wind) and לשון סתר (hidden tongue) implies that just as the north wind is a hidden

---

63. Paul Haupt, 'The Original Meaning of Sheol', *JBL* 36, no. 3-4 (1917): 258.
64. Johannes Petrus M. van der Ploeg, 'Prov. 25:23', *VT* 3 (1953): 189.

(unexpected) source of rain that arrives to expectedly, so secret speech suddenly causes damage from an unexpected location, perhaps a trusted person. The text is thus translated as follows:

> [23] The north [hidden] wind produces rain,
>   and a 'hidden' tongue, [produces] angry looks.
> [24] It is better to live in a corner of the roof
>   than in a house shared with a contentious wife.
> [25] Cool water on a failing throat,
>   is good news from a far country.
> [26] A muddied spring or a polluted fountain
>   is the righteous slipping before the wicked.

4.2.3.3. Literary considerations.

4.2.3.3.1. *General observations.* Proverbs 25 belongs to a larger composition, Prov. 25–27, which is a composite whole attempting to create literary contexts and hermeneutic clues for independent sayings within which they can be understood.[65] As indicated by the mention of wisdom collectors in 25:1, Prov. 25–27 is simply a collection of ancient Hebrew wisdom sayings. The chapters contain not one proverb, but rather a number of proverbs held together by a short wisdom poem to form a new whole, which contains minor units (25:2-27; 26:1-12, 13-16, 17-28; 27:1-22, 23-27).

It is therefore possible that these units were either adapted or created *ad hoc* to play a role in the larger proverbial composition. They were brought together by scribes who selected and structured the proverbs in the standard order in which they are found in collections.[66] This implies that each section is literarily distinct from the other, but has been edited with a view to forming a literary whole (chs. 25–27) in which they reveal more insights from the artful juxtaposition of the individual units. The poet-compiler has also identified and arranged sub-units within these units according to the function they convey in the whole unit.

Our passage, Prov. 25:23-26, is a literary sub-unit of 25:2-27, which is now known as a 'small wisdom book'. This phrase was coined by Bryce, who argued that Prov. 25:2-27 is a distinct literary unit on the basis of its Egyptian parallels and internal stylistic and thematic features. The whole passage is introduced by vv. 2-5, dealing with the book's two principal subjects, the king (vv. 2-3) and the wicked (vv. 4-5), which are further

---

65. Raymond C. van Leeuwen, *Context and Meaning in Proverbs 25–27* (Atlanta: Scholar Press, 1988), 31.
66. Ibid., 37.

developed in vv. 6-15 (the king) and vv. 16-26 (the wicked). For Bryce,[67] the first section (vv. 6-15) of the 'book' deals with the relationship between the courier and his superior, while the second (vv. 16-26) involves various wicked people.

Bryce's argument about the literary unit of Prov. 25:2-27 is widely accepted, though some have questioned the rubrics he assigned to the different sections. Van Leeuwen convincingly pointed out that it is not clear how issues such as 'Sayings' and 'Admonitions' in vv. 6-15 can be subsumed under the 'rubric' of the king or how the hateful friend in v. 17 is a danger *per se*.[68]

Nevertheless, Bryce has carefully identified the main contours of Prov. 25:2-27, especially in his identification of the sub-units of the texts. The identified rubrics can be named differently, as follows. First, 25:2-27 involves another kind of wisdom poems – next to chs. 1–9 – about the court hierarchy and the conflict of the righteous and the wicked. Second, the passage is doubly introduced by vv. 2-3 and 4-5, prior to its two main units: a decalogue of proverbs for courtiers (vv. 6-15) and general human conflicts (vv. 16-26), before ending with a conclusion (v. 27).

Clearly, the literary context of 25:23-26 is 25:16-26, which contains admonitions and sayings related to human matters. Proverbs 25:16-26 involves two sub-units: 25:16-22, which relates to conflict resolution, and 25:23-26, which highlights unexpected conflicts.[69] The following section develops the literary matters of 25:23-26.

4.2.3.3.2. Literary structure of Proverbs 25:23-26. This sub-unit of Prov. 25:16-26 consists of two proverb pairs (vv. 23-24 and vv. 25-26) using water-related metaphors as vehicles to depict unexpected matters. The pairs are organised in such a way that the water metaphor of v. 23 (A) points to the referent in v. 24 (A'), and the water image of v. 25 (B) points to the referent in v. 26 (B'). Verses 23-24 (AA') involve unexpected conflicts due to bad speech, while vv. 25-26 (BB') contrast restoration of a weary person with a wavering righteous person.

Since Prov. 25:23-26 refers to unexpected human conflicts, all the water-related images or metaphors used must be related to this subject in some way. The structure of the text can be presented as follows:

---

67. Glendon E. Bryce, 'Another Wisdom-'Book' in Proverbs', *JBL* 91 (1972): 151.
68. Van Leeuwen, *Context and Meaning*, 24.
69. Bruce K. Waltke, *The Book of Proverbs: Chapters 15–31* (Grand Rapids: Eerdmans, 2005), xiii.

A	North wind producing rain…and a sly tongue bringing an angry look (v. 23)
A'	Bad weather is better than sharing a house with a nagging wife (v. 24)
B	Cold water for a weary person is good news from a distant land (v. 25)
B'	A muddied spring/fountain is a wavering righteous person (v. 26)

Table 4. *The Structure of Proverbs 25:23-26*

Verse 23 is termed an unexpected 'cause and effect proverb' related to arguments of value.[70] One of the basic insights of the wisdom books is that of reward and punishment (see Prov. 26:27 or Sir. 27:27). However, this notion is denied by Job and furthered by Jonah – the claim being that God lets the wicked live, thereby implying the reversal of rules. The same idea is behind Prov. 25:23, where 'north wind' acts against expectations by producing rain that would result in damage just as an unexpected sly speech results in the darkening of the face of the victim.

Verse 24 presents the 'better than' chiasmus of natural-versus-human pattern in which the man ironically prefers to be exposed to a rainstorm rather than being exposed to the 'rainstorms' of bad speech from a contentious wife. This is what Perry calls 'the argument of value', in which all values are either positive or negative – there are no neutral values; it can be termed 'plus versus minus'.[71] Both bad weather and sly speech are negative values, but being exposed to bad weather is more endurable than being exposed to a tempestuous wife.

Verses 25-26 present the argument of value as well. The metaphor of life-giving cool water for a weary person being like good news from faraway is contrasted with the muddied spring or polluted fountain, which is a vehicle for a slipping righteous person before the wicked. All the water-related metaphors reflect abruptness of the referents. This book attempts to determine whether these water images offer ecological wisdom when the text is read through an ecological lens.

4.2.3.4. *Ecological insights of water images in Proverbs 25:23-26.*

4.2.3.4.1. *The rains brought by the north winds as sly tongue's effects (vv. 23-24).* The first proverbial pair uses the theme of unexpected rains deriving from the north wind in order to criticise conflicts arising from a backbiting tongue (v. 23). As such, v. 23a portrays life-threatening rains caused by the north wind, whereas v. 23b highlights angry faces as the

---

70. Theodore A. Perry, *Wisdom Literature and the Structure of Proverbs* (University Park: Penn State University Press, 1993), 75.

71. Ibid., 71.

effect of a backbiting tongue. The word used for rain is גשם, which is related to the October–December heavy rainfalls accompanied by storms. These rains can bring about flash floods that provoke land erosion, especially if occurring at an unexpected time.[72]

The rainfall pattern in Palestine was generally linked with the west winds, which provided gentle rains that were well distributed throughout the growing season. Conversely, untimely and unexpected rains resulted in damage to crops during their most vulnerable stage of growth, as well as violent soil erosion.[73] In this sense, Delitzsch thinks that the expression 'north wind bringing rains' in Prov. 25:23 is geographically inaccurate in Palestine and so should be replaced by the northwest wind.[74] This interpretation overlooks the text's intention of highlighting the idea of unexpectedness.

Indeed, the Israelites expected the west, not the north wind, to bring rain (Lk. 12:4). The cold north wind (Job 37:9) normally cleared the skies (prevents the rainfall) and brought good visibility. Accordingly, the merchants of Ugarit and sea captains prayed for it 'while they were waiting to set out with heavily loaded ships for the main trade targets in the South and Egypt'.[75] Hopkins states it clearly when he says that:

> [The eastern Mediterranean] cyclones bring rain-bearing winds from the southwest and west and are followed by anti-cyclones generating winds out of the northeast and east that bring clear skies.[76]

No rainfall could then be expected from the north wind. The KJV has attempted to resolve this by translating 'the north wind that drives away rain'. As Van der Ploeg observes:

> Lorsque, en Palestine, souffle le vent du nord, tout le monde sait qu'il ne pleuvra pas.[77]

Yet, the proverbs ought to be understood as a riddle whose meaning should be guessed. The relevance of the metaphor in Prov. 25:23 is precisely that rain from a north wind is hidden (רוח צפון תחולל גשם), while

72. Bimson, 'Has the Rain a Father?' 1.
73. Hillel, *The Natural History*, 157.
74. Franz Delitzsch, *Biblical Commentary on the Proverbs of Solomon* (Grand Rapids: Eerdmans, 1950), 168.
75. Cecilia Grave, 'The Etymology of Northwest Semitic ṣapānu', *UF* 12 (1980): 228.
76. Hopkins, *The Highlands*, 80.
77. Van der Ploeg, 'Prov. 25:23', 189.

unexpected and similarly hidden slander brings unexpected damage (סתר נזעמים לשון), an angry face.

The present-day reference to a rainstorm as 'angry weather' unwittingly confirms the metaphor of Prov. 25:23 likening a rainstorm to an 'angry face'.

In other words, just as the rainstorms/clouds darken the sky, slander darkens the face of the victim. The verb תחולל attributes the power of fertility to the north wind, begetting rains (גשם) the way living beings procreate (Deut. 32:18; Isa. 51:2). However, the Polel form of the verb and the abruptness of the rains (גשם) suggest life-threatening aspects denoting that the north wind causes damaging rains just as a backbiting tongue produces an angry face.

'Face' is plural in Hebrew – פנים – denoting that a backbiting tongue does not affect a single being only, but causes problems for many, destroying friendly relations. A slanderous tongue also excites suspicion and enmity in various areas, just as damaging rain causes crisis in society (failure of crops, land erosion, flooding of a human settlement).

Rainfall is a significant climatic factor in the physical existence of people in Israel and agricultural life. The vitality of rainfall for Israel is shown in its various Hebrew words (גשם, מלקוש, יורה, מטר). Genesis 2:5 is explicit that no vegetation had sprung forth because 'the Lord God had not caused it to rain upon the earth'. Proverbs 25:14 compared clouds and wind without rain to one who boasts of a gift never given.

However, the advantage or disadvantage of the rain depended on its season.[78] Accordingly, Deut. 11:14 reports that if one fears the Lord, then 'he will give the rain (מטר) for your ground in its season (בעתו), the early rain (יורה) and the latter rain (מלקוש), and you will gather in your grain, your wine, and your oil'.

Otherwise, unexpected heavy/violent rain occurring in mid-summer, for instance, may damage the crops. Proverbs 25:23 uses the Hebrew word גשם to refer to the heavy winter rains that soak the ground and replenish the cisterns needed for agriculture and survival.[79] The issue is that here they occur at an unexpected time (from the north wind), and thus are potentially just as life-threatening as slanderous speech.

In Prov. 25:23, the damaging result of hidden speech is as life-threatening – causing an angry face on the victim, ופנים נזעמים – as untimely heavy rains (גשם) from the north wind, which result in the failure of crops and ruin.[80] The NIV has rendered the verse as follows: 'Like a north wind

---

78. See Lev. 26:4; Esd 10:13; Jer. 5:24; Ezek. 34:26.
79. King and Stager, *Life in Biblical Israel*, 87.
80. Waltke, *Proverbs 15–31*, 333.

that brings unexpected rain is a sly tongue which provokes a horrified look'. Just as unexpected heavy rains (גשם) are by nature life-threatening, so is a sly secret speech. The metaphor has thus been informed by the idea of untimely rains as a threatening force.

That is why in v. 24 the man prefers to be exposed to a real rainstorm rather than being exposed to the 'rainstorms' of bad speech from a contentious wife. The sage ironically highlights the life-threatening potential of water in a figurative comparison between the north wind and exposure on a corner of the roof. In other words, it is 'better to live in a corner of the roof, unprotected from the rain, than to live within the shared house unprotected from her'.[81]

The point is that the life-threatening effects of bad weather and sudden heavy rains are more bearable than the 'bad weather' that can be caused by a contentious wife. Both the rains and backbiting, sly speech are damaging (v. 23), but being exposed to the bad weather of the north wind's rain is more supportable than living in a house with a tempestuous wife (v. 24). Still, hostile speech is as unexpected and unwelcome as the heavy rains from the north wind. When someone finds out that a secret slanderer is working against them, he or she shows it by his/her angry look, just as the sky is dark (angry) with clouds when a storm is threatened.

Implicitly, Prov. 25:23-24 is a call for changes in behaviour, just as farmers expect the north wind not to bring heavy rains, but to clear the sky. In this sense, rain during the time of harvest is a metaphor for honour attributed to the fool in Prov. 26:1: it is damaging. The New American Standard Bible translates v. 1 as 'So honour is not fitting for the fool'. Just as snow in summer and rain in harvest time are inconvenient/useless, giving honour to a fool will result in boasting and the destruction of others. The text testifies to the awareness of life-threatening aspects of rain occurring at an unexpected time.

4.2.3.4.2. *Metaphor of cold water for a thirsty person (Prov. 25:25).* This verse equates the relief brought by cold water to a weary person with hearing good news from a distant land. While giving water in Prov. 25:21 is an act of charity extended even to an enemy, here in Prov. 25:25 it is a remedy. In Prov. 25:21, giving water is a way of restoring a hurt person in a relationship. Proverbs 25:25, on the other hand, focuses on the life-giving role of 'cold water' to revive a 'weary person' (נפש עיפה). Exodus 17:1-6 shows that for the Israelites, lack of water was equated with death.

---

81. Malbim, *The Commentary*, 262.

In Prov. 5:15, the words מים קרים (cold water) imply the same refreshing function of flowing/running water in a well.

The Hebrew word עיפה in Prov. 25:25 means that the man is completely deprived of energy due to thirst, and so unable and/or unwilling to continue living. The word עיפה derives from the root עיף, which often occurs in Qal form in the Hebrew Bible and refers to a situation of becoming tired.[82] In Gen. 25:29 the word is associated with hunger, while it is connected with exhaustion due to both hunger and thirst in 2 Sam. 17:29. In Judg. 4:21, the verb עיף occurs next to the verb מות in the expression ויעף וימת, referring to the loss of consciousness before death. Proverbs 25:25 implies that the weary person needs water to 'revive' himself and thus refers to the life-giving function of water (see Job 22:7).

This is, in fact, what occurs in Exod. 17:1-6 and Num. 20:11, where Israelites refuse to continue their walk in the wilderness unless Moses gives them water to drink. People in a state of dehydration can no longer endure physical exertion and so need to be given revitalising and life-giving water. Water is thus seen as a life-giving entity, whose presence or absence is closely linked with life or death. As stated earlier in the analysis of Prov. 5:15-20, cisterns, wells, springs and streams were all seen as essential for life in the arid land of Palestine. A prolonged period of drought resulted in food crisis and death.

Proverbs 25:25 equates the life-giving water that revitalises the weary with the spiritual remedy given to a person anxious about a situation in a distant land (מארץ מרחק) that he cannot control or even reach. The root רחק contains within its meanings a sense of distance and remoteness from someone or something, though it usually occurs in reference to the land.[83] It can be assumed that the person is mentally incapable of continuing due to his anxiety about a situation in a distant land.[84]

Modern readers who are exposed to all kinds of hi-tech means of facilitating access to information cannot understand the ecological significance of the metaphor if they do not put themselves in the biblical context, where news travelled upsettingly slowly and was delivered with great difficulty. There was no certainty that news sent from a distant country would arrive at its destination,[85] or that it would be transmitted in good

---

82. BDB, 746.

83. See Gen. 22:4; 37:4; Exod. 2:4; 20:21; 24:1; 1 Sam. 26:13; Ps. 38:12; Prov. 25:25; Isa. 13:5; 46:11; 59:9; Jer. 6:20; 23:23; Ezek. 23:40 etc.

84. Waltke, *Proverbs 15–31*, 335.

85. Travel and especially pedestrian travel was difficult in Palestine. Lurking bandits and wild animals made walking so hazardous that travelling on foot could result in death and the loss of the information being carried.

time. In many cases news would take the form of vague and fragmentary reports, the information having been transmitted by passing merchants rather than a specially commissioned courier. In the light of this, we can quite understand why the coolness of the snow in the day of harvest is equated with the refreshing power of a reliable messenger in Prov. 25:13. McKane correctly states that:

> Just as the cold water revives the stamina of the harvesters, banishing their fatigue and giving them new zest for their work, so a messenger who is completely trustworthy puts new life (*nepheš*) into his master... [T]he reliable envoy is a spring of living water to his principal.[86]

In reference to the latter exilic context of the text, Prov. 25:25 may be informed by the nostalgia of an exile, and the craving for news from home (Judah), which is like a parching thirst. The long interval of this news and the means by which it was supplied reinforce the ecological significance of cold water as refreshing to the weary person. The relief to the latter, when receiving good news, is as refreshing as a draught of cool water to a fainting, weary person.

4.2.3.4.3. Metaphor of polluted springs/fountains (v. 26). In v. 26 the text moves to compare the pollution of sources of water (springs or fountains) to a righteous person slipping before evil. The irresolute righteous person is equated with muddied spring and polluted fountain. Springs or fountains, as natural sources of water, were regarded as arising from the cosmic subterranean ocean to bring life and fertility on earth (see Ps. 104:10-11). In this sense, they acted as agents of hope and determined human settlements (Exod. 15:27; Num. 33:9; Deut. 8:7; 1 Kgs 18:5), providing sustenance and focal points of social life.

The reference to a muddied, bubbling spring refers to the intentional or deliberate befouling of an important supply of water. The Niphal נרפש (from the root רפש) in v. 26a means 'to muddy water by trampling', as is the case in Ezek. 32:2 and 34:19, where the same verb form occurs. Relatedly, 2 Chr. 32:3-4 records how, in preparation for Sennacherib's invasion of Jerusalem, Hezekiah blocked all the springs in the vicinity.

Although Prov. 25:26 displays clear traces of anthropocentrism – springs serve as a source of water *for people* – the verse displays an ecological awareness of the relevance of a spring in ancient Palestine. To befoul a desert waterhole is one of the most unforgivable criminal acts

---

86. William McKane, *Proverbs: A New Approach* (London: SCM, 1970), 586.

for the Bedouin, who move their flocks on routes punctuated by precious water sources.[87] The Hophal משחת, which literally means 'was caused to be ruined by', suggests also that the fountain, another source of vital water, has been cruelly polluted or ruined by people.

The two images of muddied springs and polluted fountains describe the deadly effects of an irresolute life lacking righteousness, and thus the dangers posed to others. When a righteous person behaves according to his inner nature (Prov. 18:10) and with a commitment for serving the community, Prov. 10:11 says that he/she is a 'fountain of life'. In contrast, the wicked are linked with violence. That is why Ps. 104:35 prays that the wicked be removed from the earth, and why Job 24:18 says that their place is on the surface of waters since their portion on the earth is cursed.

The metaphor is probably informed by knowledge of the grave consequences associated with ecological wickedness. Importantly, it can be used in the modern world to discourage worldwide pollution of sources of water. A wavering righteous person will disappoint the community, just as a muddied spring or a polluted fountain will naturally disappoint, imperil and become a source of life-threatening water for the many – plants, animals and humans alike – who rely on it for their survival.

The metaphor of Prov. 25:26 also resonates with the principle of the intrinsic value of water as life, which is equated to the intrinsic value of a righteous person. By nature, a spring or a fountain was regarded as a 'collective' source of life (Ps. 104:10-13) to the point that it is often used as a metaphor for wisdom (Prov. 16:22), the fear of the Lord (14:27) or the words from the righteous one's mouth (Prov. 10:11; 13:14; Sir. 21:23). Therefore, the pollution of a spring/fountain is not related to its innate inner character, but is instead caused by an external agent. This is presupposed by the use of the Niphal form, נרפש, for a muddied spring, and by the Hophal form, משחת, for a ruined fountain (v. 26).

4.3. Water and Water-related Phenomena in Proverbs 3:19-20 and 8:22-31

4.3.1. Introduction

In contrast to the previous texts, in which water is a metaphor (vehicle) for something else, Prov. 3:19-20 and 8:22-31 present water as a physical entity. These texts can be seen as the loci of the theology of creation in the book of Proverbs, and the wisdom books more broadly.[88] Publications

---

87. Hopkins, *The Highlands*, 250.
88. Clifford, 'The Theology of Creation', 85.

on these texts concern the role of Wisdom in Creation. This section is not interested in repeating the debate related to this matter, but looks at the ecological significance of water-related entities in this text.

4.3.2. *Water and Water-related Phenomena in Proverbs 3:19-20*

4.3.2.1. *Introduction.* This section explores the ecological potential of water and water-related phenomena appearing in Prov. 3:19-20. I will first explore general literary matters before retrieving ecological wisdom regarding the life-giving and life-threatening potential of water and water-related phenomena in this text. I am not going to explore the theme of wisdom and creation.

4.3.2.2. *General literary considerations*

4.3.2.2.1. *Translation of Proverbs 3:19-20.* I have adopted the translation of the NRSV. However, unlike the NRSV, the Hebrew word שמים (v. 19) is translated below as 'sky', not heaven. The reasons for this rendering will be given in the eco-theological analysis of the text. My preferred translation reads:

> [19] The LORD by wisdom founded the earth; by understanding he established the sky; [20] by his knowledge the deeps broke open, and the clouds drop down the dew.

4.3.2.2.2. *The position of Proverbs 3:19-20 in Proverbs 1–9.* Proverbs 3:19-20 is part of the first section of the book of Proverbs, chs. 1–9, setting forth a number of father–son (teacher–disciple) teachings. In its immediate context, Prov. 3:19-20 fits in the first text about creation theology in the book of Proverbs, namely 3:13-20. This wisdom poem has three strophes: the first strophe (3:13-17) portrays the happiness (אשרי) that comes to those who find Wisdom; the second (3:18) personifies Wisdom as a tree of life, a major symbol of fertility in the ancient Near East;[89] the last strophe depicts Wisdom's role in creation (3:19-20).

Therefore, the praise of Wisdom culminates in Prov. 3:19-20, where YHWH uses Wisdom to create and sustain the world. This strophe, which is rhetorically different from vv. 13-18, seeks to underline that YHWH used his Wisdom both in securing the earth from the life-threatening chaos waters and in supplying the life-giving water that fertilises the cosmos. The rhetorical structure of 3:19-20 is seen in the following section.

---

89. Perdue, *Wisdom Literature*, 50.

4.3.2.2.3. *Structure of Proverbs 3:19-20.* Biblical scholars agree that Prov. 3:19-20 originally evolved as an independent unit, but came to be placed in its current position in order to underline the means and merit of Wisdom's efficacy.[90] The unit presents its striking rhetorical structure as follows:

A	YHWH by Wisdom (חכמה) founded (יסד) the earth (ארץ) (v. 19a)	
B	Establishing (כונן) the sky (שמים) by understanding (תבונה) (v. 19b)	
A'	By his (YHWH) knowledge (דעת) the deeps (תהומות) burst open (בקע) (v. 20a)	
B'	And the clouds (שחקים) drop (ירעפו) dew (טל) (v. 20b)	

Table 5. *The Rhetorical Structure of Proverbs 3:19-20*

The above structure presents itself as an instance of alternating parallelism.[91] This poetic construction sees lines 1 and 3, and lines 2 and 4, working together to communicate the author's message. In Prov. 3:19-20, A relates to A' in the sense that the secured earth and the deeps belong to the lower sphere of the created order, while B and B' concern the upper sphere of the created order. Hence, the תהומות may now burst forth its water without turning the created order into chaos because they act according to God's דעת, or design, of the world.[92] Likewise, the sky sends forth its water, in the form of dew, toward earth via the clouds to fertilize the earth.

The AA' pairing implies also the life-threatening quality of water (תהומות) from which the earth is secured. Likewise, the establishment of the sky (שמים) by God's knowledge calls to mind the vault set up to hold above-waters, thereby preventing them from collapsing and turning the created order into chaos.

4.3.2.3. *Eco-theological reading of Proverbs 3:19-20*

4.3.2.3.1. *Life-giving quality of water in Proverbs 3:19-20.* In v. 19, the word בחכמה (by Wisdom) would be understood as God's attribute, but it could also be read as a quality immanent in creation in the sense that 'creation was raised by God to a state of wisdom or understanding'.[93]

---

90. Gerhard von Rad, *Wisdom in Israel* (London: SCM, 1972), 151; Brown, *The Ethos*, 284.

91. Willis, 'Alternating', 49.

92. דעת must read here as המכח or even the Egyptian *Ma'at* in the sense of world order. See Roger N. Whybray, *The Composition of the Book of Proverbs* (Sheffield: Sheffield Academic, 1994), 37.

93. Von Rad, *Wisdom*, 155.

This is in agreement with the hymn of Ps. 104:24, 'You have made all your works in Wisdom', and with Sir. 1:9, which states that God has 'poured Wisdom out upon all his works'.

The three Hebrew words for Wisdom (חכמה, תבונה, דעת) serve to underline that there is Wisdom in the limitation of the unruly life-threatening water from which earth is secured (AA', vv. 19a and 20a) and in the falling of the life-giving water from the sky (שמים) to the earth via the clouds (BB', vv. 19b and 20b). In Prov. 3:19, the earth and skies are securely established, and even the life-threatening deeps 'burst open' (v. 20a) only at YHWH's דעת (knowledge) to fertilise the earth.

Contrary to Gen. 7:11, which uses the verb בקע to describe the beginning of a disastrous flood, Prov. 3:20a attributes a positive aspect to the cosmic deluge by underscoring the restorative and life-giving role of the waters (תהומות) in favour of the earth. The sage is likely alluding to Gen. 2:4b, where the mist from the subterranean deeps burst open to fertilise the land. YHWH refreshes and revitalizes earth by the life-giving water from both the deeps (v. 20a) and dew drops (v. 20b). This verse patently juxtaposes the beneficent water flowing from the sky with the released depths, each working for life on earth.[94]

The word שחקים (v. 20b) means clouds that give water in the form of dew or rain (see my comments on Job 36:28). The Hebrew word used here for the falling of dew on earth is ירעפו. In Elihu's speech in Job 36:28, ירעפו signifies 'to pour down', while in Ps. 65:12 it means to flow. In this sense, the verb does not merely refer to the dripping of dew (טל), but to the fact that YHWH regularly waters the earth. In Canaan's rainless summer, the land was heavily dependent on dew. That is why the pair 'rain and dew' usually occur together in many parts of the Bible (see Appendix A).

4.3.2.3.2. Life-threatening potential of water in Proverbs 3:19-20. The Hebrew verbs יסד (to establish) the earth (ארץ) and כונן (to secure) the sky (שמים) imply driving the waters off the earth and keeping them within limits that they must not transgress. These Hebrew verbs present God as the ultimate architect who lays down a strong foundation and secures a building of walls and pillars, and supports the sky with a roof constructed over the cosmic sea to hold the waters back.[95]

The text denotes the common cosmogonic ideas of the time in which the earth was conceived as a mass resting on an ocean (Pss. 24:2; 136:6), and as having foundations and being supported by pillars beneath the ocean (in

---

94. Waltke, *Proverbs 1–15*, 262.
95. Perdue, *Wisdom Literature*, 51.

Sheol) (Isa. 51:33; Job 9:6; Amos 9:2-3). Likewise, above the earth, the sky was thought of as a material expanse (רָקִיעַ) fixed in its place by God (Gen. 1:6; Isa. 20:22) and supported by pillars (Job 26:11) so that the water above would not meet the water below and turn creation into chaos.[96]

As explained earlier, the word שמים (sky) etymologically means 'what relates to water'. In this sense, in the ancient Near East, the solidity of the dome (רקיע) and the blue colour of the sky (שמים) were assumed to be closely linked with the holding back of the upper-waters, and thus preventing the cosmic sea from breaking out and overwhelming the created order. Just as in Gen. 1, Prov. 3:20a is aware of the unruly waters in specific limits within the created order. By the verbs to 'secure' and 'establish', the sage implies that in wisdom God protects his creation from being overwhelmed by the life-threatening chaos waters. As such, by means of God's דעת, the channels were cleaved open to permit some water to come up from the great cosmic ocean into springs on the earth.[97]

In v. 20a, תהומות burst open according to God's דעת, which is a life-giving action. It should be known, however, that תהומות normally refers to the primeval deep with life-threatening potential. It is linguistically the equivalent of Tiamat, the Akkadian chaos monster threatening to devour the gods. The verb בקע (v. 20a) may thus infer the mythical image of Marduk 'splitting open' the chaos monster to protect the world from being flooded by chaos.[98] תהום or תהומות was a dangerous place, symbolised by the chaos monster living in its depths.

Proverbs 3:20a states that תהומות is kept in check to act according to God's דעת (v. 20a), by letting some water flow within designed channels to the land and thus diminishing the volume of water. Were this not the case, תהומות would uncontrollably send forth its life-threatening water against the created order. Such a thing happened once before, during the flood (Gen. 7:11). Then, תהומות both poured down waters through the windows of the vault (above the limit of water) and flowed up through the springs: all the springs of the great deep (כל־מעינת תהום רבה) were cleaved open (נבקעו) and the waters rushed up, turning creation into chaos.

Proverbs 3:20a implies that if the waters are not kept in their appointed place, they are potentially life-threatening. In this sense, the expression תהומות נבקעו (the deeps burst open) in Prov. 3:20a probably refers to the

---

96. The function of רקיע is to separate the waters from waters (literally: מבדיל בין מים למים, Gen. 1:6b).

97. John A. Emerton, 'Spring and Torrent in Psalm 74:15', *VTSup* 15 (1966): 127.

98. Perdue, *Wisdom Literature*, 51.

creation of channels for this water since v. 19 presumes the original act of creation in Gen. 1:1-2.[99] God's act of wisdom does not annihilate the life-threatening waters of תהומות, but creates channels so that some water can flow from the deep into the springs on the land.

4.3.2.3.3. *Eco-theological synthesis.* It is fascinating to see that the text contains the opposing ideas of water as the enemy of the created order (life-threatening quality) and water playing a major role in the sustenance of life in the created order (life-giving quality). The text speaks to the principle of the intrinsic worth of water. For Prov. 3:19-20, water is life-giving when it flows within fixed limits (i.e. according to wisdom/ principle that God used to establish the created order).

Water will then flow from the ground (below) and the dew from the clouds (above) to fertilise the land. However, the primeval deeps (life-threatening waters) continue to flow upwards and are held back by the sky, preventing them from overrunning the created order. It is by wisdom, the principle of the created order, that creation is maintained in order.

4.3.3. *Water and Water-related Phenomena in Proverbs 8:22-31*

4.3.3.1. *Introduction.* This section explores the ecological potential of water in Prov. 8:22-31. It should be noted that, unlike virtually all scholarly discussions dealing with 8:22-31, the discussion offered in this section does not focus on Wisdom and Creation. Instead, the present exploration is made on the ecological insights of water, which is the dominant feature of the cosmos in 8:22-31.

4.3.3.2. *Translation of Proverbs 8:22-31.* The following translation is that of the NRSV:

> [22] The LORD created me at the beginning of his work,
>   the first of his acts of long ago.
> [23] Ages ago I was set up, at the first,
>   before the beginning of the earth.
> [24] When there were no depths, I was brought forth,
>   when there were no springs abounding with water.
> [25] Before the mountains had been shaped,
>   before the hills, I was brought forth—
> [26] when he had not yet made earth and fields,
>   or the world's first bits of soil.

99. Emerton, 'Spring and Torrent', 125.

> [27] When he established the heavens, I was there,
>> when he drew a circle on the face of the deep,
> [28] when he made firm the skies above,
>> when he established the fountains of the deep,
> [29a] when he assigned to the sea its limit,
>> so that the waters might not transgress his command,
> [29b-30aα] when he marked out the foundations of the earth,
> [30aβ-b] then I was beside him, like a master worker;
>> and I was daily his delight, rejoicing before him always,
> [31] rejoicing in his inhabited world and delighting in the human race.

4.3.3.3. *Wisdom and creation in Proverbs 8:22-31*. Proverbs 8:22-31 is the central part of the whole ch. 8 of the book of Proverbs. It is preceded by 8:4-21, where Wisdom explains her value and vital nature, and is followed by 8:32-36, which returns to the sapiential theme of vv. 4-21 that orders one to listen to Wisdom, for on this depends life or death.[100]

The artistic structure of this central section has impressed scholars. The beginning (vv. 22-23) and the end (vv. 30-31) both concern Wisdom's relationship with YHWH, while the poetic body (vv. 24-29) narrates the active role of Wisdom in the formation of the cosmos. Like *Ma'at* in Egypt, Wisdom is here given a special position *vis-à-vis* all creatures, a position of firstborn (ראשית) emphasised also in Job 28. Proverbs 8:22-31 therefore presents the following chiastic structure:[101]

A	YHWH creates Wisdom in primordial time (vv. 22-23)
B	Situation before creation (When there were no...) (vv. 24-26)
B'	Creation ordered by YHWH (When he...) (vv. 27-29)
A'	Wisdom's intimacy with YHWH (vv. 30-31)

Table 6. *The Structure of Proverbs 8:22-31*

The poem presents an alternating parallelism where line 1 points to line 4 (AA'), while lines 2 and 3 antithetically correlate (BB'). While the pair AA' points to Wisdom's intimacy with God, BB' contrasts the precreation situation with the situation after/during the creation. What is striking is that the good and the not-good elements of creation are determined by aspects of waters: while vv. 24-26 concern the situation before the chaos

---

100. Von Rad, *Wisdom*, 151.
101. This structure is adapted from the model by Richard J. Clifford, *Creation Accounts in the Ancient Near East and in the Bible* (Washington, DC: Catholic Biblical Association of America, 1994), 183.

waters (life-threatening), vv. 27-29 depict the boundaries set up to control the waters, thereby securing the created order. In this sense, both the first (AA') and the second (BB') pairs close with the mention of 'earth' (ארץ, vv. 26a and 29c). Waters of life and death are the dominant features of the poem.

4.3.3.4. *Life-threatening potential of water (vv. 24-26)*. Similar to Gen. 2:4b, Wisdom's creation poem in Prov. 8:22-31 starts with the negative (not yet) situation of waters' absence: depths and wellsprings. The hills and mountains are added to the list of lack (vv. 24-25). While the priestly creation account (Gen. 1:1–2:4a) starts with watery chaos everywhere (על־פני), Prov. 8:22 deals with the time before the deeps came into existence. Wisdom is termed as the first of God's deeds: she existed even before the watery chaos, the primeval deeps.

The expression באין־תהומות (when there were no deeps) in v. 22 would thus seem to refer to a situation before the primeval deeps, contrary to Gen. 1:2. Raymond[102] argues that תהומות here means 'springs' as in Deut. 8:7, rather than 'primeval depths', as the idea that there was a time תהומות did not exist would be strange in the Old Testament. Still, the springs have their origins back in תהומות. The answer resides in the meaning of the verb קנה in v. 22 and ראשית in v. 23 in relation to Wisdom.

In accordance with Vawter,[103] one could argue that the verb קנה points to the idea that here wisdom is said to have pre-existed the created order and therefore would be outside it, though it subsequently became instrumental in the production of the created order. God possessed wisdom as an attribute or faculty that he used to order elements of creation, including the תהומות. The word תהומות in v. 23 does not thus indicate temporal precedence, but rather the 'principle' or the model by which creation was made.[104]

Wisdom is intrinsically linked with the created order. It is implied here that God possessed Wisdom before his dealings with the waters in v. 24: he had not yet shaped the רקיע or allowed controlled springs of water to irrigate the earth. Similarly, he had not yet shaped the mountains that would hold up the earth from the sea (Jon. 2:6). All were hidden in the life-threatening primeval deeps before God's creative work. In vv. 24-26, one can thus notice that the presentation of elements of creation follow

---

102. Reymond, *L'eau*, 175.
103. Bruce Vawter, 'Proverbs 8:22: Wisdom and Creation', *JBL* 99, no. 2 (1980): 213.
104. Jean de Savignac, 'Proverbs', *VT* 4 (1954): 429.

the movement from below the earth to above it: from the underground depths (v. 24a), to the springs leading to earth's surface (v. 24b) to the visible mountains rooted in the depths (v. 25a), the hills (v. 25b) and the land (v. 26).

All the enlisted spheres (springs, mountains, hills and earth) have direct links with the life-threatening primeval waters, תהומות. When the waters of תהומות retreated after the flood event, spheres of nature appeared in this logical order (Gen. 8:4-12); all were previously engulfed in the life-threatening waters of תהומות. It is for this reason that the following verses, vv. 27-29, deal with several limitations placed on water, ones related to the shaping, establishing, supporting and stabilising of the earth, since the unbound תהום is a lurking danger for the created order.

4.3.3.5. *Life-giving quality of water (vv. 27-29).* Verses 27-29 positively depict the forming of the cosmic order in a way that is similar to that found in the Priestly creation account of Gen. 1:1–2:4a: the sky, the waters and the earth. The limits of the deep and the sea are set up, while the sky is secured and the underground springs are stabilised. The section also concludes with the earth's foundations, which are established by the creator (v. 29b). With these limits imposed, the waters of the deep are no longer in service of death but of life.

Within vv. 27-29, the sage seems to imply that life arose on earth when the primal deeps were restricted within boundaries and let out again in the form of springs (v. 28). In v. 29, an edict is given by God to the life-threatening primordial deep, keeping it from turning the creation order into chaos. When located within these boundaries, the waters are in the service of life in the created order. It is by Wisdom that God secures, restrains and arranges the created order by maintaining the waters within limits.[105]

4.3.3.6. *Eco-theological synthesis.* The main purpose of the Proverbs text is to explain the presence of Wisdom during these primordial events. Nevertheless, even though it is not intended to be a technical depiction of the process, the poem echoes the Gen. 1 account of the separation of the waters. Unlike the priestly creation account, the cosmos of Prov. 8:22-31 does not point towards a perfect creation. The watery domains are depicted with both life-giving and life-threatening potential.

---

105. Dell, *Proverbs*, 143.

Therefore, vv. 27-28 list the limits being imposed on the chaos water (תהומות): the fixing of the sky (שמים), the circumcision of the deep (תהום), the strengthening of the clouds (שחקים), the intensification of the fountains (עינות) and the decree that sets the limits of the sea (ים). With the setting up of the skies – שמים: literally, what relates to water – as well as the deeps limited, the cosmos becomes a bastion of security against the life-threatening potential of תהום.

God is therefore the perfect architect, sinking the pillars of the earth in the water in order to launch an arena of life and to survive the threatening pressure of the watery chaos.[106]

4.4. *Comparative Conclusion*

This chapter has involved the analysis of two categories of texts: texts that use water as metaphor, namely Prov. 5:15-20; 9:13-18 and 25:23-26, and wisdom poems where water appears as a physical entity, namely 3:19-20 and 8:22-31. In the first category, the aim was to explore the possibility of retrieving ecological wisdom of water used as a vehicle for human matters. The analysis tried to uncover the life-giving and life-threatening potential of water and water-related phenomena that had gone unnoticed, ignored or muted by anthropocentric readings of the passages. In the second category, the attempt consisted of focusing on water and water-related phenomena that are often muffled in studies about the role of Wisdom in creation in Prov. 3:19-20 and 8:22-36.

Therefore, the analysis observed that Prov. 5:15-20 displays a number of water-related phenomena with the life-giving potential. The private wells and cisterns, along with springs and fountains, are all a true depiction of the erotic aspect of water that gives life. The text suggests that only private cisterns and wells are in the service of life. Additionally, the restriction against not spilling the spring/fountains on public areas denotes the idea that bad behaviour will lead inter alia to water depletion. Proverbs 5:15-20 also presumes that the public area contains life-threatening water which is not fit for consumption. Thus, the text is informed by the ecological idea of proper water management.

Proverbs 9:13-18 explicitly deals with both aspects of water as a life-giving and life-threatening entity. While Folly's water is sweet for a while, denoting the romantic (life-giving) aspect of water, her path ultimately leads to the depths of Sheol (life-threatening water). It was shown that the words עמקים שאול (depths of Sheol) are the equivalent of the depths of

---

106. Brown, *The Ethos*, 276.

an abyss since the word מעמקים (depths) refers to life-threatening waters similar to תהום or ים inspiring death of the created order. In this sense, both aspects of water are present in the metaphorical language of the text.

Finally, Prov. 25:23-26 proved to be the most insightful text in terms of a clear illustration of both aspects of water as giving life and death. The metaphor of the north wind that brings forth rain in v. 23 is informed by the life-threatening aspect of unexpected heavy rains (גשם), which result in land erosion, the failure of crops and thus the ruined hopes of Israelite farmers. The text has thus been informed by an agricultural world in which the rain from the north wind is hidden and potentially damaging, just as a backbiting tongue is hidden and thus potentially destructive. (The idea of water's unpredictability will be emphasised further in the following chapter, dealing with Qoheleth.)

By contrast, Prov. 25:25 denotes the life-giving functions of water, while v. 26 implies both the life-giving and life-threatening aspects. In v. 25, the metaphor compares the revitalising power that cold water has on the weary (almost dead) with the relief of receiving good news from a distant land. Verse 26 expresses the feeling of deception that arises when encountering a (deliberately) muddied spring or polluted fountain, which is compared to the feelings that arise when witnessing a wavering person's righteousness before the wicked. As polluted water, the spring or fountain is no longer a source of life, but instead a life-threatening entity.

Proverbs 3:19-20 and 8:22-31 both highlight in their own way the life-giving and life-threatening potential of water. With the references to the primeval deep and the dew drop fertilising the earth, along with the limitations placed on the waters in the skies and underneath the earth, both wisdom poems underline that while water is a lurking danger in the created order it is nevertheless a vital element for the continuance of life in the universe.

Chapter 5

WATER AND WATER-RELATED PHENOMENA IN THE BOOK OF QOHELETH

5.1. *Introduction*

The book of Qoheleth makes many references to water and water-related phenomena. The book is primarily anthropocentric, focusing on 'what is good for humans to do under the sun during the few days of their life' (2:3). The few passages that do make reference to water and water-related phenomena include 1:4-11; 2:4-6 and 11:1-6. These verses have apparently nothing to do with water itself as a subject, but are used as enigmatic details in Qoheleth's philosophical understanding of human experience.

While Qoh. 1:4-11 and 11:1-6 use water metaphors to comment on human issues, 2:4-6 is an autobiography outlining Qoheleth's sources of pleasure. It is notable that the water supply in parks is included in the list.

I will from the outset state that this chapter is somewhat ambitious, as it attempts to retrieve ecological wisdom from texts that seem to have no bearing on environmental matters.

5.2. *Introduction to the Book of Qoheleth*

5.2.1. *Socio-historical Context of the Book of Qoheleth*

This sub-section does not attempt to replace previous scholarly studies of the book of Qoheleth, but instead draws on them in order to investigate hidden ecological insights about water and water-related phenomena in the book. Despite the arguments of traditional Jewish and Christian exegesis, it is now accepted that Solomon was not the author of the book of Qoheleth. The famous nineteenth-century scholar Franz Delitzsch even said: 'If the book of Koheleth were of Solomonic origin, then there is no history of the Hebrew language'.[1]

---

1. Franz Delitzsch, *Commentary on Song of Songs and Ecclesiastes* (Grand Rapids: Eerdmans, 1968), 1990.

Today, the scholarly consensus is that the composition of the book of Qoheleth took place in Jerusalem at some point during the second half of the third century BCE, during the Ptolemaic reign.[2] An earlier theory which dated Qoheleth to the Persian context on the basis of supposed Aramaisms in the text has been largely overturned by insights from the discovery of scroll fragments of the book (4QQoh^a) at Qumran that favour the mid-second century BCE.[3]

It is believed that Sirach probably knew and used the book of Qoheleth about 190 BCE.[4] Several reasons can be put forward in support of this later date, including: Qoheleth's sceptical views about human life, the *Carpe diem* ideas, and the many parallels to Hellenistic ideas, such as 'under the sun' (ὑπὸ τὸν ἥλιον) or futility/frustration (ματαιοτης).[5]

Qoheleth's context was characterised by the Ptolemaic reign of force and persuasion, which avoided interfering in local customs of conquered nations. Bagnall summarises the principle that led the Ptolemaic governance quite succinctly: 'Let the cities run their own affairs so long as they satisfy whatever obligations they have to the crown'.[6] Despite its absolutism, the Ptolemaic reign was a period of peace, agricultural and economic productivity, and various profits for Israel.[7]

The *Letter of Aristeas* can be cited as evidence of such a profitable time in Israel's history. The letter lists the natural and economic abundance of Palestine during this period:

> Their country is plentifully wooded with numerous olive trees, and rich in cereal crops and pulse, and also in vines and honey. Date palms and other fruit trees are beyond reckoning among them. They have plentiful cattle of all varieties, and their pastures are lush... For the country is adapted for commerce as well as agriculture and the city is rich in crafts and lacks none of the things imported by sea...[8]

---

2. Perdue, *Wisdom Literature*, 161–2.
3. Frank M. Cross, 'Oldest Manuscripts from Qumran', *JBL* 74, no. 3 (1955): 153–62.
4. Thomas Krüger, *Qoheleth: A Commentary* (Minneapolis: Fortress, 2004), 20.
5. Koh, *Royal Autobiography*, 15; Perdue, *Wisdom Literature*, 177–8.
6. Roger S. Bagnall, *The Administration of the Ptolemaic Possessions Outside Egypt* (Leiden: Brill, 1976), 9.
7. Elias J. Bickerman, *The Jews in the Greek Age* (Cambridge, MA: Harvard University Press, 1988), 70.
8. Moses Hadas, *Aristeas to Philocrates (Letter of Aristeas)* (New York: Harper, 1951), 147.

However, the opportunity of a splendid life of plenty was reserved for a relatively small group of people. In many cases, the peasantry had to cope with marginal subsistence since the exportation and heavy taxation system served local officials only, and thus created frustration among most of the rural populace. Qoheleth's sceptical and ambiguous rhetoric serves as a critique of this socio-historical context.

5.2.2. *The Use of Nature Languages in Qoheleth*

Qoheleth belongs to the five *Meggilloth*, the five short scrolls read during Jewish festivals. As a result of Qoheleth's earthly nature, the book came to be associated with Sukkot (the tabernacles festival), a festival celebrating the conclusion of 'the fruit harvest and the onset of the rainy season in the seasonal cycle of the land of Israel'.[9] This is derived from many passages in the book, including Qoh. 9:1, which states: 'Go, eat your bread with pleasure…for God has already approved your works'.

The book of Qoheleth represents a 'crisis' in Israel's wisdom tradition in that the book attacks the dogma of conventional wisdom, namely, God's sense of justice, the romantic view of nature and the value of human life. In a sense, the book as a whole creates various contradictions, stating problems rather than solving them, inferring that the readers must hold many of Qoheleth's observations in tension.[10]

For Qoheleth, the cosmology of conventional wisdom did not offer the proper responses to the issues he raised about discovering what is good in human experience. This, it seems, was because creation itself has many ambiguities.[11] Qoheleth is, therefore, unable to draw on insights he perceived in nature to construct vital models and compelling articulations of faith and ethical life. Unlike the traditions of Genesis, Psalms, Isaiah and Job, which claim that nature displays clear order, creation in Qoheleth is characterised by *hebel* (הבל).

Countless scholarly explanations and translations have been offered for the word *hebel*, and here is not the place to revisit them. What can be noted is that the book of Qoheleth contains over half of all the uses of term in the Hebrew Bible (38 instances in Qoheleth; 73 occurences in total).

---

9. Marvin Sweeney, *TANAK: A Theological and Critical Introduction to the Jewish Bible* (Minneapolis: Fortress, 2012), 438.

10. Michael V. Fox, *Qoheleth and his Contradictions* (Sheffield: Almond, 1989), 11.

11. Leo G. Perdue, *Wisdom and Creation: The Theology of Wisdom Literature* (Nashville: Abingdon, 1994), 193.

The literal meaning of the word is 'vapour' (Isa. 57:13), though prevailing understandings of *hebel* include vanity, absurdity, meaninglessness and futility. Importantly, no single scholarly suggestion for the meaning of *hebel* quite encompasses the full range of meanings seemingly intended by the use of the term within Qoheleth. Aware of this, Whybray suggests 'futility' in most instances, but 'brevity' for 6:12; 9:9 and 10:10.[12] It seems that Ogden's translation of *hebel* as 'enigmatic' or 'ambiguous'[13] would fit with the socio-historical and literary contexts of the book. For Qoheleth, life is ambiguous or enigmatic: it is complex and manifold; no single natural phenomenon, either positive or negative, can fully explain it.

As a result of this, nature in Qoheleth cannot simply be framed, using Brown's words, as 'the dying cosmos',[14] nor, adopting Whybray's thesis, as a 'romantic cosmos of regularity'.[15] Instead, nature seems to be a mixture of both. In other words, it is not that a positive (romantic) *or* a negative meaning of nature is intended, but that the reader needs to see both aspects as the true depiction of life. Qoheleth's cosmos is characterised by futility and regularity.

5.3. *Water and Water-related Phenomena in Qoheleth 1:4-11*

5.3.1. *Introduction*

References to water-related phenomena are mainly found in Qoh. 1:7. However, in order to understand this verse fully, it is important to analyse it in the context of the passage to which it belongs, namely 1:4-11, since v. 7 has meaning only in relation to the 'ambiguous' cosmological poetry of the text. With this in mind, the present section offers a literary analysis before an ecological interpretation is attempted.

5.3.2. *Literary Considerations*

This section discusses the artful ambiguity of the Hebrew text of Qoh. 1:4-11 and issues of its literary delimitation.

5.3.2.1. *Artful ambiguity in Qoheleth 1:4-11.* Qoheleth 1:4-11 is part of the literary unit which starts in v. 1 and ends in v. 11. This unit has been read either as a depiction of the endless or pointless repetitions in

---

12. Roger N. Whybray, 'Qoheleth, Preacher of Joy', *JSOT* 23 (1982): 89.
13. Graham S. Ogden, *Qoheleth* (Sheffield: JSOT, 1987), 15.
14. William P. Brown, *The Seven Pillars of Creation: The Bible, Science, and the Ecology of Wonder* (Oxford: Oxford University Press, 2010), 177.
15. Whybray, 'Ecclesiastes 1:5-7', 105.

nature (negative focus),[16] or as about the regular cycles of nature inviting wonders (romantic perspective).[17] Although scholars tend to favour either a romantic or a negative reading, I consider both aspects to be part of Qoheleth's enigmatic work. I am in agreement with Whybray, who says:

> When an author [Qoheleth] truly leaves several alternatives open, we should refrain from foreclosing on any of them. Then we should treat the openness as a significant (and not merely symptomatic) datum of the text.[18]

This assumption is based on Good's observation that the style, not the content, of the unit contains some artistic clues that can affect the meaning of the text. Good argues that in Qoh. 1:2-11 'every expression appears to have more than one possible meaning'.[19] The text contains several expressions with a broad semantic range, which makes the passage an ideal world of ambiguity.[20] The whole problem originates in the translation of הבל, which is the main metaphor that encompasses the meaning of the whole book.

Not only is there an unresolved debate about the meaning of הבל in v. 2, but also the grammatical style of the text poses the question whether the expression 'הכל is הבל' refers to absolutely everything – including God and piety – or just everything under the sun, as introduced in v. 3. Verse 3 is particularly enigmatic. One may ask whether the rhetorical question requires a 'No' or 'Yes' answer. Others could see v. 2 as the earlier response or that the question does not need to be answered. Does the word עמל in v. 3 refer to hard work, limited to any kind of labour, or the wealth that results from one's labour (Ps. 105:44)? Stylistic ambiguities can be added.

When we turn to the main core of the text, vv. 4-8, the situation is even more enigmatic. Whybray has argued that the text does not point to the futility of human life cycles, but rather to the regularity of life cycles exemplified in the images of nature in vv. 4-7.[21] By contrast, the majority of scholars think that vv. 4-7 are not a mere nature poem, but rather serve to highlight the pointlessness of human activity.

---

16. Brown, *The Seven Pillars*, 179.
17. Whybray, 'Ecclesiastes 1:5-7', 108.
18. Michael V. Fox, 'The Use of Indeterminacy', *Semeia* 71 (1995): 175.
19. Edwin M. Good, 'The Unfilled Sea: Style and Meaning in Ecclesiastes 1:2-11', in *Israelite Wisdom: Theological and Literary Essays in Honour of Samuel Terrien*, ed. John G. Gammie et al. (Atlanta: Scholars Press, 1978), 64–5.
20. Lindsay Wilson, 'Artful Ambiguity in Ecclesiastes 1:1-11', in *Qoheleth in the Context of Wisdom*, ed. Antoon Schoors (Leuven: Uitgeverij Peeters, 1998), 358.
21. Whybray, 'Ecclesiastes 1:5-7', 108.

This world of ambiguity is the literary context in which the water-related phenomena of v. 7 occur. A re-reading of Qoh. 1:4-11 reveals that both views about the text are possible. Ambiguity does not mean an infinite number of meanings, but 'an indefinite number of subsets (different component "meanings"), some of them overlapping or with fuzzy partitions between them'.[22] What is interesting in ambiguous texts is that no single meaning can claim to be the absolute truth of the passage.

Spangenberg has argued that the book of Qoheleth is characterised by marks of irony which have the potential to mislead the reader as they point to two possible meanings.[23] This is no more than what Good named as an enigmatic style. In irony or enigma, both readings are possible, and not only sequentially or as variants or alternatives, but also simultaneously, at the moment of reading. Sometimes one has to combine both readings in order to have the full 'meaning' of the text. Alter states that failure to respect this indeterminacy and openness of the text would lead us:

> To say whatever we wanted about it, and we would end up, tediously, talking only about ourselves, as certain contemporary critics are inclined to do.[24]

Thus, ironic/enigmatic texts pave the way for substantial freedom in the reader's (re)construction of many potential unspoken meanings since arriving at a definitive meaning of a real ironic text is almost impossible, while definitive misunderstanding is a distinct possibility.[25] By definitive misunderstanding, I am referring to a situation whereby one opts for a single reading of a text to the exclusion of other possible voices in that text. In this sense, the cosmological depiction of human life in Qoheleth involves both romantic and negative images of nature, including water.

5.3.2.2. *Delimitation of Qoheleth 1:4-11.* Qoheleth 1:4-11 belongs to the prelude to the whole book (1:1-11), which, along with 11:9–12:14, forms the frame of the book.[26] Both parts of this frame are poems on cosmology and anthropology, and are characterised by the repetition of the major *leitmotif* (all is הבל) at the opening (1:2) and close of the book (12:8).

---

22. Fox, 'The Use of', 175.
23. Izak Spangenberg, 'Irony in the Book of Qoheleth', *JSOT* 72 (1996): 61.
24. Robert Alter, *The Pleasures of Reading in an Ideological Age* (New York: Simon & Schuster, 1990), 237.
25. Carolyn J. Sharp, 'Ironic Representation, Authorial Voice, and Meaning in Qohelet', *Biblical Interpretation* 12 (2004): 48.
26. Perdue, *Wisdom Literature*, 205.

Qoheleth 1:4-11 is divided into two mains parts – cosmos (vv. 4-7) and humanity (vv. 8-11) – each revealing a well-organised structure. Qoheleth 1:4-11 as a whole is read either as being about 'regularity' in creation that lasts forever versus human death, or as concerning the wearisomeness of creation reflecting the pointlessness of human life and toil.

An ecological re-reading of these verses (vv. 4-11), based on the meaning of הבל as enigmatic in the frames (Qoh. 1:2 and 12:8) of the book, shows that both meanings of nature may be implied in the text. Nature is both purposeful (positive) and wearisome (negative), just as human life is complex and puzzling.

5.3.3. *Ecological Insights of Qoheleth 1:4-11*

5.3.1.1. *Wearisomeness of nature.* This section first examines the wearisomeness of nature in general, before pointing to the wearisomeness of water in particular in Qoh. 1:4-11.

5.3.1.1.1. *Wearisomeness of nature in general.* This kind of reading establishes, first of all, a link between vv. 3 and 4, in the sense that v. 4 views the fleeting nature of human life or life-span (דור) against the background of the eternal existence of the earth (והארץ לעולם). In other words, Qoheleth questions why the earth stays 'forever' but human generations 'go and come'.

This reading views Qoh. 1:4–11 as expressing the futility of human life compared to pointless repetitions visible in nature (vv. 5–7). Humans go and come in steady succession – reflecting both linear (historical) and cyclical (repetitive) time – just as the sun rises and sets, the wind blows in circles and the rivers flow in unending courses to the sea.[27]

For Qoheleth, the cyclical nature movement of nature is a wearisome motion that knows no end, leads to no change and is meaningless.[28] The comparison between humans and nature is exciting: just as humans go (הלך) and come (בא) (v. 4), so the sun rises (בא) (v. 5), the wind goes (הלך) (v. 6) and the streams come (ללכת, הלכים) (v. 7). The frequent use of the verbs שוב (vv. 6, 7) and סבב (three times in v. 6) denotes endless repetition, while the repeated שם emphasises the sameness of end-points and starting-points.[29] In this sense, Qoheleth concludes that there is nothing new under the sun (v. 9).

---

27. Ibid., 210.
28. Young-Jin Min, 'How Do the Rivers Flow (Ecclesiastes 1:7)', *BT* 42 (1991): 229.
29. Jennie Barbour, *The Story of Israel in the Book of Qoheleth: Ecclesiastes as Cultural Memory* (Oxford: Oxford Academic, 2012), 49.

In other words, like the endless movement of the three physical forces (sun, wind and water), humans fruitlessly search for meaning and insights. Brown has simply termed nature in Qoheleth a *dying cosmos* in the sense of 'a world without pause and effect, a world without history... and future'.[30] Qoheleth acknowledges that there is indeed activity in the universe, but it is devoid of *telos* (a goal) and filled with toil.

5.3.3.1.2. Wearisomeness of water (v. 7). Proponents of the wearisomeness of nature in Qoh. 1:4-11 prefer the following translation of v. 7:

> All streams run to the sea, but the sea is not full; to the place to which the rivers flow they flow again and again (שבים ללכת).[31]

This translation understands the verb שבים to mean 'going', not 'to return'. In reading שבים as a ceaseless, futile movement, Qoheleth depicts the waters of the earth as circling back to their point of origin, changing nothing. The movement of water in Qoheleth is devoid of any visible purpose, in contrast to Ps. 104, where God is behind the life-giving waters (rains and streams) that revitalise the earth and its inhabitants.

It is understood that the Dead Sea has informed the mention of the unfilled sea in Qoh. 1:7a. It would have been a common observation for the writer of Qoheleth that, while the Jordan River flows constantly into the Dead Sea, the Dead Sea never fills up – even though no rivers flow out of it (v. 8). In a similar way, human eyes and ears are never satiated. Longman III thinks that many Hebrew words in vv. 4-7, such as הלכים (flow), מקום (place) and שבים (return), reflect the message of pointlessness in terms of 'sameness in the midst of illusory change'.[32]

5.3.3.2. Wonders of the regularity of nature.

5.3.3.2.1. Wonders of nature in general: romantic reading. The romantic interpretation starts by removing any possible continuation between v. 3 and v. 4, viewing v. 3 as an editorial addition that is better connected with v. 2 to form a summary of the book of Qoheleth as a whole. As such, the meaning of דור in v. 4 is much discussed. Rather than reading דור as connoting 'human life-span' as in other Semitic languages and elsewhere

---

30. Brown, *The Seven Pillars*, 179.
31. Krüger, *Qoheleth*, 47.
32. Tremper Longman III, *The Book of Ecclesiastes* (Grand Rapids: Eerdmans, 1998), 71.

in the Old Testament, proponents of this reading link דור with a more general sense such as duration, age or period.³³

The meaning is thus connected with passages where the sense of דור as human life is improbable. These passages include Isa. 41:4, where YHWH calls the דרות from the beginning, and Isa. 51:9, in which דרות עולמים refer to 'unspecified periods' (future or present). It is, therefore, believed that this idea of דור as simply connotiong 'period' has informed Qoh. 1:4. Therefore, Whybray reads the word עולם in v. 4 as consisting of a succession of endlessly repeated cyclical processes in nature (דור הלך ודר) which are illustrated in vv. 5-7.³⁴

In other words, the word דור does not contrast the ephemerality of humanity with the permanence of the earth; instead, the word דור points to the cyclical movements of nature depicted in vv. 5-8.³⁵ Accordingly, v. 4 contains only verbs in the participial form (הלך, בא and עמדת) underlining the unchanging nature and regularity of these phenomena.

The activities of the sun (השמש) in v. 5, the wind (הרוח) in v. 6 and the water-related phenomena (הנחלים, small rivers, and הים, sea) in v. 7 are not seen as showing the futility of these aspects of nature, but the wonders of their controlled regularity. In other words, vv. 5-7 depict not human futility, but 'wonders of nature elements' acting according to the 'limitations imposed on them by their allotted natures and functions, which necessitate their constant cyclical repetition'.³⁶

According to the romantic reading, יגעים (v. 8), the word that sums up the cosmological part of the unit (vv. 4-7) is rendered not as 'wearisome' but as 'labour'. The notion of the purposefulness of the effective activity of nature elements is thus supported as a strong possible meaning in Qoh. 1:8. It is said that the literary and historical context of the text suggests the sense of all things being in constant activity – something which supports the permanent existence of earth.

Verse 8 is understood as perfectly summarising the idea of the regularity of the catalogue of activities in nature depicted in vv. 5-7. It emphasises the fabulous wonders of nature that leave humans in a situation of contemplation. It is as if vv. 4-7 intend to leave humans speechless when they contemplate nature with their eyes and ears. The text makes clear that human senses are incapable of mastering its mysteries: לא־יוכל איש לדבר

---

33. Victor P. Hamilton, 'דּוֹר (Generation)', *NIDOTTE* 1:930–1.
34. Whybray, 'Ecclesiastes 1:5-7', 106.
35. Ogden, *Qoheleth*, 91.
36. Whybray, 'Ecclesiastes 1:5-7', 105.

(no man is able to speak). In other words, when observing the rhythms of the sun, wind and water, they remain beyond human understanding, and so leave one at a loss for words.

The verb שואף in v. 5, relating to the movement of the sun, is read positively in relation to its sense as 'panting with eagerness and desire' in Ps. 119:13 and Job 7:2. As to the movements of the wind (v. 6), Whybray affirms that Qoheleth intends to mean that the 'wind has its own fixed circuit and can be relied on to remain within it, always returning (שוב) eventually to the direction from which it started'.[37]

A consideration of how this perspective reads the movement of water in v. 7 in particular, follows.

5.3.3.2.2. Wonders of water in v. 7. Romantic readers prefer the rendering of שבים as 'to return', suggesting that water returns to the place from which it flows in order to flow afresh. In such a light, v. 7 is read as follows:

> All streams run to the sea, but the sea is not full; to the place from which the rivers flow they return.[38]

In other words, v. 7 is understood as describing a cyclical beneficent movement of water of the rivers that, having flowed into the sea, returns (שבים) to their source to repeat the natural process. In this sense, Lohfink adds that Qoheleth's poem 'praises the cosmos as glorious and eternal in this image of cyclic return'.[39] Water is seen as positively circulating and providing life-giving water to the places it passes before flowing into the sea.

Ibn Ezra states that the sea is not full because there is a mist (אד) regularly rising from the sea to the sky (Job 36:27), which forms the clouds before falling earthwards as rain.[40] Qoheleth probably imagined the hydrological cycle as follows: the rivers flow to the sea; the sea is linked to the subterranean water, perhaps via channels; and the water below, in turn, provides water to the rivers (נחל).[41] This is an amazing hydrological cycle that invites wonder!

---

37. Ibid., 108.
38. Ibid.
39. Norbert Lohfink, *Qohelet: A Continental Commentary* (Minneapolis: Fortress, 2003), 40.
40. See Roger N. Whybray, *Ecclesiastes* (Grand Rapids, MI: Eerdmans), 42.
41. Nili Samet, 'Qohelet 1,4 and the Structure of the Book's Prologue', *ZAW* 126 (2014): 99.

In the Bible, נחל often denotes a torrent or wadi that flows only intermittently and during certain parts of the year (Isa. 34:9). Qoheleth 1:7 would then be seen as referring to the repeated annual flow of the wadi. To oppose this meaning, romantic readers suggest that נחל does not always refer to an intermittent flow of water. They continue that the use of the participle הלך here as the subject of הנחלים suggests, as is the case in previous verses, unending flowing rivers rather than wadi.[42] This interpretation has the support of Reymond, who declares of Qoh. 1:7 that:

> La continuité du mouvement de l'eau qui s'écoule a aussi servi de point de départ pour plusieurs comparaisons. Elle a permis à l'Ecclésiaste de montrer la vie dans ce qu'elle a de toujours identique à elle-même: tous les fleuves vont continuellement vers la mer sans que celle-ci se remplisse.[43]

This reading is possibly reflected in the *Letter of Aristeas*, which was probably written after the composition of Qoheleth. The letter talks about the abundance of Palestine during the Ptolemaic period, with a specific focus on a natural circulating water system (the River Jordan) providing fertility to much of the land before being emptied into the sea. Hadad states the following:

> The country enjoys everything in abundance, being well watered everywhere and possessing great security. Around it flows the river called Jordan, whose stream never fails… About the time of harvest the river rises, like the Nile, and irrigates much of the land. The stream empties into another river in the district of Ptolemais, and this flows into the sea.[44]

Briefly, the romantic reading regards v. 7 as continuing the cyclical process of nature in vv. 4-6. It is argued that the introduction of another kind of phenomenon here would be unnatural and would weaken the force of the argument. Indeed, the repetition of a series of key words such as שוב, הלך or מקום in these verses suggests that these verses are intended to be bound in the same ideal.

5.3.4. *Critical Conclusion and Assessment*

This conclusion concerns both ecological insights about nature in general, and water in particular in Qoh. 1:4-11.

---

42. Whybray, 'Ecclesiastes 1:5-7', 112.
43. Reymond, *L'eau*, 111.
44. Hadas, *Aristeas*, 147.

5.3.4.1. *Nature in general.* Both the romantic (purposeful) and negative (goalless) ideas are inherent in the artful enigmatic and ambiguous features of the text. Either dissociating or linking vv. 3 and 4 in order to determine the meaning of דור, the Hebrew word דור in v. 4 has both human and natural cycles in mind. The earth remains the same despite the constant cycles, either goal-directed or wearisome, of human generations and nature phenomena.

From the text's deliberate artful ambiguity, neither the wearisomeness of nature alone (negative) nor the romantic meaning of nature alone can be supported. The ambiguous status of the book does not present one single meaning of the text, but instead presents two or more possible meanings. The delayed identification of the subject in the first half of v. 6, for instance, leads one to think that v. 6 still speaks about the sun (v. 5) whereas the focus has already shifted to the wind.

Furthermore, the Hebrew verb שואף, depicting the movement of the sun in v. 5, alternately occurs in the Old Testament both positively – panting with eagerness or desire (Ps. 119:131; Job 7:2) – and negatively – panting with weakness like a woman in labour (Isa. 42:14; Jer. 14:6). The artful ambiguity of the Hebrew text presupposes that both aspects are true to life. The sun joyously panting across the sky depicts a positive aspect of life, while its toils across the sky in futile movement refer to unsuccessful results in life. Both readings are inherent in the text, and opting for one instead of the other is being a victim of Qoheleth's enigmatic style.

5.3.4.2. *Water and water-related phenomena in verse 7.* Romantic and negative aspects of water clearly feature in v. 7. The point that the sea does not get full despite the constant flow of rivers streaming into it, makes clear that the flowing of the rivers into the sea is a goal-directed process (positive), though one lacking efficiency as the sea is not filled. The rivers, which like human generations are in constant movement (by the use of the verb הלך in both vv. 4 and 7), contrast with the sea as a stable point of reference (like the earth in v. 4).

There are debates about how best to understand the flowing of the streams of נחלים in v. 7. Pessimistic readings prefer the usual meaning of נחלים as wadi flowing intermittently and during parts of the year (rainy seasons). However, other occurrences of נחלים show it as an overflowing stream or continuous water flow. This is the case in Amos 5:24, which, calls for justice/righteousness that flows continuously in the country, just as the streams of נחל constantly bring greening to the region.

In my view, both meanings of the word are possible in the mind of Qoheleth. The romantic view – water returning to its source to flow afresh – echoes Ps. 104:10-16, where the purposeful movement of the streams provides life-giving water to the plants, beasts, birds and the earth. In accordance with the meaning of נחלים in Amos 5:24, v. 7 also implies the life-giving effects that an ever-flowing stream causes in greening the region where it flows. By contrast, if read as pointing to the wearisomeness of nature, v. 7 could possibly be linked with Job 12, where the use of water by God to destroy earth is claimed by Job as a pointless action.

It has to be observed that Qoheleth implies both aspects of water. This is likely due to the complexity of the matter he is describing – namely life. Nature is puzzling and enigmatic since, on the one hand, there are many regular, life-giving cycles in nature (positive), while, on the other hand, there are many pointless repetitions (negative). The reason that neither humans nor rivers ever achieve a final goal despite regular activity is given in v. 8: humans cannot successfully speak about life just as it is difficult to have a full understanding of nature forces, including the water-related phenomena.

This is in accordance with Qoheleth's intention of re-questioning wisdom tradition. It is possible that, just as in the book of Job, Qoheleth asserts that the truth about the world order – which is sustained by *Ma'at* in Egypt, *Me* in Sumer and חכמה in Israel – is very complex, to the point that its human perception is often confused and confusing. For Qoheleth, the wisdom of the world order is so complex and unfathomable that Sir. 24:28-29 can state:

> [28] The first man did not know wisdom fully, nor will the last one fathom her.
> [29] or her thoughts are more abundant than the sea, and her counsel deeper than the great abyss. (NRSV)

Nature is both wearisome and purposeful, which makes it an appropriate metaphor for depicting the puzzling and enigmatic nature of human life in its complexity. Each reading alone fails to do justice to the historical context of the message of Qoheleth, which is a world of opportunities and frustrations. Without denying that there is order (life-giving aspects) in the world (Ptolemaic/Hellenistic world), the use of ambiguity here shows that Qoheleth wants to teach that there is also confusion and pointlessness or life-threatening aspects in this order. The ambiguous flow of water can be couched in the following statement:

Rivers come from a source, which may be remote, inaccessible or intimate; they flow incessantly, ever-changing and always the same; they bring life and are the economic base of inimical empires, and are consequently occasions of death, displacement and anguish, the constitutive trauma of the Hebrew Bible.[45]

Eco-theological explorations of Qoh. 1:4-11 will be much rewarded if they take both aspects of water into consideration. The ambiguous style of Qoh. 1:4-11 does not mean that the meaning of the text is uncertain; rather, it teaches that the meaning is 'richer when it affirms two aspects which may be in tension with each other, but which are both equally true to life'.[46] Neither the life-giving potential of nature/water (supported by the romantic focus of Whybray and Lohfink), nor the pessimistic (life-threatening) view of nature/water (Murphy, Perdue and Brown) alone give justice to the fullness of Qoheleth's reflection about the realities of life.

5.3.4.3. Eco-theological retrieval of the text. Anthropocentric perspectives on Qoh. 1:4-11 ignore the ecological significance of water in this text in favour of discourses about human matters. Our ecological awareness has led us to find that the text presents insightful ecological wisdom of water and water-related phenomena. There is a kind of ambiguous relationship between human life and nature/water in the artful ambiguity of Qoh. 1:4-11. Human beings sometimes do experience nature/water as pointless (particularly when it is acting against them), but at the same time nature/water acts purposefully – especially when it serves the created order.

The unfilled sea in v. 7 highlights this double meaning. As indicated previously, the word שבים in v. 7 means both 'to return', implying cyclic life-giving movement of water (as in Ps. 105), and 'to go', recalling the pointless movement of water which benefits neither humans nor other earth members. The interpretation of the movement of water as both wearisome and purposeful denotes water as an uneasy and puzzled entity that has puzzled realities similar to those of human life.

Therefore, the purposeful use of ambiguity in v. 7 underlines the intrinsic value of water acting on its own, whether for human interest or not: the movement of water, either wearisome or positive, is to be understood as part of the created order just as the way of life is embedded

---

45. Francis Landy, 'Fluvial Fantasies', in Ben Zvi and Levin, eds., *Thinking of Water in the Early Second Temple Period*, 437.
46. Wilson, 'Artful', 364.

with frustrations and order. The interpretation of movement of water as both wearisome and purposeful explains the experience of ambiguity and uneasiness linked with a position of human vulnerability or strength *vis-à-vis* realities of life. As in the natural world, so too in human life there is complexity.

The next section points to the life-giving function of water in Qoh. 2:4-6.

5.4. *Water and Water-related Phenomena in Qoheleth 2:4-6*

5.4.1. *Introduction.* Water occurs here in the context of Qoheleth's boasting about his wealth. Generally, 'making pools to water the forest' and 'irrigation system of the garden and parks' are read as being among the measures taken by Qoheleth in his pursuit of the meaning in pleasure. While agreeing with this interpretation, this chapter investigates whether Qoheleth's projects related to water systems and reservoirs presume the ecological relevance of water given the aridness of Palestine.

This section critically analyses Qoh. 2:4-6 in relation to other ancient Near Eastern autobiographic inscriptions about parks, cisterns and reservoirs as well as biblical texts highlighting the garden theme and water supply. Thereafter, it focuses on the literary analysis of the text before then exploring its ecological aspects.

5.4.2. *Translation of Qoheleth 2:4-6*

This following translation is that of the NRSV:

> [4] I made great works; I built houses and planted vineyards for myself;
> [5] I made myself gardens and parks, and planted in them all kinds of fruit trees.
> [6] I made myself pools from which to water the forest of growing trees.

5.4.3. *Literary considerations.* Qoheleth 2:4-11 belongs to the part of the book that deals with the historical quest of Qoheleth to master life and to determine the good in human life.[47] The good that Qoheleth discovers is the ironic *Carpe diem* situation. The wider literary context of the passage is Qoh. 1:1–2:26, with its main concerns of the unfathomability of human life.[48]

---

47. Perdue, *Wisdom Literature*, 205.
48. Koh, *Royal Autobiography*, 26.

Despite arguing that the 'royal fiction' is limited to Qoh. 1:12–2:11, Loader admitted that Qoh. 1:12–2:26 is a logical literary unit enclosing Qoheleth's self-introduction, the announcement of his royal experiment, and their results.[49] The unit is framed by the claim that God is responsible for giving humans the grievous task that keeps them occupied (1:13), and concludes with God giving human beings the possibility to enjoy it (2:24-26).

The central part of the royal fiction encompasses the announcement of Qoheleth's royal experiment in the pursuit of pleasure. In his search for what was good for mortals to do under the sun during the few days of their life, Qoheleth made great works, including constructing vineyards, gardens, parks, irrigation systems and reservoirs of water (2:4-6). Qoheleth also claims to have gained fabulous wealth in the form of slaves, flocks, silver, gold, provinces, singers and concubines (2:7-9), but deemed these as *hebel* and chasing of the wind (v. 11).

It is worth noting that significant similarities exist between the seven 'great works' (vv. 4-11) that Qoheleth achieved and the seven sections/days of creation in Gen. 1:2–2:4a. While God deemed everything that he had made to be 'very good' (or pleasing) and rested on the seventh day 'from all his work that he had done' (Gen. 1:31 and 2:4a), Qoheleth assesses all that his 'hands had done and the toil spent in doing it' as *hebel*.

Therefore, if Qoh. 2:4-11 does indeed suggest Genesis creation traditions, then Hertzberg is on the right track in affirming that the royal voice mentioning the making of gardens, parks, pools of water and irrigation of forest denotes that Qoheleth toiled to create the delights of the paradise of Gen. 2–3.[50] The ecological potential of water and water-related phenomena in vv. 4-6 are thus the same as texts reflecting the garden motif (Gen. 2 and Song 4:12-15), and mentioning irrigation systems (Neh. 3:15). However, the difference here in Qoh. 2 is that they are encompassed in the idea of *hebel*.

The following section analyses Qoh. 2:4-6 in relation to ancient Near Eastern texts that record royal autobiography alongside matters that can be understood to touch upon ecological matters, notably issues of water supply.

---

49. James A. Loader, *Polar Structures in the Book of Qohelet* (Berlin: de Gruyter, 1979), 35–9.

50. Hans W. Hertzberg, *Der Prediger* (Gütersloh: Gerd Mohn, 1963), 87.

5.4.4. Socio-literary Analysis of Qoheleth 2:4-6

5.4.4.1. *Qoheleth 2:4-6 versus ancient Eastern inscriptions.* The recitation of a king's 'great works' (achievements) is a major feature in royal inscriptions in the ancient East. Lists of great royal works typically include references to the building of memorial statues, temples, the kings' palaces, defence, civil works and the rebuilding of cities. The inscriptions often include the monarch's boastful comments about deeds performed on behalf of his people: economic wealth, peace in the land, the abundant harvest of crops and occasional mentions of livestock.

The Mesha inscription is particularly interesting, as it presents striking similarities with Qoheleth's list. The inscription lists the repairing of parkland walls and the building of a water reservoir with an additional irrigation system.[51] However, unlike Qoheleth, Mesha's projects are listed as part of Moab's efforts to renovate the country after their supposed break from Israelite dominion:

9   ...I rebuilt Baal-meon, and I made a reservoir in it...
21 ...I have rebuilt Qarhōh, the parkland walls and the walls...
22 of the acropolis, and I rebuilt its gates and repaired its towers, and
23 I repaired the king's residence, and I made retaining walls for the reser[voir at the spr]ing inside
24 the town...

In the agrarian societies of the ancient Near East, royal building projects often sought to 'make the land fruitful'; the creation of an irrigated pleasure-garden was often a sign of this.[52] Qoheleth appears to have adopted this literary convention, though there is a significant difference in content between the self-centred, hyperbolic depiction of his achievements in Qoh. 2:4-9 and those found in the West Semitic inscriptions.[53]

While extra-biblical inscriptions (Azatiwada, Hadad, Kilamuwa and Mesha) boast of the good that they had done for their people in terms of securing peace and prosperity of the land, Qoheleth lists the extent of his private wealth and efforts in the pursuit of pleasure. Qoheleth boasts of building palaces 'for me' (לי), just as the vineyards which he planted were

---

51. Herbert Donner and Wolfgang Röllig, eds., *Kanaanäische und Aramamaïsche Inschriften* (Wiesbaden: Harrassowitz, 1964), 168–69 (inscr. 181, lines 9 and 23).

52. Douglas Green, 'When the Gardener Returns: An Ecological Perspective on Adam's Dominion', in Toly and Block, eds., *Keeping God's Earth*, 272.

53. Koh, *Royal Autobiography*, 79.

לְ. The gardens and parks were created לְ, and the pools or reservoir of water/irrigation systems were לְ (vv. 4-6). Qoheleth is not talking about public works, but projects for his 'self-pleasure'.

The self-pleasure approach is also found in the Tell Siran inscription,[54] which is a tribute to Amminadab, king of the Ammonites. The text presents syntactic similarities with Qoh. 2:4-6, as illustrated in the following noteworthy quotation:

> May the product of Amminadab, king of the Ammonites, the son of Hissil-'El, king of the Ammonites, the son of Amminadab, king of the Ammonites – the vineyard and the orchard and the park and <the> pools – give pleasure for many days and for years far off.[55]

While Mesha's inscription shows that the king provided or repaired irrigation systems for the sake of his people, the Tell Siran text calls for the orchards, parks and their pools of water to bring everlasting pleasure only to the king. Like the Tell Siran inscription, Qoheleth's royal fiction speaks not of water systems dedicated to the betterment of the land of Israel, but rather personal water systems. The relevance of the ego-approach of Qoheleth has to be understood as a critical view on prevailing practices.

The critical portrayal of the text may also imply that, in addition to Solomon (the monarch traditionally seen as the author of Qoheleth), other Hellenistic rulers and their representatives in Judea pursued projects serving their own ends. A notable example would be Tobia Joseph, an ego-centric man who based his happiness on his personal wealth and 'built his son Hyrcanus a palace with park and irrigation system' between 182 and 175 BCE.[56] It is implied in the text of Qoheleth that in his pursuit of personal happiness, Qoheleth did not care about the happiness or pain of the people he used to realise his great works (4:1-3).

The text is informative for contemporary readers because it can be seen to criticise present-day abuses of resources, including water resources, to serve the happiness and interest of those in power or of small groups of people. While water is seen to have life-giving potential, it is used for the happiness of one person to the detriment of many. Despite his wealth, Qoheleth concludes that he has still achieved no gain (v. 11) – only *hebel*

---

54. Henry Thompson and Fawzi Zayadine, 'The Tell Siran Inscription', *BASOR* 212 (1973): 9.

55. Robert B. Coote, 'The Tell Siran Bottle Inscription', *BASOR* 240 (1980): 93.

56. Krüger, *Qoheleth*, 66.

and striving after wind. Qoheleth's autobiography is, therefore, a critical commentary against the unbalanced distribution of resources, including the supply of water.

5.4.4.2. *The 'Eden water theme' in Qoheleth 2:4-6.* The word Eden in Gen. 2:8 refers to a well-watered land, and not a field as it is often proposed.[57] This meaning is supported by the Tell Fakhariyah inscription which is written in early Aramaic and Assyrian scripts. Its Aramaic text praises Hadad who *m'dn* the regions, or who provides an abundance of water.[58] The corresponding word of *m'dn* in the Assyrian version is *muṭaḥḥidu*, referring to the attractiveness of a royal ornament[59] as assumed in Qoh. 2:4-6. The LXX has rendered the Hebrew words גן־עדן by παράδεισος in Gen. 2:15, a place of plentiful water.

Qoheleth provided his human-made gardens with irrigation pools to ensure the necessary water for the growth of the fruit trees. The mention of עץ כל־פרי (every kind of fruit trees) calls to mind Gen. 1:11, which speaks of the land yielding any kind of fruit trees (עץ פרי). In so doing, Qoheleth not only poses as a king, but even as God trying to create a garden (גנה) and parks (פרדסים) in a land where water is very scarce.[60]

The provision of water in royal gardens/parks is also attested in extra-biblical texts arising from the Achaemenid period:

> Plants gathered from all over the empire were planted in carefully planned gardens. Sections of the parks were laid out as lush woodlands, well supplied with water, forming orderly and fertile oases in the midst of barren landscapes. These forested sections also served as game reserves, stocked with animals (lions, tigers, bears), where kings and courtiers hunted, allowing the former to exhibit his physical prowess.[61]

The making of this kind of garden involved a number of measures related to water supply, including the lining and maintenance of water channels or aqueducts connected to the major basins or pools to ensure the regularity of water to mollify the arid climate of the immediate surroundings.

---

57. Alan R. Millard, 'The Etymology of Eden', *VT* 34 (1984): 103-4.
58. Richard S. Hess, 'Eden', *Bible Review* (1991): 32.
59. Millard, 'The Etymology', 104.
60. Arian Verheij, 'Paradise Retried: On Qohelet 2:4-6', *JSOT* 50 (1991): 114.
61. Amélie Kuhrt, *The Persian Empire: A Corpus of Sources from Achaemenid Period* (London: Routledge, 2010), 272.

Ironically, Qoheleth appears to state that these pleasurable gardens and parks never brought him satisfaction. However, it must be admitted that Qoh. 2:4-6 can be read as 'referring to a failed attempt on the part of Qoheleth at creating something like Paradise'.[62] While God saw that everything he had done was very good in Gen. 1:31, Qoh. 2:1 states:

> Then I considered all that my hands had done and the toil I had spent in doing it, and again, all was vanity [*hebel*] and a chasing after wind, and there was nothing to be gained under the sun. (NRSV)

Qoheleth is upset not by the enterprise itself – which he did with pleasure (v. 10) – but the fact that it did help him to obtain or appreciate the fullness of life. Although Qoheleth is not fully satisfied with the pleasures wealth affords, they are still the best that life has to offer.

5.4.5. *Ecological Significance of Water in Qoheleth 2:4-6*

Anthropocentric readings of Qoh. 2:4-6 simply ignore the significance of water in this text in favour of reading the text as part of Solomon's measure of pleasure. However, our ecological awareness has led us to discern the significance of water in Qoheleth's garden projects. References to a well-irrigated garden in Qoheleth remind us of the relevance of water in the ancient Near Eastern physical world, where drought was synonymous with death.[63]

In a dry land like Palestine, water and trees are two visible signs of life and beauty. Ansari stated that in hot and dry places, gardens (i.e. water and plants) are symbols of freshness: 'they are examples of paradise on the earth'.[64] Water was then, as now, central to the life of a garden. As such, various methods were involved in distributing water from the main supply to various reservoirs for water storage – an insurance against drought – and were placed at the inlet of the irrigation system of gardens and parks.[65]

---

62. Verheij, 'Paradise Retried', 115.

63. Louis Jonker, 'Manasseh in Paradise? The Influence of ANE Palace Garden Imagery in LXX 2 Chronicles 33:20', in Ben Zvi and Levin, eds., *Thinking of Water in the Early Second Temple Period*, 340.

64. Mojtaba Ansari, *Principles of Islamic Traditional Architectural Design* (Tehran: Tarbiat Modares University Press, 1989), 109.

65. Shin T. Kang, 'Irrigation in Ancient Mesopotamia', *AWRA* 8, no. 3 (1972): 622.

The idea of the king creating a fertile garden out of barren land is akin to bringing order out of chaos. In other words, it is as if the king duplicates the divine paradise on earth. This was a powerful statement in the ancient East, symbolising authority, fertility and legitimacy. Gardens, especially 'royal gardens', were seen as mythological symbols of the city – to the point that Jewish readings (Midrash) interpret the Garden of Eden as the depiction of the Promised Land.[66] That is why the portrayal of the Promised Land in Deut. 11:8-15 presents similarities with the Garden of Eden in terms of water availability and land fertility.

Qoheleth intentionally uses here the words גנה and פרדסים instead of גנן. Although the biblical lexica do not significantly differentiate גנה and גנן, the latter refers to a garden or park, which was intended for enjoyment and pleasure, while the former can mean both a garden for agricultural production and a place for enjoyment.

The Hebrew word פרדסים – a loanword from the Persian *paradaida* and the Greek παραδεισος – refers to specially watered parks and pleasure gardens (Cant. 4:13). In Qoh. 2:4 it is supplemented by גנות, denoting the idea of 'enclosure'. Deriving from the root גנן (to close), גנות suggests private property. In the context of Qoheleth, פרדסים and גנות denote not only a place for pleasure, but also an investment. In fact, the usage of the Greek word παραδεισος during the Ptolemaic period referred to an ecologically and economically productive orchard yielding every kind of fruit tree and botanical environment enabled by water availability.[67]

Although Qoheleth realises that all his effort is *hebel*, the text nevertheless reflects the water management attitudes in the mind of the writer. One can read in the language of Qoh. 2:5 the idea of making the arid land fruitful by proper water management. As a great king, Hezekiah also listed his achievements in terms of making pools and a conduit of water to supply the city (2 Kgs 20:20; Sir. 50:4-6) along with vineyards and gardens, as well as irrigations channels and reservoirs. In other words:

> The botanical garden, filled with exotic trees and flowing streams, was the parade example of the king's life-giving role as gardener, and visible proof that his wise rule brought fertility and fruitfulness to his whole land.[68]

---

66. Paul Morris, 'Exiled from Eden: Jewish Interpretations of Genesis', in *A Walk in the Garden: Biblical, Iconographical and Literary Images of Eden*, ed. Paul Morris and D. Sawyer (Sheffield: JSOT, 1992), 118.

67. Dominic Rudman, *Determinism in the Book of Ecclesiastes* (Sheffield: Sheffield Academic, 2001), 15.

68. Green, 'When the Gardener Returns', 273.

Water is seen as having intrinsic worth by creating life in the desert. It becomes clear that Qoheleth's water irrigation works testify to his awareness about water management and sanitation as the key for a fertile and delightful environment.

5.5. Water and Water-related Phenomena in Qoheleth 11:1-6

5.5.1. Introduction

There are various interpretations of this enigmatic passage of Qoheleth. Interpretations include an exhortation for liberality, an agricultural invitation to sow, an invitation for fishing, *Carpe diem*, and an allusion to maritime trade. The intention of this section is not to argue for or against any of these interpretations, but to scrutinise the underlying worldview that may have informed the use of water-related images in this ambiguous passage. The ideal is to attend to the language Qoheleth uses without moving too quickly into a discussion of what the text means.

Figurative and anthropocentric interpretations often fail to recognise that the nature images on the surface of Qoh. 11:1-6 are what the author chooses to show us first and most clearly. In his excursus on Qoh. 12, Fox points something out that is also valid for Qoh. 11:1-6:

> Rather than thinking of the imagery as an expendable outer garb, we should compare it to the visible surface of a painting. The imagery *is* the painting. We can discuss the painting's symbolism, emotive overtones, ideological message, and so on, but only as projections of the surface imagery, not as substitutes for it. To understand the poem we must first look carefully at the surface the author shows us.[69]

Accepting this, we can assume that Qoh. 11:1-6 echoes an agricultural context. This assumption draws on various considerations. First, the book of Qoheleth was read during an agricultural festival, *Sukkot*. Second, a number of authors also think that Qoh. 11:1 echoes both the Hapi hymn and the Egyptian practice of sowing by casting the seed from the boats during the Nile inundation so that when the waters retreat the grains in the alluvial soil spring up (Isa. 32:20). Third, vv. 2-6 deal directly with agricultural details.

The present section includes: a translation of Qoh. 11:1-6, an analysis of our text with regard to the extra-biblical sources and, finally, an ecological analysis of Qoheleth's words.

---

69. Michael V. Fox, 'Aging and Death in Qohelet 12', *JSOT* 42 (1988): 57.

5.5.2. Translation

With the exception of v. 5, the following translation is that of the NRSV:

> [1] Send out your bread upon the waters, for after many days you will get it back.
> [2] Divide your means seven ways, or even eight, for you do not know what disaster may happen on earth.
> [3] When clouds are full, they empty rain on the earth; whether a tree falls to the south or to the north, in the place where the tree falls, there it will lie.
> [4] Whoever observes the wind will not sow; and whoever regards the clouds will not reap.
> [5] *Just as you don't know the way of the wind[70] or how bones grow in a pregnant woman's womb, so you don't know the work of God, the maker of everything.*
> [6] In the morning sow your seed, and at evening do not let your hands be idle; for you do not know which will prosper, this or that, or whether both alike will be good.

5.5.3. Literary Considerations

I am of the opinion that vv. 3-6 develop the theme of vv. 1-2 in Qoh. 11:1-6. The unit is framed by four imperatives: שלח (send out, v. 1), תן (divide, v. 2), זרע (sow, v. 6a) and אל־תנח (do not slack off, v. 6b) – all denoting agricultural thoughts. The text is clearly different from Qoh. 11:7–12:7, which is much more apocalyptic.

Qoheleth consists of five sections: vv. 1-2; 3; 4; 5 and 6. Verses 1-2 and 6 frame the unit in terms of substantial exhortations, while the rest of the verses form the argument of the enigma. Several nature key-words are used to connect the sections to one another: עבים (clouds, vv. 3 and 4), רוח (wind, vv. 4 and 5), זרע (sow, vv. 4 and 6). The argument consists of highlighting human ignorance *vis-à-vis* the variations of nature forces, mainly the water-related phenomena, which are potentially life-giving or life-threatening, especially in the Israelite agrarian context. Human ignorance is reinforced via the repetition of the phrase 'you do not know', which appears (in different forms) in vv. 2 and 5a (לא תדע) and vv. 5b and 6 (אינך יודע).

---

70. The phrase מה דרך הרוח כעצמים בבטן המלאה literally means 'the way of the wind like the bones in the womb get full (complete)?' The NRSV has prefixed ב instead of כ to the word עצמים in order to justify the translation of the verse as being about הרוח entering the embryo. The problem is that this reading breaks the idea of nature images that starts in v. 1 and continues up to v. 6. The *lectio difficilor* of the MT is thus to be preferred.

5.5.4. Ecological Significance of Water in Qoheleth 11:1-6

5.5.4.1. *Water ambivalence in Qoheleth 11:1-2.* Loader[71] argues that Qoh. 11:1-6 is about risk and assurance. The positive imperatives in vv. 1-2 (send your bread...divide your means and sow your seed) draw on the inscrutability of water in an agricultural context, denoting that anything, either positive or negative, can occur. Whether vv. 1-2 refer to charity[72] or business,[73] the idea behind the text is about risk and assurance in an agrarian worldview.

The metaphor reinforces the idea of risk since לחם denotes something that is ready for consumption (1 Sam. 17:17). It is unpredictable whether bread upon the water will be found or not, but one has to do it. The imperfect form of the verb in v. 1 suggests that 'the bread in the "source domain" *may or may not be rediscovered*'.[74] The Complete Jewish Bible simply translated the second part of v. 1 as: 'eventually you will reap a return'.

Qoheleth 11:1 can, thus, possibly be linked to the Egyptian sage Ankhsheshonqy: 'do a good deed and throw it in the water; when it dries you will find it' (19.10). While it is difficult to fix precisely the dating of either text, both are aphorisms and it is possible to use one to shed light upon the other.[75] Since both texts are believed to have been written during the Ptolemaic period, the underlying idea behind the text could be the same.[76] The sage Ankhsheshonqy might have had in mind a water-related realm in which rediscovery was not easy to imagine; possibly a Nile context is envisaged.

Some have linked vv. 1-2 with the Egyptian Hapi hymn, which speaks of sowing during the Nile's inundation – an act not without risk. The hymn praises the personified inundating Nile River for its life-giving function in watering the land, something that leads directly to the provision of bread and the sustenance of human beings. The hymn also warns that 'whoever observes the wind will not sow, and whoever regards the clouds will not reap'.[77] Egyptians could and did take a real risk when sowing by casting seed from a boat during the Nile inundation, though the risk was evidently

---

71. Loader, *Pollar Structures*, 66.
72. Krüger, *Qoheleth*, 192.
73. Hubbard, 'Principles', 346.
74. Christopher Whitwell, 'The Variation of Nature in Ecclesiastes 11', *JSOT* 34 (2009): 87 (original emphasis).
75. Ibid.
76. Lichtheim, *Ancient Egyptian*, 159.
77. James L. Crenshaw, *Ecclesiastes* (London: SCM, 1988), 178.

justified when the grains germinated and began to grow in the rich alluvial soil.[78] Whether Qoheleth had such an idea in mind is by no means certain, though the link between the texts does seem clear.

It is, therefore, possible that the idea of finding bread after many days in Qoh. 11:1 alludes to the period between the Egyptian *Akhet* season – month of inundation – and the *Peret* season – the second season, signalling the forthcoming alluvial soil from the waters and the rise of vegetation from the newly replenished soil.

5.5.4.2. *Water volatility and the agrarian life (vv. 3-4 and 6)*. In vv. 3-4 and 6, Qoheleth points to the two most important agricultural events of the year: the coming of the clouds and the arrival of the winds, whose variations may lead farmers to delay sowing and harvesting. In Palestine, the timeframe for sowing is between the coming of the rains and a time that allows grain to develop fully before the next dry season.[79] However, Hopkins has observed that sometimes the period of rain alternates with intervals of dry weather, making it difficult to determine when the rainy season actually begins.[80]

The statement 'when the clouds are full (אם־ימלאו העבים) it will rain' testifies to an awareness of clouds being water-carriers. In Qoh. 11:3-6, rain is the key-word and its relevance is emphasised by the fact that vv. 3-4 are literally wrapped by 'clouds' and the agrarian ideas of sowing and reaping in v. 6.

The point is that upper-waters pass via the firmament (רקיע) into the clouds before being emptied on earth. In the Old Testament world, it was believed that there was a great reservoir of water above, which was held by the solid vault (רקיע) that has doors capable of opening or shutting as required (Gen. 8:2; Isa. 24:18). If these doors were opened and the water descended on earth without the intermediary assistance of clouds, the effect was devastating, destructive and life-threatening (Gen. 7:11).

Therefore, water in the clouds and the arrival of rain at the expected time (Deut. 11:14) were signs of the life-giving potential of water. In this sense, Prov. 16:15 compares the king's mercy with the clouds that bring the spring rain. The Hebrew word גשם (v. 3a) refers to those heavy winter-rains that occur in October–November. Having knowledge of the regularity of these rains was vital for farmers and their decisions about

78. Gerald E. Kadish, 'Seasonality and the Name of the Nile', *JARCE* 25 (1988): 187.
79. King and Stager, *Life in Biblical Israel*, 68–89.
80. Hopkins, *The Highlands*, 215.

when an when not to sow. However, the גשם rains are not seen so positively in Qoh. 11:3-6, but are instead seen as potentially life-threatening, linked with the hesitation to reap.

In the Hellenistic era, the observation of the clouds, mainly in agriculture, served the purpose of forecasting the weather.[81] In this sense, it is normally understood that v. 3 says that one can predict the future by watching nature. While this is the first impression Qoheleth's ironic words give, quickly he emphasises the randomness of nature in vv. 4-6. For Qoheleth, one may know things about the laws of nature (i.e. when the clouds are full they pour rain on earth, v. 3), but one has no control of the event (one does not know when it will rain, v. 4) and its outcomes (v. 6). In other words, 'nature may give one the impression of predictability, but it is in fact not completely predictable'.[82]

Possibly, Qoheleth ironically questions the techniques that claim to predict the future, especially in agriculture, from the observation of nature. Qoheleth is not a monolithic thinker who takes nature as being always predictable. He presents what is commonly known before concluding with an opposite statement. Qoheleth introduces the idea that no one can predict what things, whether good or bad, will occur (vv. 1-2), and concludes with the same statement (v. 6). Despite some sign of reliability, nature (water) is still a mystery, which makes it a life-giver and a life-threatener.

It comes as no surprise that Qoh. 11:3-6 features among parts of the book that were read during *Sukkot*, possibly addressed to farmers who hesitated in taking any risk when sowing/reaping and who were in search of perfect weather conditions. The NJPS accurately translated v. 4: 'if one watches the wind, one will never sow; if one observes the cloud one will never reap'. Hopkins[83] explains the capricious rain pattern in Israel as follows:

> The timing of the first rains is not constant. If the rainy season were to begin early, the farmer could plant early and risk the night frost in the hills, a lengthy rainfall pause before the heart of the rainy season, or a heavy spring rain that might beat down precociously tall stalks, hoping for a good harvest from a long growing season. If the rains began late, then the farmer would be forced to plant at a later than optimal time and would risk in a diminished season immature grains at harvest.

---

81. Krüger, *Qoheleth*, 194.
82. Seow, *Ecclesiastes*, 345.
83. Hopkins, *The Highlands*, 215.

Therefore, for Qoheleth, searching for the right time to sow/reap by contemplating the clouds is indeed responsible, but the right time could be missed as nature/water is sometimes unpredictable. The text emphasises humans' incapacity for mastering all details of the natural world (v. 5). In view of Qoheleth's basic idea of the inscrutability of the future, human actions will remain risky.

For Qoh. 11:3-4, whether the rains began early, late or at the normal time, the unpredictability of the rainfall regime bears risk regardless of the moment chosen for planting. Qoheleth's irony denotes that the clouds may or may not pour the גשם down earthwards and, thus, farmers sometimes have to take risky decisions.

As noted already, during the Ptolemaic period Egyptians identified the seasons for sowing and reaping based on the regularity of the Nile. In Palestine, however, the return of the rain was uncertain and varied from year to year – the rains could arrive too late, they could be insufficient or they could even fail to arrive at all.[84] While major variations/deficiencies in nature were viewed as questions of the divine, Qoheleth attributes such events to the unpredictability of nature, which is inherently mysterious.

Thus, the search for the right time or appropriate season will result in endless delaying of agricultural activities, and perhaps hedging against great errors occurring when one reaps/sows at the wrong time.[85] Water-related phenomena (clouds and rains) are, therefore, seen with life-giving and life-threatening potential, which is attached to their unpredictable status.

5.5.4.3. *Eco-theological wisdom of Qoheleth 11:1-6.* Anthropocentric perspectives on the text are mainly formulated on an understanding of the text in terms of risk and assurance. Human-focused reading generally bypass the significance of the water-related metaphors that are used to convey this message. Just as in Qoh. 1:4-11, water and water-related phenomena are here presented in terms of their potential of ambivalence and unpredictability, which may cause life or death.

Given that water is implied as having both life-threatening (risk) functions – since the expression על־פני המים usually occurs with negative connotations (Gen. 1:2; Job 24:18) – and life-giving aspects – since bread upon the waters will be found after many days – Qoh. 11:2 encourages measures of security regarding potential disasters. The idea of dividing

---

84. Christophe Levin, 'Drought and Locust Plague in Joel 1–2', in Ben Zvi and Levin, eds., *Thinking of Water in the Early Second Temple Period*, 197.

85. Hubbard, 'Principles', 343.

the seed into seven/eight (v. 2) parts denotes that a single sowing at what seemed the right time would not be seen as guaranteeing success given the unpredictability of nature (water) appearing with the potential to cause life or threat.

It is, therefore, not a mistake to link Qoh. 11:1-2 with the ambivalent character of the Nile inundation. The Nile is life-threatening in the manner and forces of its inundation, but its flooding results in the fertility of the land and a supply of plentiful water that could be stored in reservoirs for the dry season. The words על־פני המים in Gen. 1:2b, for instance, usually refer to the life-threatening primeval deep, but at the same time they allude to the situation prior to the fertility of the land because when they retreated the land yielded fruits (Gen. 1:9-12). Qoheleth 11:1-2 has both ideas in mind.

Furthermore, while water in the clouds was a sign of life-giving water for agricultural life if it occurred at the expected time (Deut. 11:14), גשם in Qoh. 11:3-4 is not seen as vital rain, but as potential life-threatening rain that is linked with the hesitation to reap. Qoheleth gives the impression that it will surely rain (v. 3), but quickly emphasises the uncertainty of nature (v. 4).

5.6. Conclusion

This chapter focused on the potential of water and water-related phenomena in three main texts: Qoh. 1:4-11; 2:4-11 and 11:1-6. In the first text, we realised that both the romantic and wearisome views of nature are in the mind of Qoheleth given the puzzling nature of the theme he wants to describe: life. We saw that in Qoh. 1:4-11, the same word in the text can cover both positive aspects of nature (life-giving water in regular cycles) and apparent negative (pointless) aspects of nature, which are two realities of human life.

As for Qoh. 2:4-6, we found that the text echoes the portrayal of the Garden of Eden in which water plays a life-giving role. One can read in the language of Qoh. 2:5 the idea of making the arid land fruitful by means of the proper management of water even though this is done from an anthropocentric/egocentric perspective and interest. By ensuring his parks have water, by providing natural irrigation systems in the garden to provide the necessary water for cultivation, Qoheleth poses as God in Gen. 2:15.

Finally, the enigmatic text of Qoh. 11:1-6 suggests that water and water-related phenomena have the potential to cause life and death. The positive imperatives in vv. 1-2 (send your bread...divide your means and sow your seed) draw on the inscrutability and unpredictability of water in an agricultural context by denoting that anything, be it life-giving or life-threatening, can occur. For Qoh. 11:1-6, despite some signs of reliability, water remains a mystery capable of causing life or death, especially in the context of agrarian activities.

Chapter 6

WATER AND WATER-RELATED PHENOMENA
IN THE DEUTERO-CANONICAL WISDOM BOOKS

6.1. *Introduction*

This chapter deals with the life-giving and life-threatening potential of water and water-related phenomena in the Deutero-canonical wisdom books, namely the Wisdom of Jesus Son of Sirach (hereafter Sirach) and the Wisdom of Solomon (hereafter Wisdom). This study is limited to eco-theological perspectives on water and water-related phenomena in Sir. 24:23-34 and 43:13-26 as well as Wis. 11:2-14. Wisdom 19:1-12 is also analysed to shed light on Wis. 11:2-14 because it mirrors the theme of water used to rescue and to destroy in Wis. 11:2-14.

6.2. *Water and Water-related Phenomena in Sirach 24:23-34 and 43:13-26*

6.2.1. *Introduction*

This section attempts an ecological interpretation of Sir. 24:23-34 and 43:13-26, respectively, depicting water as a metaphor for the Torah/Wisdom and a real cosmic entity. The analysis draws intertextually on other Old Testament books. Special attention is given to geographical and hydrological insights of the ancient world, as well as the socio-historical clues of the Hellenistic time that may enable the ecological retrieval of the texts.

6.2.2. *Introduction to the Book of Sirach*

6.2.2.1. *The date and context of Sirach.* Sirach, also called Ecclesiasticus, is unique among the Old Testament Wisdom books by explicitly naming its author: Jesus Ben Sira. The book can be dated to about 180 BCE and was originally written in the Jerusalemite form of Hebrew used during the Hellenistic times.[1] It seems that Ben Sira wrote or published his work before the threats of Antiochus IV since the book contains no direct or indirect mention of the sufferings of the pious Jews.[2]

Sirach reacted to Hellenism, though not in an unduly critical way. This is likely because the danger that Greek philosophy posed to traditional Judaism was not as great in Palestine as it was elsewhere. Ben Sira did not intend to offer a systematic polemic against Hellenism, but rather to convince Jews and some Gentiles that the inspired books of Israel, and not the intellectual literature of Hellenism, are the fountains of true wisdom. This ideal is clearly rooted in Sir. 24:23-34, in which the Torah overflows with wisdom like the vital water of the six rivers. Furthermore, Sirach is depicted as a rivulet channelling the water of wisdom's streams into the garden and far away.

6.2.2.2. Texts and versions of Sirach. It is generally agreed that Ben Sira wrote his book in Hebrew sometime between 200 and 175 BCE in Jerusalem. This text, called HTI, was translated into Greek (GI) by Ben Sira's grandson in Alexandria. Between 50 BCE and 150 CE, HTI underwent expansion and alteration, resulting in a variety of textual recensions.[3] The final product of this process is known as HTII. The Greek version (LXX) is the most reliable since it contains the entire book, even though it exists in two major recensions: GI and GII.[4] For our purposes, the Hebrew versions are preferred as they share the culture and language of the original manuscript (HTI).

The Hebrew text is divided into parts in six different, medieval, Cairo Genizah manuscripts (A, B, C, D, E and F). Fragments of the work were found at Qumran (2Q18; 11QPsa), and 26 fragments, including a lengthy and short section of Sir. 39:27–44:71, were found at Masada (M). The analysis of Sir. 24:23-34 offered here is based on the Hebrew text, while the reading of Sir. 43:13-26 relies on the Sirach scroll from Masada. In addition, the eco-theological analysis combines the insights of the LXX and those of the Hebrew language.

6.2.2.3. Literary structure of the book. The current form of Sirach should rightly be seen as the fruit of the efforts of (a) later editor(s). Its structure consists of three well-integrated and clear parts: chs. 1–24; 25–43 and

---

1. Jessie F. Rogers, 'Wisdom and Creation in Sirach 24', *JNSL* 22, no. 2 (1996): 142.
2. Skehan and Di Lella, *Wisdom*, 10.
3. Rogers, 'Wisdom', 142–3.
4. Perdue, *Wisdom Literature*, 235.

44–51.[5] Each part of the book concludes with a poem or hymn: ch. 24 (a psalm of wisdom praise), 41:15–43:33 (a hymn on creation), and 51:13-20 (a poem on Ben Sira's search for wisdom).

Curiously, Sir. 24:23-34 contains two units (vv. 23-29 and 30-34) that conclude the initial poem (Sir. 1–24; compare the hymn of personified Wisdom in Prov. 1–9), while Sir. 43:13-26 belongs to the final poem of the second part (Sir. 42:15–43:33). Taken together, these poems (Sir. 1–24 and 42:15–43:33) form a literary *inclusio* in the two parts, setting forth themes of wisdom and creation.[6] Both Sir. 24:23-34 and 43:13-26 belong to the literary units that deal with creation theology in the book of Sirach.

6.2.3. *Water and Water-related Phenomena in Sirach 24:23-34*

6.2.3.1. *Introduction.* It should be observed that Sir. 24:23-34 contains two distinct literary units. The first, Sir. 24:23-25, presents the Torah and Wisdom in the metaphor of the six vital rivers of the ancient Near East. The second, Sir. 24:30-34, portrays Ben Sira as a rivulet channelling water into the garden and beyond. These two units will be analysed separately even though the second continues the water imagery of the first.

6.2.3.2. *Position of Sirach 24:23-34 within Sirach 24.* Sirach 24 is a long poem about Wisdom's self-praise consisting of three distinct units. The first unit, Sir. 24:1-22, is a first-person Wisdom speech rhetorically similar to Prov. 8:22-31. The second, Sir. 24:23-29, is a six-line stanza in which Wisdom and Torah are identical. The last section describes Ben Sira's role as a wisdom teacher metaphorically, comparing it to a rivulet channelling water (Sir. 24:30-34).

Sirach 24:23-29 is, therefore, the core part of Sir. 24. It is characterised by a third-person speech, introduced by v. 23, equating the Torah with Wisdom. Verses 25-27 further compare the Torah with the abundant and life-giving waters of the rivers of the paradise in Gen. 2:11-14 (the Pishon, Tigris, Euphrates and Gihon), to which Ben Sira affixes the Jordan and Nile. With their periods of flood, these rivers symbolise the idea of the refreshing fullness of life of the torrent of Wisdom. Verses 28-29 declare the mystery of Wisdom over the millennia. Finally, Sir. 24:28-34 is a kind of application of the insights of Sir. 24:23-29.

---

5. John J. Collins, *Jewish Wisdom in the Hellenistic Age* (Louisville: John Knox, 1997), 45–6.

6. Perdue, *Wisdom Literature*, 234.

6.2.3.3. *The Hebrew text of Sirach 24:23-29.* The original Hebrew text (HTI) does not contain v. 24. It is believed that a pious Jew added this at a later date. In GII v. 24 reads as follows:

> Do not grow weary of striving with the Lord's help, but cling to him that he may reinforce you. The Lord Almighty alone is God, and apart from him there is no saviour.

Given that GII is a later Greek recension based on Hebrew translations (HTII), and in light of the fact that this pious statement breaks the rhetoric and literary patterns of the poem that is imbued with water-related images, many modern translations ignore it.

However, with the exception of v. 27b, I have opted to follow the NRSV's translation. Many modern translations are based on GI, omitting και (and) before Gihon in order to equate the Nile with Gihon as in Jer. 2:18. The Greek word και occurs in GII, translating the Hebrew ו before כגיחון (and as Gihon) in HTI, and thus giving a perfect balance to vv. 25-27 in terms of one river in each of the six lines of vv. 25-27. The text reads as follows:

> [23] All this is the book of the covenant of the Most High God,
>   the law that Moses commanded us
>   as an inheritance for the congregations of Jacob.
> [25] It overflows, like the Pishon, with wisdom,
>   and like the Tigris at the time of the first fruits.
> [26] It runs over, like the Euphrates, with understanding,
>   and like the Jordan at harvest time.
> [27] It pours forth instruction like the Nile[7]
>   and like the Gihon at the time of vintage.
> [28] The first man did not know wisdom fully,
>   nor will the last one fathom her.
> [29] For her thoughts are more abundant than the sea,
>   and her counsel deeper than the great abyss.

6.2.3.4. *Literary structure of Sirach 24:23-29.* As the following discussion makes clear, the poem presents itself as a chiastic structure. It should be noted that the reading offered here has not, to my knowledge, been offered elsewhere.

---

7. The Greek translation misunderstood the Hebrew word יאור as 'light' instead of 'the Nile', combining thus the verb אאיר (for shining), used in v. 32b, to underline the role of Sirach to send forth teachings to shine like the dawn. However, the Syriac Peshitta understood the Hebrew word יאור in v. 27a as 'the Nile'.

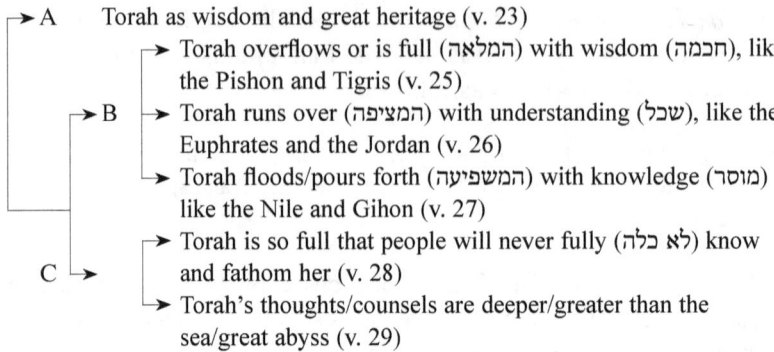

Table 7. *The Literary Structure of Sirach 24:23-29*

Sirach 24:23-29 presents itself as an ABC structure. A contains the main subject, which is the Torah (v. 23). B is made up of three parallel verses (vv. 25-27), each containing two rivers and one agricultural season. B as a whole depicts the significance of the Torah's wisdom in terms of the life-giving water of the six rivers that fertilise the land at specific times (the times of first fruits, harvest and vintage). In the Hebrew text, the syntactical patterns are constructed in such a way that the beginnings (ה) and endings (בימי־) of lines in vv. 25-27 almost carry identical resonance.[8]

C conveys the idea of the abundance of wisdom from the Torah. This wisdom is deeper than the depths of the sea and greater than the abyss. Like these water-related phenomena, the Torah is so profound and abundant that, despite all scribal efforts, its meaning has not been exhausted. Just as people never fully discern the mysterious character of these water-related phenomena, so it is for wisdom. B and C are, therefore, the description of the vitality of the subject of A.

Sirach 24:23-29 has deliberately positioned the Pishon as the first river and Gihon as the last in order that the other two rivers, the Nile and the Jordan, appear as additional streams of the paradise.[9] The Nile and the Jordan are the two prominent rivers of the Semitic region, and for the Jewish author they deserve to be ranked among the cosmic rivers that transport water out from Eden toward the whole earth (Gen. 2:10). In this metaphor, Ben Sira suggests that water is a central condition for life and refreshment.

---

8. Patrick W. Skehan, 'Structure in Poems on Wisdom: Proverbs 8 and Sirach 24', *CBQ* 41 (1979): 379.

9. Sheppard, *Wisdom*, 69.

6.2.3.5. *Wisdom as life-giving water (vv. 23-27).* In the following eco-theological analysis of Sir. 24:23-27, the focus is on the significance of the various key-words (verbs, nouns and seasons) used to compare the Torah's wisdom with the vital water of the six rivers. Thereafter, the eco-theological significance of water stated in vv. 28-29 is retrieved.

6.2.3.5.1. *Brimful like Pishon and Tigris (v. 25).* The Torah is said to be full (המלאה) of Wisdom (חכמה) like the Pishon and Tigris at the time of new crops, namely in spring when rivers are at their highest water level.[10] The Hebrew word for the verb 'to be full' is מלא, while Wisdom is חכמה (see HTI, v. 25). מלא is the same verb used in Gen. 1:28, when God conferred the blessing of fullness and fertility on human beings. Thus, Sir. 24:25 testifies to the awareness of the life-giving waters of the Pishon and Tigris that procure fertility at the time of new crops. This fullness is equated with the fertility that Wisdom procures to her listeners.

Sirach 24:25-27 calls attention once again to Ps. 1, which contrasts the wicked with those who meditate on the Torah of God. In Ps. 1:3, the righteous are like trees planted by streams of water (על־פלגי מים) that yield their fruits in season and whose leaves do not wither.

Pishon and Tigris are among the four rivers of Gen. 2:10-14 that channel water from Eden to fertilise the garden. The hydrological information of the ancient Near East tells us that an irregularity in the flow of the Tigris could cause devastating floods in some years and disastrous droughts in others.[11] In this sense, Sir. 24:25 puts the emphasis on 'overflows with wisdom', which envisages the life-giving function of the Tigris when it is brimful at the time of new crops.

6.2.3.5.2. *Running over like the Euphrates and the Jordan (v. 26).* In Sir. 24:26, the poetry shifts from the idea of *fullness* to that of 'movement towards'. Here, the Torah is not only full with Wisdom (v. 25a), but runs over like the Euphrates with understanding and like the Jordan at harvest time. The water-related images are crucial. Physically speaking, the Euphrates flows some 2,235 miles from east central Turkey, through the north-eastern parts of Syria and the central areas of Iraq towards the Tigris, with which it forms the Shatt-al-Arab.[12]

---

10. Skehan and Di Lella, *Wisdom*, 336.
11. Carl Rasmussen, *The Zondervan NIV Atlas of the Bible* (Grand Rapids: Zondervan, 1989), 66.
12. Skehan and Di Lella, *Wisdom*, 336.

In Isa. 3:7, the Euphrates is called הנהר, to mean the river *par excellence*. The words הנהר הגדל (the great River) in Deut. 1:7 highlight the same ideal. Jeremiah 51:36 names the Euphrates 'the sea' (ים), imagining that only God can dry up its multiple fountains. This river made a big impression on the Israelites, who were less familiar with large seas and oceans. As such, Isa. 8:6 contrasts its mighty floods with the water of Shiloh that flows gently (לאט) without disastrous effects. In addition, the fact that Sargon II boasted about having crossed the Euphrates during its inundation proves that people in the ancient Near East feared the flooding of this river.

However, Sir. 24:26 softens the mighty 'floods' of the Euphrates with the Hebrew word שכל (understanding), which is rendered in GI as σύνεσιν (with understanding), providing them a positive role. Although the floods of the Euphrates are life-threatening in form, they result in the fertility of the land. This is what Sir. 24:26, in my opinion, equates with 'flowing with understanding'. In other words, the righteous will depend on the Torah for a responsible ethical life, just as life in the Euphrates and Jordan valleys was dependent upon the floods for irrigation to maintain physical life.[13]

The Jordan River was ancient Palestine's best known and most vital river. Following the etymology proposed by Köhler,[14] Jordan is the junction of two Iranian words: *Jār* (year) and *dan* (river). Thus, the Jordan River is defined as the river that flows the whole year. As a result of this reliability, the Jordan valley has long attracted human settlement. It is for this reason that Lot chose the Jordan valley as his preferred settlement. As Gen. 13:10 records, the Jordan valley was irrigated everywhere (כלה משקה) similar to the garden of YHWH (כגן־יהוה) and the land of Egypt (כארץ־מצרים).

However, just like the Euphrates, crossing the Jordan was not easy. Especially after heavy rains, the river has a significant flow, with the rushing water forming violent waves. Given this, it is no surprise that 1 Chr. 12:16 praises the army officers who crossed the Jordan during its period of inundation. At the same time, it should not be forgotten that the great floods of the Jordan made and continue to make possible abundant vegetation not just on its banks, but across the whole Jordan valley. The contrast with the dry, arid highlands could not be more stark.[15] In biblical

---

13. John G. Snaith, *Ecclesiasticus or the Wisdom of Jesus Son of Sirach* (Cambridge: Cambridge University Press, 1974), 125.
14. Ludwig Köhler, 'Der Jordan', *ZDPV* 62 (1939): 115–20.
15. Reymond, *L'eau*, 94.

times, the valley was one of the few places that could yield a great number of large trees for house building (2 Kgs 6:2). With this, we have a further demonstration of the life-giving, fertilising role of the floods.

The comparison in Sir. 24:26 of the Torah with the water of these two rivers focuses less on the form of their flooding and more on their providence of life-giving water for the agricultural activities. The primary concern is not with describing the flood waters, but on making clear what the floods bring to the land: fertility. The Hebrew phrase בימי אביב (at harvest time), which is translated in Greek as ἐν ἡμέραις θερισμοῦ, sufficiently underlines the point. When used elsewhere in the Bible,[16] the term ἐν ἡμέραις means 'a day appointed for a special purpose'. In Sir. 24:26, the appointed day is the harvest time, which benefits from the inundations of the Euphrates and the Jordan just as the Torah's listeners will benefit from understanding, which will overflow from it at 'an appointed time' of life.

6.2.3.5.3. *Flooding like the Nile and Gihon (verse 27)*. Sirach 24:27 says that the Torah floods with knowledge like the Nile, and like the Gihon at the time of vintage. In the LXX version of Jer. 2:18, the Gihon is identified with the Nile. The same idea is found in the GI version of Sir. 24:27b, which deliberately omits καὶ (and) before ὡς Γηὼν (like the Gihon) (cf. GII). Moreover, ו (and) occurs in the Hebrew text (HTII) and the Syriac Peshitta. Possibly, the original Hebrew text (HTI) contained 'and' before 'like', which would give a perfect balance of one river in each of the six lines of vv. 25-27.[17]

The annual flooding of the Nile was never seen as a threat because it always resulted in the fertility of the land. When the water retreated after the inundations, it left behind a marshy and fertile land ready for agriculture (Exod. 2:3 and Isa. 19:6). Every year, the floods deposited rich black silt and thus provided the Egyptians with fresh arable land and supplied the country with a great volume of water that could be distributed via canals and kept in reservoirs for later use.[18]

The great volume of water from the Nile flood (about 700 million cubic metres a day) also aided agriculture by slowly washing salt from the soil. In addition, the silt from the Nile delivered the raw material used in the Egyptian ceramic industry and in mud brick production.

---

16. See Lk. 17:24; Acts 28:23; 1 Cor. 4:3; Rev. 16:14.
17. Skehan and Di Lella, *Wisdom*, 337.
18. Salima Ikram, *Ancient Egypt: An Introduction* (Cambridge: Cambridge University Press, 2010), 6.

The Nile inundation was so significant for ancient Egyptians that their calendar system was based on it.[19] Of course, while people judiciously kept their settlements away from the flood plains, the floods were always viewed as God's providence for the renewal and re-creation of the land. For Egyptians, the god responsible for the inundation of the Nile, and with it the production of life-sustaining bread, was the hermaphrodite deity Hapi. This deity was so important that a representation of Hapi was engraved on a pillar at Ramses II's temple at Abydos (Upper Egypt).[20]

Sirach 24:27 clearly has this idea in mind. The life-giving water of the Nile inundation, which renewed and re-created the land, providing bread for the Egyptians, is equated with knowledge flowing from the Torah to irrigate and nourish people's lives. The reference to Nile 'floods with knowledge' (v. 27a) refers to the river rising at the right time (after a long dry season lasting from February to June), when the dry land actually longs to be hydrated, fertilised and nurtured.

Gihon has the same fertilising role. This Edenic river is mentioned in 2 Chr. 32:2-4 as being dammed by the people of Jerusalem in order to prevent their enemies from having access to its life-giving water. In Ps. 110:7, the king will drink from the brook (נחל) – Gihon – as he shows pride in his victory over the enemy. Gihon is, thus, not simply refreshing and life-sustaining, but also the medium of divine assistance in the defence of Zion. In this sense, Gihon did not only guarantee Jerusalem's water supply, but is also the location of King Solomon's coronation (1 Kgs 1:38).

Furthermore, the act of channelling the waters of Gihon in order to supply the city of David features among the great achievements of King Hezekiah (2 Chr. 32:30). It is generally agreed that the Gihon source and stream provide the physical background for the Temple source and river in the vision of Ezek. 47:1-12, where the river originates from the sanctuary and provides evergreen flora along its banks.

Thus, Sir. 24:27ab has two cultures in mind: Egypt and Israel. While the inundation of the Nile resulted in the fertility of the land of Egypt, in Israel the Gihon's flowing waters fertilised nearby vineyards and the city

---

19. The Egyptian calendar year was divided into three basic seasons: *Akhet* or inundation (June–October); *Peret* or coming forth/growing, when the land rose from the water and could be cultivated (October–mid-February); and *Shemu* or drought, when the crops ripened and were harvested (February–June). See Ikram, *Ancient Egypt*, 8.

20. See Hillel, *Natural History*, 34.

of Jerusalem.[21] The abundant life-giving waters of these two rivers typify the life-giving power of Wisdom. Water is seen as an intrinsically life-giving entity.

6.2.3.6. *Wisdom as deeper/greater than a sea/abyss (vv. 28-29).* The expressions 'the first human' and 'the last human' imply that Wisdom is beyond all human beings and their attempts to attain her (v. 28). Therefore, v. 29 compares Wisdom to water that is 'deeper than the sea' and greater than the abyss. Strikingly, v. 29 presents the following well-balanced structure:[22]

A	Her thoughts
B	Her counsels
A'	More abundant than the sea
B'	Deeper than the great abyss

Table 8. *The Structure of Sirach 24:29*

Sirach's use of these water entities to illustrate the inexhaustibility, vastness and unfathomability of Wisdom is ecologically insightful. The two Hebrew words for water, namely מים and הבר סוהת, are rendered in Greek as θαλάσσα (sea) and ἀβίσσου μεγάλης (great abyss), referring to two mythological water entities that were feared by ancient people because of their vastness and pre-existence in the primeval times.

However, unlike Sir. 46:23-26, the text does not focus on the life-threatening potential of these water-related phenomena, but rather on the comprehensiveness/universality that Wisdom possessed before being fixed in Israel (24:5-6). The point is that just as no one can contain the sea and the abyss, so no one can master the full extent of the Torah's wisdom.

This universal dimension is pictured in terms of these cosmic waters. The mention of the names of rivers found in various places of the ancient Near East suggests the universality of Wisdom. The metaphor of the greatness of the sea in Sir. 24:28-29 underlines the ecological idea that just as for Wisdom there will always be something that we ignore about water. Water is something bigger than us, something we cannot fully control, yet also without which we cannot live.

---

21. Perdue, *Wisdom Literature*, 247.
22. James L. Crenshaw, 'The Book of Sirach', *NIB* 5:758.

6.2.3.7. *Sirach 24:23-29 as a metaphor for the Promised Land.* The naming of the six rivers in the text denotes Ben Sira's Midrashic reading of the Old Testament traditions related to the Promised Land, which is seen as a well-watered paradise.[23] In Gen. 15:18, God promised a land 'from the river Egypt [Nile] to the great river Euphrates'. In Deut. 11:8-15, the 'land beyond the Jordan' is depicted in terms of an irrigated land that is assured for Israel by obedience to the Torah. The Nile, Euphrates and Jordan are the great river boundaries of the Promised Land full of water.

This Torah, located within Israel (Sir. 24:8), is equated with Wisdom and portrayed in terms of the six vital rivers (Sir. 24:23-29). Through the naming of Pishon, Tigris, Gihon and Euphrates, as well as the Nile and Jordan, Sir. 24:23-29 recalls an Eden-like Promised Land where the Torah abounds with wisdom.[24] The wealth of Wisdom is likened to the great rivers that periodically overflow with life-giving water to nurture the land. Water, here, is a powerful ecological metaphor of fertility and abundance.

6.2.4. *Water and Water-related Phenomena in Sirach 24:30-34*

6.2.4.1. *Translation of Sirach 24:30-34.* Once again, the NRSV translation is preferred for the purposes of this study. Verse 34 represents the concluding statement in praise of Wisdom in Sirach 24:

> [30] As for me, I was like a canal from a river,
>   like a water channel into a garden.
> [31] I said, 'I will water my garden and drench my flower-beds'.
>   And lo, my canal became a river, and my river a sea.
> [32] I will again make instruction shine forth like the dawn,
>   and I will make it clear from far away.
> [33] I will again pour out teaching like prophecy,
>   and leave it to all future generations.
> [34] Observe that I have not labored for myself alone,
>   but for all who seek wisdom.

6.2.4.2. *The literary structure of Sirach 24:30-34*

A	I (Sirach) am like a canal to water my garden	(vv. 30-31a)
B	My canal became a river, and my river a sea	(v. 31b)
A'	I will spread forth instruction (water) afar off	(vv. 32-33)
B'	I labored not for myself, but for all wisdom seekers	(v. 34)

Table 9. *The Literary Structure of Sirach 24:30-34*

23. Sheppard, *Wisdom*, 70.
24. Ibid., 71.

The above structure presents an ABA'B' formulation. AA' offers an antithetical parallel in which the idea of A is contrasted with that of A'. In A, Sirach has in mind the use of the life-giving waters for his purposes, while in A' he realises that the abundance of water should be shared with others. Further, BB' conveys the idea of a canal that became a mighty river and a sea whose life-giving waters are available for all wisdom seekers.

6.2.4.3. *The idea of abundance and sharing.* Sirach 24:30-34 is concerned with the idea of fullness and sharing of the life-giving water that reflects Torah's wisdom. Sirach proudly compares himself to a canal or a rivulet that has a disseminating role, just as the four cosmic rivers that originated from Eden irrigate the garden in Gen. 2:10-13. In vv. 30-31, Sirach has in mind, in the first instance, the use the life-giving water to irrigate a small garden for his own interest – as in Qoh. 2:4-6. Then, suddenly, his canal became a river and a sea, suggesting a cosmic dimension of wisdom. In Gen. 2:10, the river that originated from Eden at first watered the garden, before suddenly dividing and becoming four (abundant) branches that water the whole land. Both texts underline the idea of abundance and water distribution.

In Sir. 24:30-34 the metaphor sheds light on the referent and vice versa. The text highlights the ecological idea that wisdom/water is not destined to belong to one individual. Importantly, Sirach teaching is not viewed as a personal invention; rather, his wisdom is simply that of the Torah, of which he was the first to benefit, and which has to be spread far afield for the benefit of others (vv. 32-33).[25] This idea recurs in v. 34, where Sirach realises that his labour benefited all the seekers of wisdom. Whatever we do about water, we must make sure our actions do not undermine the free flow of this valuable commodity to its other users.

6.2.5. *Eco-theological Synthesis of Sirach 24:23-34*

6.2.5.1. *Intrinsic worth of water.* Anthropocentrism is muffled in Sir. 24:23-29. The Torah is depicted as naturally flowing with worth, just like the waters of the six rivers. The Earth Bible principle of purpose is also underlined in that the rivers are presented as flowing with wisdom at specific times. In a sense, Sir. 24:23-29 is a kind of Midrashic interpretation of Gen. 2:10-14 in which four rivers (Pishon, Gihon, Tigris and Euphrates) naturally channel water from Eden to fertilise the whole earth.

---

25. Skehan and Di Lella, *Wisdom*, 337.

In recalling Gen. 2:10-14, one could argue that Sir. 24:25-29 is informed by the idea of water management. I would agree with Tsumura that the initial situation in Gen. 2 'is not a lack of water but a lack of adequate control of it'.[26] The four rivers here in Sir. 24:25-27 are vehicles for the same idea of water management. Sirach claims that these rivers naturally rise and spread water all over the land, just as the Torah rises with wisdom to irrigate its listeners.

The themes of fullness, irrigation and flooding occur in vv. 25-27 and are certainly part of the water management process that helps to make the land fertile and enables the supply of food and drink for the human and animal inhabitants. The Torah is, therefore, depicted as following the same process in its role as nourisher of Wisdom to its listeners. For Sirach, Torah is available all the time for those who want life. That is why, during the early twentieth century, Jews began to view the Bible as their most significant asset and heritage, as well as their greatest contribution to humankind.[27]

The other two rivers, the Jordan and the Nile, point to essential water-based images for the people living in Canaan and Egypt respectively. The Nile is the source of Egypt's agricultural fertility and it is upon this watercourse that the economy of the entire country depends. The Jordan River is the best-known river in Israel. Any comparison of the Torah with the flooding of these two important rivers, on which so many people depended for their survival, would have had significant resonances. Any action that polluted or harmed these rivers was viewed as a criminal and unforgivable deed (Prov. 25:26). The question may be posed: What are we doing with our rivers today?

By comparing the Torah to these rivers, the author invites his/her listeners to view and preciously hold onto Scripture as a valuable and life-sustaining resource and as a worthy inheritance. In their periods of flood, the six rivers of Sir. 24:25-27 serve as metaphors for the abundance and fertility of life-giving streams of wisdom, understanding and knowledge poured out in the Torah. For Sirach, water is a symbol of life and it should be regarded as such and valued for its intrinsic worth.

6.2.5.2. *The mystery of water.* Verses 28-29 underline the idea that there will always be something about water that is beyond human knowledge. Wisdom is deeper than the sea and greater than the abyss. The point is that the life-giving treasure of wisdom pre-existed and will remain forever just

---

26. Tsumura, 'A Biblical Theology', 169.
27. Yaakov Shavit and Mordechai Eran, *The Hebrew Bible Reborn: From Scripture to the Book of Books* (Berlin: de Gruyter, 2007), 3.

as these bodies of water were viewed as pre-existent and perennial. In this sense, Sir. 24:30-34 continues the water-related metaphor of irrigation. Sirach depicts himself as watering a garden, but later realised that the fullness of the life-giving water cannot be kept for oneself, but is a flood that needs to be shared with others.

6.2.6. *Water and Water-related Phenomena in Sirach 43:13-26*

6.2.6.1. *Introduction.* The passage is part of a large unit in Sirach focusing on creation, namely 42:15–43:33. Sirach 43:13-26 is the only text in this unit referring to water as a physical substance.

6.2.6.2. *Literary considerations.*

6.2.6.2.1. *Translation of Sirach 43:13-26.* The Hebrew text preserved in the scroll from Masada (containing Sir. 39:27–43:30) is severely damaged from vv. 20 to 30 of ch. 43. As such, the most ancient Hebrew source for Sir. 43:13-26 is of little use for this study. The following translation relies on the NRSV, which has reconstructed the Hebrew text with the aid of material from the LXX:

> [13] By his command he sends the driving snow,
>   and speeds the lightning of his judgment.
> [14] Therefore the storehouses are opened,
>   and the clouds fly out like birds.
> [15] In his majesty he gives the clouds their strength,
>   and the hailstones are broken in pieces.
> [16] When he appears, the mountains shake.
>   At his will the south wind blows;
> [17] The voice of his thunder rebukes the earth;
>   so do the storm from the north and the whirlwind.
> He scatters the snow like birds flying down,
>   and its descent is like locusts alighting.
> [18] The eye is dazzled by the beauty of its whiteness,
>   and the mind is amazed as it falls.
> [19] He pours frost over the earth like salt,
>   and icicles form like pointed thorns.
> [20] The cold north wind blows,
>   and ice freezes on the water;
> it settles on every pool of water,
>   and the water puts it on like a breastplate.
> [21] He consumes the mountains and burns up the wilderness,
>   and withers the tender grass like fire.
> [22] A mist quickly heals all things;
>   the falling dew gives refreshment from the heat.

>²³ By his plan he stilled the deep
> and planted islands in it.
>²⁴ Those who sail the sea tell of its dangers,
> and we marvel at what we hear.
>²⁵ In it are strange and marvelous creatures,
> all kinds of living things, and huge sea-monsters.
>²⁶ Because of him each of his messengers succeeds,
> and by his word all things hold together.

6.2.6.2.2. Position of Sirach 43:13-26 in Sirach 42:15–43:33. Sirach 42:15–43:33 is an architecturally focused poem concerning God's glory in creation. This passage is divided into five sections, each centring on an aspect of God's creation. The first section is an introductory poem praising God's work as 'full of his glory' that reflects his presence and purpose in creation (42:15-25). The second concerns God's glory reflected in the planets: the sun, stars, rainbow, and particularly the moon's role in setting the signs for days and seasons (43:1-12).

Sirach 43:13-26 is the centre of the poem and serves to highlight God's power in employing water-related and weather phenomena (storm, cloud, dew, snow and frost) for good or for harm. The fourth section shows that God is 'the all' (43:27-31), before the fifth declares human inability to grasp fully the wisdom of the creation order (43:32-33).

The poem can be understood not merely as a display of wisdom, but also as a lesson in spiritual discipline with a view to nurturing a sense of God's presence through the contemplation of God's works.[28] The works of God are desirable and sparkling (Sir. 42:22). The sense of delight and joy deriving from contemplation is fully unveiled in the depiction of water-related and weather phenomena in 43:13-26.

Sirach 43:13-26 presents creation less as God's 'work' and more as the 'play' of God.[29] The order of creation, the complex complementarity it exhibits, and its purposiveness serve to inspire the sense of beauty and delight (43:26).

6.2.6.2.3. Literary structure of Sirach 43:13-26. After depicting the wonders of the stars and the rainbow in vv. 1-12, Sirach turns to various water-related phenomena in vv. 13-26, which is the text to be explored in this study. In vv. 13-17b, the text deals with warm weather as evidence

---

28. Newsom, *The Book of Job*, 224.
29. Daniel Migliore, *Faith Seeking Understanding: An Introduction to Christian Theology* (Grand Rapids: Eerdmans, 1991), 93.

of God's power, while vv. 17c-20 describe cold weather bringing forth snow and ice. Verses 21-22 depict rainstorms and life-giving dew, while vv. 23-26 deal with the marvels of the deep.

Newsom notes that by concluding with the deep, the poem takes water as its central image and completes a movement through various forms of moisture that nourish the earth – from droplets of water falling upon the earth, to the mighty expanse of water in the sea.[30] Interestingly, Sirach 43 talks about distinct water-related phenomena, whether life-giving or life-threatening, as contributing to what makes creation delightful.

6.2.6.2.4. *Sirach 43:13-26 and Psalm 104.* Sirach 43:13-26 and Ps. 104 both offer lists of cosmic phenomena. What is striking in Sirach, however, is not the list itself, but the way in which it is developed. Psalm 104 makes use of a similar cosmological list, but it only briefly depicts each element of creation. The merit of Sirach's poem is the lengthy, ecologically observed and brilliant portrayal of each natural phenomenon.

With regard to water-related phenomena, for instance, neither Job 38 nor Ps. 104 give a detailed depiction of the winter storm and its effects. By contrast, Sirach expresses his delight in the movement of snow in terms of bird flight, with the settling of snow compared to the swarming of locusts. Thus, Sirach is able to denote the purposefulness of this water-related phenomenon. The fine colour of frost is likened to salt poured out, while the crystalline shapes it forms are equated to blossoms. Ice on ponds/pools is seen as a kind of breastplate. With apparent delight in the description itself, Sirach responds with poetic richness and variety that contribute to highlight the beauty of the universe.[31]

Unlike Job 37:17, which highlights the invincible, life-threatening power of the sun, Ben Sira balances the image by concluding with a reference to the dripping clouds and dew restoring the parched mountains (Sir. 43:22). Thus, one of the distinctive features of Sir. 43:13-26 is its detailed description of specific traits of water-related natural phenomena. Such attention is lacking in Ps. 104 and even Job 38.

6.2.6.3. *Significance of water in Sirach 43:13-26.*

6.2.6.3.1. *Destructive water and water-related phenomena (vv. 13-17b).* The thunderstorm with its acolytes, namely lightning, winds, rain clouds and hail, are depicted as having the life-threatening potential to execute God's judgment on the world. The life-giving potential of water is also

---

30. Newsom, *The Book of Job*, 224.
31. Crenshaw, 'The Book of Sirach', 834.

discerned in God's forceful unleashing of the 'storehouse of the clouds' that soar like vultures (πετεινά, from the Hebrew word, עַיִט, meaning 'bird of prey') which are naturally bloodthirsty birds (v. 14b).

In Qoh. 11:3 it is stated that when the clouds (עבים) are full (ימלאו), they empty rain (גשם) on the earth. In other words, the עבים are the natural carriers of the life-giving rainwater that fertilises the earth. However, in Sir. 43:15, God strengthens (ἰσχύω, from Hebrew חזק, 'make hard') the clouds (νεφέλη or עבים in Hebrew) not to produce life-giving rainwater (as in Job 36:27 and Qoh. 1:3), but in order to produce a life-threatening natural phenomenon – the waters of the clouds are frozen and converted into a block of ice in the sky from which destructive hailstones are carved.

Water-related phenomena in this section are seen as highly life-threatening entities capable of sending woe on earth and making it writhe (43:16a, 17a). Just as God's mighty power makes the south wind blow, so too the whirlwind, hurricane and storm wind are under his control (43:17b). In various prophetic texts (e.g. Isa. 29:6; Jer. 23:19), these winds accompanied rainstorms and occurred in the context of God's anger and judgment. Naturally, rainstorms alternated with southerly desert winds and tempests, resulting in the various misfortunes of every kind in Israel.[32] The water-related phenomena are here depicted with life-threatening potential.

6.2.6.3.2. Cool water and water-related phenomena, vv. 17c-20. In contrast to the life-threatening water-related phenomena in vv. 13-17b, which typify God's anger, God's snow is compared to flying birds (43:17c) and swarms of locusts (v. 17d). The comparison is not so much on the essence of the flying creatures (especially the locusts), but on their beauty and orderly settling (Prov. 30:27). Therefore, Sir. 43:18 is impressed by the wonder and whiteness of the snow. Likewise, God pours frost out like salt; it is beautifully shining like blossoms on the thorns (v. 19). This is an interesting water imagery suggesting both threat and beauty.

All water-related phenomena depicted here typify beauty and delight. The Bible does have many ambiguities as to the role of frost. Some texts present frost as a life-threatening water-related phenomenon. Zechariah 14:6, for instance, portrays the day of the Lord as lacking the threat of frosty weather, while Ps. 78:47 views frost as lethal, capable of destroying a sycamore. Other texts focus on the fragility of frost (Sir. 3:15; Wis. 5:14), while a few texts present it as God's messenger (Ps. 148:8).

---

32. Hillel, *The Natural History*, 31.

Other texts view frost as beautiful and lovely. In Exod. 16:14, when the dew evaporated, the Israelites saw a flaky substance which they deemed as fine as frost on the ground. Sirach 43:19a belongs to this category of texts given the idea of delight and shining in v. 19b. Although Sirach is only interested in the shining of the frost, frozen water is a natural source of hydration for some wild plants, especially the thorn bush (v. 19b), which uniquely depends on the life-giving water of the rain, dew and snow.

Snow is for Sirach a positive element of creation. Like frost, snow is a symbol of purity and freshness in the Bible. Psalm 51:7 compares the whiteness of the snow to the purity of the heart. In Jer. 18:14, the permanence of the snow that brings freshness to Lebanon is contrasted with Israel abandoning YHWH, who is the source of living water.

Thus, it seems that the idea of snow flying like birds and settling down like swarms of locusts (Sir. 43:17cd) implies the natural irrigation of the ground by the snow. Settling like swarms of locusts implies 'a natural purpose'. Proverbs 30:27 depicts locusts as well-ordered fauna that purposefully settle into rank. Naturally, locust outbreaks are linked with plague and affliction because locusts consume all the vegetation of the invaded land (see Joel 1:1-4). Desert locusts are distributed over a total area of 20 million square kilometres – 20 per cent of the earth's surface.[33]

It seems that Sir. 43:17d is less interested in the theme of plague, and more in the beauty of the outbreaks of the locusts covering the earth like refreshing snow. Sirach 43:17d has in mind the same idea as Isa. 55:10, which portrays snow and rain as invading the earth from the sky and not returning (through evaporation) until the earth has been fertilised:

> [10] For as the rain and the snow come down from heaven, and do not return there until they have watered the earth, making it bring forth and sprout, giving seed to the sower and bread to the eater, [11] so shall my word be that goes out from my mouth; it shall not return to me empty, but it shall accomplish that which I purpose, and succeed in the thing for which I sent it. (Isa. 55:10-11, NRSV)

Finally, Ben Sira delights in the blowing of the cold north wind (v. 20). This wind blows and freezes the ponds solid and clothes each pool with a breastplate. Sirach delights in the colourful sight of a frozen pond (v. 20b). Previously in the analysis of Prov. 25:23-26, I noted that the cold

---

33. Ronald A. Simkins, *Yahweh's Activity in History and Nature in the Book of Joel* (Lewiston: Edwin Mellen, 1991), 108.

north wind was a sign of rainless weather which was suitable for the ship-captains as it brought good visibility in the sky. For seafarers, the north wind was, thus, welcome as a life-giving/life-preserving meteorological phenomenon. Here, Sir. 43:20 is impressed with the effect of the wind on the pool.

6.2.6.3.3. *The life-giving quality of dew (vv. 21-22).* Sirach next turns to the life-giving and restorative quality of dew. The dripping clouds and dew have the potential to bring to life the withering, burnt up and dried mountains (v. 21). Like the rain that falls in October–November, dew was an important source of moisture during the dry season in ancient Israel. Dew was thus considered as a divine blessing (Gen. 27:28), and a lack of dew was seen as a curse (Gen. 27:39). The mention of dew restoring the withering mountains implies that Sir. 43:22 is aware of the fact that dew was a very significant source of moisture during the dry season.

What is interesting in Sirach and elsewhere in the Bible is that both rain and dew are valuable gifts from God. Therefore, in Gen. 27:28 the expression 'dew of heaven' occurs in relationship with 'fatness of the earth' in order to underline the life-giving potential of this water-related phenomenon that is a blessing for Jacob. In Dan. 4:25, however, Nebuchadnezzar is cursed to live outside the human sphere and to bathe in the 'dew' with wild animals. This text does not deny the life-giving potential of dew, but underlines the shame of a king eating wild grass that is yet to be nurtured by the dew of the sky.

6.2.6.3.4. *The abyss and sea under control (vv. 23-26).* The most interesting part of the poem is the depiction of the sea, the deep and the sea-monsters (רהב) in vv. 23-26. In Job 26:12 and Ps. 89:9-10, Rahab is presented in parallel to the sea (ים), which is, in turn, parallel to the deep (תהום) in Job 28:14 and 38:16. Rahab, the sea and the deep denote chaos and the antithesis of the created order in biblical traditions, as depicted in Gen. 1:2; Isa. 51:9-10 and Ezek. 27:1. Like Job 38:8-11, Sir. 43:25 presents the sea and the deep as having life-threatening potential, one that is kept in check by God.

The phrase 'those who go to the sea' also occurs in Ps. 107:23 and relates to the extent and life-threatening aspects of the deep. The poem is informed by the livelihoods of those living and working in the coastal regions of Canaan. The sea and the seafaring way of life were familiar to the people of Israel, whose land ran from sea to sea – from the Great Sea (Mediterranean) in the west to the Lower Sea in the south. The Israelites would have experienced foreign ships loading or unloading their cargoes, and would naturally have enquired about aspects of maritime life.

While primarily agrarian, the Israelites, by experience, observation or hearsay, knew of the vastness of the sea, its depths (Ezek. 28:2), its wildness and remoteness, and often strange teeming creatures therein, including the mighty ones (Gen. 1:20-21). In this pre-modern world, the Israelites gave names to the latter sea monsters – Rahab, Leviathan, Taninin and Yam – that were capable of lifting and lowering the waters as well as causing violent waves and winds. Therefore, when stilled, these sea and river deities could provide calm seas, gentle winds and safe passage. On other occasions they could sweep ships off course, smash them or even swallow them.

For Sirach, God's plan/word (λογισμός) keeps both the mighty waters and the sea monsters in check. God places the islands in the deep and fills its cosmic waters with a variety of living beings, including the sea monsters (v. 25). As in Ps. 104, these water-related phenomena are not a threat to creation, but instead play a delightful role in it. This observation chimes with the notion that 'each element of creation functions according to its purpose'.[34] The sea and Rahab, which in ancient myths typified chaos (cf. Ps. 74:13-14), are portrayed as part of YHWH's design.

In Sir. 43, neither the sea itself nor the things living in it could loosen God's grip and turn creation into primeval chaos. For Sir. 43:25, the sea is benign, teeming with God's countless, stupendous and amazing creatures. The sea contains all kinds of life, including Rahab. Just as in Ps. 104:25-26, these creatures were created not to pose a threat, but to play in the deep. Sirach goes beyond Ps. 104 by saying that each of the sea creatures, including Rahab, is called a 'messenger' (ἄγγελος) created to fulfil a particular role in creation (vv. 25-26).

6.2.6.4. *Eco-theological synthesis.* In highlighting the sense of delight and beauty of water-related phenomena, Sirach affirms the intrinsic worth of nature. For him, water and nature bring wonder. Sirach 43:13-26 wants to show that even familiar water-related phenomena such as snow, ice, frost and dew, when perceived as objects of wonder, 'are temporarily estranged, made new and surprising'.[35] Sirach sees a world that has a place for humans, but is not designed primarily for their benefit. Sirach 43:13-26 is not about 'utilitarianism'; instead, it is a contemplation of water-related phenomena and their intrinsic aesthetic value.

Sirach 43:13-26 offers a rich, balanced reflection on elements of nature. The life-threatening heat of the sun is balanced by the healing power of the life-giving water which comes in the form of dripping clouds and dew

---

34. Perdue, *Wisdom Literature*, 256.
35. Newsom, *The Book of Job*, 226.

(vv. 21-22). The threat of storm and hail is balanced by the wonders of the purposeful settling of snow and the benign view of the sea teeming with God's countless amazing beings (vv. 13-20, 23-26). Indubitably, the depiction of water-related phenomena in the poem of Sir. 43:13-26 is expressing the complexity of the living world.

As expressed in Ps. 104, chaotic waters are under God's control and have been so arranged for life-serving purposes (vv. 25-26). Still, Sirach is aware that these forces, while tamed, have not been abolished completely – they remain a potential danger to the created order, especially for seafarers (v. 24). However, Sir. 43:13-26 invites those disposed to seeing nothing but chaos in the world and the deeps to look again with a wide-angle lens. When we look at the world through the eyes of Sir. 43:13-26, then chaos, in comparison to the goodness of the whole picture of the created order, is associated with wonders and miracles.[36]

In a non-utilitarian and non-anthropocentric perspective on nature, Sirach understood that even the deep and the sea-monsters that were symbols of threat against the created order are now God's messengers ($\alpha\gamma\gamma\epsilon\lambda\acute{o}\varsigma$, v. 26). All the cosmic elements of nature listed in Sir. 43:13-26 are instruments of God's power, used by him in his dominion over the earth, and sometimes employed by him to punish and establish order. Sirach is full of joy and delight in contemplating the wonders of these watery images.

The fact that Sirach looks at the cosmological beings with joy and praise has profound theological implications. Although the poem is not a theodicy in any rational sense of the word, it nevertheless expresses the goodness of creation and of the God who is known through it.[37] Sirach suggests that via a non-utilitarian contemplation of the beings of creation, including water, one can grasp the glory of their Creator. In other words, every experience of nature is also an experience of God.[38]

6.3. *Water and Water-related Phenomena in Wisdom 11:2-14*

6.3.1. *Introduction*

The book of Wisdom of Solomon contains many texts on creation, including water and water-related phenomena (see Appendix A). This section involves an ecological reading of Wis. 11:2-14 in which water is a substance that is simultaneously used to punish ($\dot{\epsilon}\kappa o \lambda \acute{a} \sigma \theta \eta \sigma \alpha \nu$) and

---

36. Clinton McCann Jr., 'Between Text and Sermon Psalm 104', *Interpretation* 66 (2012): 68.
37. Newsom, *The Book of Job*, 228.
38. McCann, 'Between Text', 68.

benefit (εὐεργετήθησαν). The analysis of this text draws on the exodus traditions found in Exod. 7:1-24 as these set the background of Wis. 11:2-11. In addition, a number of quotes by Philos will prove insightful for the analysis. A retrieval of ecological wisdom of the ambivalent potential of water in these texts ends this section.

6.3.2. Introduction to the Book of Wisdom

6.3.2.1. The context and date of the book. The book of Wisdom is sometimes called the Wisdom of Solomon. This latter title is a traditional inference based on the fact that the unnamed author presents himself as an ancient Israelite ruler (Wis. 7:5; 8:21; 9:7-8). Despite the tradition, modern scholarship is generally agreed that the author of the book was a rhetorician and/or teacher who received a good education in both Greek and Jewish schools, most likely in Alexandria.[39] The author wrote the book in Alexandria during the early Roman period (about 30 BCE–40 CE) when many philosophies and religions were loosely bound together by Greek culture.[40]

The context of the book includes a number of features. First, the tension between the Jews and Greeks in Alexandria under Roman rule is critical. Importantly, the book shows great concern for justice. Second, there was the attraction of Hellenistic culture, and especially Greek citizenship that offered full rights in all political, economic and cultural entities. This led some Jews to abandon their faith or to compromise with Hellenistic culture and religion. Finally, the disapproval of Greek state religion centred on the Olympian gods and the military Roman imperial control. The book of Wisdom, the *Letter of Aristeas* and Philo all criticise Greek myths, polytheism and the adoration of beauty.

In a context of religious and social disintegration, the book of Wisdom and many philosophical schools adopted a number of rhetorical features designed to teach their adherents how to live in the Hellenistic context. Wisdom drew on creation elements as a medium that God uses to sustain his people and punish their oppressors (Wis. 11:5, 15-16). In seeking to do this, water and water-related phenomena are presented in the book as agents of hope for the Israelites and woe for the enemies of Israel (11:2-14). The aim was to offer hope to the Alexandrian Jewish community who experienced severe sorrow during the reign of Gaius Caligula (37–41 CE).[41]

---

39. Perdue, *Wisdom Literature*, 286.
40. Kolarcik, 'The Book of Wisdom', 439.
41. Samuel Cheon, *The Exodus Story in the Wisdom of Solomon: A Study in Biblical Interpretation* (Sheffield: Sheffield Academic, 1997), 13.

6.3.2.2. The literary structure of the book. From 1945, the literary shape of the book of Wisdom has been a matter of debate.[42] It is widely agreed today that the book has two main parts. The first part, 1:1–11:1, depicts the praise of Wisdom, whereas the second, 11:2–19:22, presents God's care for his people during the Exodus.

This literary shape of the book presents a coherent message containing a certain eco-theological perspective. While the first part shows Wisdom as the principle of order from Adam and throughout history (see Wis. 10:1-21), the second illustrates how, in Wisdom, various cosmic domains act to punish the Egyptians and the Israelites during the exodus story.

6.3.2.3. Creation in the book of Wisdom. The worldview of the book of Wisdom is based on the belief that the human condition and destiny are all bound up with the structure of the universe. In other words, the book as a whole regards creation as the matrix within which history and salvation can be understood.[43]

It was a commonly held belief throughout the ancient Near East that the meaning of life is rooted in an inclusive cosmic order in which humans, society and gods participate. This idea is present in all cosmogonies from Sumer to Egypt via Babylonia, the priestly creation account and the exodus event in the Pentateuch.

However, by the time of the book of Wisdom's composition, this conception had become modified by the idea that nature is an 'autonomous realm'.[44] In this sense, Wis. 5:19-23 observes that creation itself joins God in the battle against the wicked. In other words, creation is not simply an instrument, but in fact acts autonomously in accordance with certain laws of nature in partnership with God to protect Israel.

Therefore, while the book continues the wisdom tradition of Israel, its conception of the cosmic character is notably closer to the scientific view of the world. It seems that the underlying conception of an impersonal cosmic order conveyed in the Egyptian *Ma'at* and חכמה in Israel underpins the worldview of the book of Wisdom. At the same time, the physical world is given an autonomy that never appears in the earlier books. Nature fights for the righteous and engulfs the wicked (Wis. 11:2-14; 19:1-9; see also Wis. 15:7; 16:24).

42. For the summary of debates, see Michael Kolarcik, *The Ambiguity of Death in the Book of Wisdom 1–6: A Study of Literary Structure and Interpretation* (Rome: Pontificio Istituto Biblico, 1991), 1–28.
43. Collins, *Jewish Wisdom*, 128.
44. Cornelius Loew, *Myth, Sacred History and Philosophy* (New York: Harcourt, Brace & Brothers, 1967), 217.

This idea appears also in other Old Testament texts, but is branded as miraculous (Judg. 5:20; Josh. 10:12). In contrast, God's interventions or miracles in the book of Wisdom are not viewed as a disruption of the structures of cosmos, but a re-arrangement of its harmony. In Wisdom, even miracles conform to regular natural laws, as shown in the depiction of water in Wis. 11:2-14 and 19:1-9.

6.3.3. *Literary Analysis of Wisdom 11:2-14*

6.3.3.1. *Midrash of the exodus story in Wisdom 11:2–19:22.* Midrash is a Jewish interpretative method that consists of taking a biblical tradition that occurs in one context and making it relevant in a new one.[45] In Wis. 11:2–19:22, which is the immediate literary context of Wis. 11:2-14, the Jewish writer makes use of a midrashic strategy consisting of five[46] syncrises contrasting the plight of the Israelites with that of the Egyptians.

The first syncrisis contrasts life-giving water from the rock with the plague of the Nile (Wis. 11:6-14). The second contrasts quails for the Israelites with the plague of small animals for Egyptians (11:15–16:15). Thereafter, the third syncrisis contrasts the raining down of manna with the plague of storms (16:15-29), while the fourth opposes the plague of darkness to the pillar of fire (17:1–18:4). Finally, the fifth syncrisis focuses on the tenth plague and the exodus (18:5–19:22).

A closer look at these antitheses reveals noteworthy insights for an eco-theological investigation. Elements of nature, including water, act in favour of Israel and against the Egyptians. It is as if the principle of life and death is inherent in the structures of the universe. In Wis. 11:2-14 and 19:1-9, for instance, the same substance – water – is depicted as being used to cause life and death.

In contrast to the military reading of the book of Exodus, the midrashic interpretation of the book of Wisdom talks about the refashioning of nature (Wis. 19:6). As shown later, the philosophical principle of interchangeability influenced the thought of Wis. 11:2–19:22. According to this Greek principle, elements of nature interchange and turn into one another completely. The mystery arises by means of transformation of the same element – becoming different at different times, and returning back to the same thing.[47] In Wisdom, water was fashioned afresh to provide

---

45. Shavit and Eran, *The Hebrew Bible*, 4.

46. Reese proposes seven syncrises instead of five. See James M. Reese, 'Plan and Structure in the Book of Wisdom', *CBQ* 27 (1965): 398–9.

47. Charles Kahn, *Anaximander and the Origins of Greek Cosmology* (New York: Colombia University Press, 1960), 119.

life-giving water to heal the cruel thirst of the Israelites (11:4), while it was also re-fashioned into a plague against the Egyptians (11:6-14 and 19:1-9). In other words:

> The very sequence of events in his description follows the pattern of the creation narrative rather than the account of the liberation of the people as found in the book of Exodus. In this way, the book of Wisdom makes a unique contribution to biblical creation theology. Instead of moving from salvation to creation – as traditional Old Testament theology claims is the fundamental focus of the Bible – the wisdom of Solomon begins with creation and moves to salvation.[48]

Therefore, the main question is whether the activity of creation in Wis. 11:2–19:22, particularly that of the water-related phenomena in 11:2-14 and 19:1-9, determines the intrinsic worth of water that gives life and poses a threat, or whether they are merely instruments with which to bless or punish humans (that is, a utilitarian view of nature). This question guides the analysis of Wis. 11:2-14 and 19:1-9.

6.3.3.2. *Translation of Wisdom 11:2-14*

[2] They journeyed through an uninhabited wilderness,
    and pitched their tents in untrodden places.
[3] They withstood their enemies
    and fought off their foes.
[4] When they were thirsty, they called upon you,
    and water was given them out of flinty rock,
    and from hard stone a remedy for their thirst.
[5] For through the very things by which their enemies were punished,
    they themselves received benefit in their need.
[6] Instead of the fountain of an ever-flowing river,
    stirred up and defiled with blood
[7] in rebuke for the decree to kill the infants,
    you gave them abundant water unexpectedly,
[8] showing by their thirst at that time
    how you punished their enemies.
[9] For when they were tried, though they were being disciplined in mercy,
    they learned how the ungodly were tormented when judged in wrath.
[10] For you tested them as a parent does in warning,
    but you examined the ungodly as a stern king does in condemnation.

---

48. Bergant, 'The Wisdom', 144.

¹¹ Whether absent or present,
    they were equally distressed,
¹² for a twofold grief possessed them,
    and a groaning at the memory of what had occurred.
¹³ For when they heard that through their own punishments the others
    were being benefited, they knew⁴⁹ it was the Lord's doing.
¹⁴ For though they had mockingly rejected him
    who long before had been cast out and exposed,
at the end of the events they marveled at him,
    when they felt thirst in a different way from the righteous.

6.3.3.3. *Double potential of water in Wisdom 11:2-14*

6.3.3.3.1. *Water used to bless and punish, vv. 2-7.* The Greek expression πέτρας ἀκροτόμου (flinty rock) in v. 4 renders the Hebrew words מים מצור (water from a rock) in Deut. 8:15, where water plays a vital role for the Israelites in the desert. The lifelessness of the desert is stated in the Greek word ἔρημον (desolate/empty) in v. 2, which is the same word employed in the LXX text of Job 38:26 for the desolate land that has to be revived by the rain.

The same reviving potential of water is reiterated here. The life-giving potential of the fluid is depicted by the Greek word ἴαμα in Wis. 11:4b, where it literally means 'to heal/to remedy'. Water, as in Prov. 25:25, is not simply a drink but a *medicine*, as a literal reading of Wis. 11:4 makes clear: 'to restore or to heal (ἴαμα) a cruel thirst (δίψης...σκληροῦ)'.

That is why the first syncrisis (Wis. 11:6-14) is introduced by the Greek preposition ἀντὶ (instead of), contrasting the life-giving water from a rock (v. 4) with the water of the Nile turned into blood (v. 6). In reaction to the Egyptian decree for shedding the blood of the Israelite male infants, the River Nile was turned into blood, thus making life impossible in Egypt (see Isa. 19:5-10). However, when the Israelites were in the wilderness, they were given life-giving water to relieve their thirst.

Verse 6-7 state that water was simultaneously a life-giving substance for the Israelites and a source of great misery to the Egyptians. These verses can thus be paraphrased as: 'When the Egyptians were troubled with clotted blood instead of a river's ever-flowing fountain, God gave the Israelites abundant water'. Philo explained that God decided to plague

---

49. The aorist ᾔσθοντο from the Greek word αἰσθάομα denotes perception (sensual, spiritual discernment or even intellectual understanding). It seems that Wis. 11:13 recalls Exod. 7:5 that reads 'the Egyptians shall know that I am the Lord…' The point is that God will make himself known through natural occurrences.

the Egyptians by means of water before anything else because they overestimated water and considered it (the Nile) to be the source of all creative power.[50]

With his new knowledge of the Nile basin, Philo depicted the river turned to blood as a regional and international pollution. Even though the plague concerned Egypt, from Ethiopia to the sea (the Mediterranean Sea), water turned into blood, as did the lakes, canals, wells, springs/fountains and all the existing water-supply of Egypt.[51] It was not only humans who suffered from the bleeding of the Nile – the fish inhabiting the watercourse also died, as their only life-giving home had become a life-threatening entity.

6.3.3.3.2. Thirst as educative and retributive, vv. 8-10. This section is a continuation of the above idea, but contrasts the aim of the Israelites' thirst with that of the Egyptians. Confident in his argument of punishment/blessing by water, the sage continues that the Israelites were allowed to thirst a little in order that they would clearly understand the sufferings the Egyptians endured when their water supply was turned into blood. The sage maintains that the aim of Israel thirsting was 'educative', but 'retributive' for the Egyptians.[52]

Many times in the Bible, water scarcity in the desert is portrayed as a reason for Israel to trust in God, the provider of the rain at the right time (Deut. 11:11). However, in Egypt, water shortage is not natural, but is due to human matters according to Wis. 11:6-10. This contrast occurs in Deut. 11:10-11, which ironically recognises the presence of water in Egypt and the dryness of Canaan – a land which depends on water from above (i.e. rain):

> [10] For the land that you are about to enter to occupy is not like the land of Egypt, from which you have come, where you sow your seed and irrigate by foot like a vegetable garden. [11] But the land that you are crossing over to occupy is a land of hills and valleys, watered by rain from the sky. (NRSV)

In the wilderness, Israel thirsted because there was no water. God gave water if Israel was obedient (i.e. educative perspective) (Deut. 11:10-15). In Egypt, the available Nile water that served for irrigation, industry and

---

50. F. H. Colson, 'Philo, Moses I and II (De Vita Mosis)', in *Philo in Ten Volumes and Two Supplementary Volumes*, ed. F. H. Colson (London: Heinemann, 1935), 327.
51. Ibid.
52. John Allen F. Cregg, *The Wisdom of Solomon* (Cambridge: Cambridge University Press, 1909), 107.

daily life was polluted and resulted in dire ecological problems all over Egypt (punitive perspective) (see Exod. 7:21).

6.3.3.3.3. *The mystery of water upon the Egyptians, vv. 11-14.* The expression ἀπόντες...παρόντες (absent...present) introduces the mystery of water. The idea is that when Israel was in Egypt and the Nile was bleeding, the Egyptians suffered. Furthermore, in their pursuit of the fugitives (Israelites), they were overwhelmed in the sea. Water was a medium of affliction for the Egyptians both in Egypt and outside, while it was a blessing for the Israelites.

This mystery of water caused great trauma for the Egyptians. They could not discern how water, which had been life-threatening to them, had befriended the fleeing Israelites.[53] The double pain of the Egyptians in v. 12 implies that the Egyptians suffered both via their own disaster of a bleeding Nile, and by the fact that the medium of their trauma – water – acted as a life-giving entity for the Israelites.

The text makes clear that the Egyptians heard the reports that the thirsty fugitives were saved from death by life-giving water flowing from the rock in the desert (v. 13). According to the Vulgate, the words εὐεργετουμένους αὐτούς must be translated 'were being benefited others', implying that the Egyptians experienced sorrow upon hearing that Israel was being continuously befriended by water.

6.3.4. *Other Forms of Water Ambivalence in Wisdom 19:1-12*

6.3.4.1. *Translation of Wisdom 19:1-12.*

> [1] But the ungodly were assailed to the end by pitiless anger,
>   for God knew in advance even their future actions:
> [2] how, though they themselves had permitted your people to depart and hastily sent them out,
>   they would change their minds and pursue them.
> [3] For while they were still engaged in mourning,
>   and were lamenting at the graves of their dead,
> they reached another foolish decision,
>   and pursued as fugitives those whom they had begged and compelled to leave.
> [4] For the fate they deserved drew them on to this end,
>   and made them forget what had happened,
>   in order that they might fill up the punishment that their torments still lacked,

---

53. Ibid., 108.

⁵ and that your people might experience an incredible journey,
    but they themselves might meet a strange death.
⁶ For the whole creation in its nature was fashioned anew,
    complying with your commands,
    so that your children might be kept unharmed.
⁷ The cloud was seen overshadowing the camp,
    and dry land emerging where water had stood before,
an unhindered way out of the Red Sea,
    and a grassy plain out of the raging waves,
⁸ where those protected by your hand passed through as one nation,
    after gazing on marvelous wonders.
⁹ For they ranged like horses,
    and leaped like lambs, praising you,
    O Lord, who delivered them.
¹⁰ For they still recalled the events of their sojourn,
    how instead of producing animals the earth brought forth gnats,
    and instead of fish the river spewed out vast numbers of frogs.
¹¹ Afterward they saw also a new kind of bird,
    when desire led them to ask for luxurious food;
¹² for, to give them relief, quails came up from the sea.

6.3.4.2. The position of Wisdom 19:1-12 in Wisdom 11:2–19:22. Wisdom 19:1-12 is part of the fifth syncrisis (Wis. 18:5–19:22) within the midrashic interpretation of the exodus event (11:2–19:22). While scholars are divided on the literary units of the fifth syncrisis,[54] there is a kind of unanimity about the content of 19:1-9, which speaks of the drowning of the Egyptians in the Red Sea, and the rescue of Israel through it. Wisdom 19:10-12 can be understood as a retrospective review of God's wonders through which nature was refashioned for Israel. Adopting this position, I am among those who believe that Wis. 19:1-5 and 6-12 form a unit depicting death and life by water.

    The syncrisis as a whole focuses on the death of the firstborn in Egypt, which leads to the exodus of Israel. However, the argument of the sage is less on the liberation of human beings, and more on the fact that the very means by which the Egyptians were punished brought blessing for Israel. In other words, in experiencing the extraordinary deliverance through the sea, the Israelites realised the way creation had continuously favoured them and punished the Egyptians.[55]

---

54. See Kolarcik, 'The Book of Wisdom', 450.
55. Ibid., 293.

At the conclusion of the *syncrisis* the rhetorician explains that elements that comprise the forces of nature changed places with one another in the same way that the notes of a harp vary the nature of the rhythm, while each note remains the same (19:18-22). The land animals became water creatures and vice versa (19:19); fire was not quenched by water (19:20); water divided to rescue Israel and the dry land yielded vegetation, while the same water engulfed the Egyptians (19:4-6).

The whole idea is about the refashioning of the forces and creatures of nature (19:6). For Wisdom, this transformation is in line with the physical constitution of creation.[56] Wisdom made use of the Greek philosophical principle of mutual interchange of elements to minimise miracles in nature.

6.3.4.3. The use of the principle of interchangeability. In his rhetoric, the Jewish author drew on the Greek philosophical principle of mutual interchange of elements in order to minimise the notion of miracles prevailing in the book of Exodus. According to Wis. 19:6, transformation in nature is brought about by an inner mutation of the universe, prompted only by God's command.[57] In their attempt to explicate divination and miracles, the Stoics employed this theory of mutual interchange to show that the gods can intervene in the cosmos without violating its laws. According to this pre-Socratic theory,

> Although the basic material substance of a thing remains the same, periodically an interchange of the elements of which it is composed occurs, resulting in an alteration in its individual combinations without a fundamental change in its substance.[58]

In this way, the rhetorician presents the exodus experience of the Pentateuch not as a liberation feat, but as the transformation or even the reshaping of creation, especially the water-related phenomena (Wis. 19:6). The rhetorician explains that the transformation of nature occurs not by miraculous intervention into the creation order, but rather by means of interchange of the basic physical elements to rescue the righteous.[59]

---

56. Perdue, *Wisdom Literature*, 317.
57. John J. Collins, 'Cosmos and Salvation: Jewish Wisdom and Apocalyptic in the Hellenistic Age', *History of Religions* 17, no. 2 (1977): 127.
58. Bergant, 'The Wisdom', 144.
59. Perdue, *Wisdom Literature*, 317.

In a similar way, Philo saw the dividing of the Red Sea as a natural fact. He commented that the south wind swept the water to enable the passage for Israel, but the north wind blew the water back and united the two sections of the sea to engulf the Egyptians.[60] Thus, having been refashioned, the Red Sea, hitherto viewed in the prophetic books as a life-threatening entity that had to be defeated, astonishingly acts here naturally as a saving entity for the Israelites.

6.3.4.4. *Alternating functions of water.* Wisdom 19:1-12 repeats the same idea of water ambivalence in Wis. 11:2-14, though here it is applied to the water of the Red Sea, which was friendly to the Israelites and cruel to the Egyptians. As in 16:25, it is not a miracle, but a transmutation of elements.[61] This idea is implicitly narrated in 1 Pet. 3:20, where the drowning of the wicked by water at the time of Noah is contrasted with the saving of the ark by water which carried it on waves. The text narrates the mystery in a language of new creation, paraphrasing the idea of Gen. 1, as follows:

> [6] For the whole creation in its nature was fashioned anew, complying with your commands, so that your children might be kept unharmed. [7] The cloud was seen overshadowing the camp, and dry land emerging where water had stood before, an unhindered way out of the Red Sea, and a grassy plain out of the raging waves, [8] where those protected by your hand passed through as one nation, after gazing on marvellous wonders. (Wis. 19:6-8, NRSV)

In contrast to Exod. 14:19, where the cloud is a pillar of darkness between two camps (the Israelites and the Egyptians), in Wis. 19:7 the cloud overshadowing the camp recalls the darkness over the deep in Gen. 1:2, as the text evokes the idea of new creation.[62] The genitive preposition ἐκ[63] in v. 7 syntactically denotes the act of separation which is confirmed by the mention of the appearance of the dry land (ξηρᾶς...γῆς), as if the land was engulfed in the waters of chaos. Philo says this is 'a great mighty work of nature, the like of which none can remember to have been seen in the past'.[64]

Later, the bottom part of the sea is romantically depicted as a 'grassy plain or green field' (χλοηφόρον πεδίον) out of the raging waves (ἐκ κλύδωνος βιαίου), implying the fruitful land of Gen. 1:11-12 (Wis. 19:7b).

---

60. Colson, 'Philo on De Vita Mosis I', 367.
61. Cregg, *The Wisdom of Solomon*, 182.
62. David Winston, *The Book of Wisdom of Solomon* (New York: Doubleday, 1979), 325.
63. See its use in Mt. 2:15; 26:27; Mk 16:3; Acts 17:33; Gal. 3:13; Rev. 14:13.
64. Colson, 'Philo on De Vita Mosis I', 361.

The text is now underlining the positive aspect of the water, which is contrasted with the life-threatening function of the same water entity that overwhelmed the Egyptians (Wis. 19:1-5). The power to give life and death is part of nature. That is why the pair ἐκολάσθησαν (to punish) and εὐεργετήθησαν (to benefit) occurs always in the frame of the exodus-related antitheses, where the same substance gives life and death at the same time.[65]

In Wis. 19:10, the earth produced gnats and the river spewed forth frogs – instead of fish as against the Egyptians – while a new kind of bird (quail) came up from the sea to feed the Israelites (Wis. 19:12). In spring, quails in the Mediterranean areas migrate in massive flocks to refresh themselves, and they are easily caught.[66] Perhaps Wisdom indicates that it was a cloud of migrating quails that came down on the camp of the Israelites. Elsewhere in the Bible, in Gen. 1:20-25, fauna was fashioned afresh in order to feed Israel and punish Egypt.[67] For Wis. 19:1-12, the alternating function of water as a life-giving and life-threatening entity accords with the order of nature (intrinsic worth), though in a transformed way.

6.3.4.5. *Eco-theological synthesis.* After a first look at Wis. 11:2-14 and 19:1-12, it could be said that God is merely using elements of nature for blessings and curses as found in Job 37:13. The anthropocentric view of nature is eloquent in the texts, evaluating water and water-related phenomena for the roles they play for Israel and against Egyptians. It is as if anthropocentrism is used to gauge the worth of water and water-related phenomena. Humans are depicted as a type of separate and unconnected block of sole consumers of the wealth of nature.

In this sense, water would be seen as possessing only an instrumental and utilitarian value and as not really valuable in their own right. Is it not for this reason that Lynn White's famous article, 'The Historical Roots of Our Ecological Crisis', blamed the biblical traditions for being responsible for ongoing ecological crises, mainly those related to the pollution of the waters of the earth?[68]

---

65. L. Mazzinghi, 'The Antithetical Pair "to Punish" and "to Benefit" (κολάζω and εὐεργετέω) in the Book of Wisdom', in *Wisdom for Life: Essays Offered to Honor Prof. Maurice Gilbert, SJ on the Occasion of His Eightieth Birthday*, ed. N. Calduch-Benages (Berlin: de Gruyter, 2014), 237.

66. Winston, *The Book of Wisdom*, 326.

67. Kolarcik, 'The Book of Wisdom', 593.

68. Lynn White, 'The Historical Roots of Our Ecological Crisis', *Science* 155 (1967): 1203–7.

However, in contrast to Elihu's speech in Job 37:13, it is emphatically stated in Wis. 19:6 that when water or water-related phenomena rescued Israel or punished Egypt, they were really acting according to the created order (evoking thus the principle of intrinsic worth), and complying with God's commands. What is ecologically interesting is that nature was changed, transformed or fashioned anew due to circumstances that developed as a consequence of human behaviour. Even though it arose in a preindustrial world, Wisdom has raised the possibility of nature being a dynamic entity.

In its use of the Greek principle of interchangeability, Wisdom has brought a specific contribution to eco-theology. The life-giving water from the rock and the bleeding Nile (Wis. 11:2-14), as well as the rescue of Israel and the submersion of the Egyptians in the Red Sea (Wis. 19:1-12), are not seen as miraculous events. Rather, Wis. 11:2-14 and 19:19 state that water and water-related phenomena are acting according to the intrinsic natural order to provide for Israel and punish Egypt.

6.4. Conclusion

This chapter attempted to retrieve the ecological wisdom of water and water-related phenomena in the Deutero-canonical wisdom books. The investigation found that these books abound with references and insights about water that eco-theological studies have missed with their inattention to these books. The study selected four texts among many that contain references to water and water-related phenomena in Sirach and Wisdom of Solomon, namely Sir. 24:23-29; 46:13-26; and Wis. 11:2-14 and 19:1-12.

The theme of Torah likened to six rivers in Sir. 24:23-29 presents water as a symbol of life since, in their time of flooding, all six rivers of Sir. 24:25-26 represent abundance and fertility. In this sense, vv. 30-34 continue the water metaphor in terms of system of garden irrigation that depicts Sirach as a gardener who realised that the fullness of the life-giving water cannot be individualised, but shared with others.

However, Sir. 46:13-26 is mostly dominated by the idea of beauty and delight. In this text, the author sees a world that is not exclusively designed for humans. In Sir. 43:13-26, it is not a matter of determining whether water is life-giving or life-threatening, which is a trait of utilitarianism, but an invitation to contemplate the water-related phenomena for their own sake. For Sir. 43:3-26, even the waters of chaos viewed in the global picture of the created order become objects of wonder.

In Wis. 11:2-14 and 19:1-12, water is used to bless Israel and punish Egypt. Despite the instrumental and anthropocentric view, which depicts humans as distinct consumers of the treasures of the earth, the texts strongly confirm the intrinsic worth of water. It is clearly expressed in Wis. 19:6 that when water and water-related phenomena rescued Israel or punished Egypt, they were actually working according to certain laws of nature.

In contrast to the exodus events in the book of Exodus, the use of the Greek principle of interchangeability aids Wisdom to minimise the miraculous intervention of God in the cosmos. In this sense, the life-giving water from the rock and the deadly, bleeding Nile water (Wis. 11:2-14), as well as the salvation of Israel and the drowning of Egyptians by the Red Sea (Wis. 19:1-12), are not seen as miraculous events. Rather, Wis. 11:2-14 and 19:19 suggest that water and water-related phenomena act according to the inherent natural order to sustain life and cause death.

Chapter 7

CONCLUSIONS:
ECO-THEOLOGICAL IMPLICATIONS OF THE STUDY

7.1. Introduction

This chapter provides the logical outcomes of our investigations. It consists of assessing the contributions and the implications of the study for the way forward. The chapter also includes understanding how the Old Testament wisdom books can aid us to address current problems associated with water.

7.2. Substantial Contributions to Eco-theology

7.2.1. Abundance of References to Water in Wisdom Books

Appendices A and B at the end of this book offer clear proof of the profusion of passages related to water in the Old Testament wisdom books, texts that have been significantly overlooked by scholars in eco-theological studies. I have shown how these books abound with references to water and water-related phenomena that should attract the focus of eco-theological scholars.

Interestingly, the Deutero-canonical wisdom books overflow with much deeper ecological wisdom about water and water-related phenomena. Further studies on these books are likely to reveal distinguished eco-theological insights that could not be explored here because no single study can thoroughly investigate more than 600 references to water and water-related phenomena occurring in the Old Testament wisdom books.

7.2.2. Insights about Waters in the Wisdom Books

7.2.2.1. Water and water-related phenomena in Job. For obvious reasons, that were given in the introductory section of the third chapter of this book, I explored water and water-related phenomena in Job 14:7-12;

36:26–37:13 and 38:22-38. Water is depicted as having the potential of life and death. Possibly, the author of the book of Job found water images suitable for dealing with existential matters because without it life is impossible, but too much of it can harm life.

Therefore, it was observed in the metaphorical text of Job 14:7-12 that water is seen as intrinsically life-giving, capable of restoring a dead plant, while human death is equated with the vanishing of a vital water supply. In an absurd idea, Job 14:11-12 compares an irreversible situation of the drying up of the perennial water supplies (rivers) with the death of human beings.

The ecological idea behind Job 14:7-12 presumes the intrinsic value and life-giving function of water. This is stated either in its power to revive the realm of flora (vv. 7-9), or in comparing human death with the vanishing of bodies of water that were considered as a permanent and perennial source of life (vv. 10-12). In its recalling of Isa. 19:5-10 concerning the drying up of the Nile and its life-threatening effects on humans, plants and animals and the land, Job 14:7-12 is a kind of perception of the intrinsic worth of water.

The speech of Elihu in Job 36:26–37:13 is dominated by features of anthropocentrism as water is used as an instrument to cause abundant food only for humans (36:28) or to punish or bless humans (37:12). Still, the careful analysis of the text revealed the intrinsic value of water that is beyond human control and exists in intimacy with God, who can use it for particular reasons. The water-related phenomenon such as the sea in 36:26–37:13 is not exposed as a created body, but as a pre-existing entity and God's partner with the potential to cause life or death.

It is also interesting to find that in Elihu's speech, some water-related phenomena have a voice. Job 37:2, for instance, shows how the voice of God is identical to the voice of a rainstorm. For Elihu, Job does not need an encounter with God's word, but with the power of God voiced through this water-related phenomenon.

Significant ecological insights are shown in Job 38:22-38, a text which decentres human beings. All the water-related phenomena depicted here are viewed for their intrinsic value and purpose. The principles of intrinsic worth and purpose are emphasised in the fact that hail and snow are not only kept in treasuries, but also designed to be used during specific 'times'. In contrast to Elihu's speech (36:26–37:13), the target of the rain in Job 38:22-38 is not just the fruitful land worked to feed people, but the wilderness which is transformed into a fertile land. The rain is not viewed as being useful for humans, but for its own value when it falls on remote land that lacks human presence.

7.2.2.2. *Water and water-related phenomena in Proverbs.* Here we investigated the life-giving and life-threatening potential of water and water-related phenomena in three metaphorical texts (Prov. 5:15-20; 9:13-18; 25:23-26) and two texts that present water in its real cosmic sense (3:19-20; 8:22-31).

In Prov. 5:15-20, the depiction of one's wife as a private well and a private cistern denotes the idea of water management and the intrinsic worth of water based on the hard work that is involved in the drilling and maintenance of a private well or cistern (5:15). The text is informed by the idea that water is life. The wife's 'water', which frames the text (vv. 15, 18b-20), implies the life-giving power attached to the well-managed water in private containers on which home life depended.

Ecologically speaking, there is wordplay between human-made (cistern) and natural sources of water (well). The text implies that life-giving water is both a natural gift and fruit of human efforts. The text teaches that the husband will experience no shortage of water, no matter the season, on condition that water (wife) as a natural gift (God's gift) be valued for its (her) own intrinsic worth, and maintained in reliable containers. The idea recalls v. 19, instructing the husband to be intoxicated by his wife's water (breasts) 'all the time' (בכל־עת) and 'always' (תמיד).

The identification of the husband's sexuality with the fountains and springs of water that must not be spread on the streets and squares also recalls a careful management of this precious natural resource. The ecological insight behind the text is that adultery will lead, inter alia, to impotence (Prov. 15:16-17) just as wrong attitudes towards water resources will lead, inter alia, to water depletion. It is now proven that water is a finite resource that cannot be replaced once depleted. That is why the modern Israeli Water Authority declares that 'every person is entitled to use water, as long as that use does not cause the salination or depletion of the water resource'.[1]

Proverbs 9:13-18 completes the idea of 15:15-20. For 9:13-18, the stolen water is sweet, but leads to Sheol. Theft and illegal appropriation of water in an arid land has probably informed the use of the water metaphor in this erotic poem. The fact that the words 'stolen water is sweet' are put in the mouth of Woman Folly and linked with Sheol implies that the sage intends to discourage this kind of behaviour as it would certainly

---

1. See Israeli Water Law and Water Authorities. Available online: http://www.sviva.gov.il/bin/en.jsp?enPage=e_BlankPage&enDisplay=view&enDispWhat=Object&enDispWho=Articals^12419&enZone=wat_law (accessed 14 May 2012).

undermine the wellbeing of the society. Sheol is connected with the life-threatening quality of water. Ecologically speaking, fraud related to water should be discouraged.

Proverbs 25:23-26 highlights the life-giving and life-threatening potential of water in terms of its intrinsic value and unpredictability, respectively. The cold north wind is seen as an agent of deadly rain whose effects are similar to those of slanderous speech (v. 23). The Israelites expected the west, not the north wind, to bring rain (Lk. 12:4). The גשם (rains), which bring life-giving water when falling at the right time, are seen here as life-threatening because they are hidden in the north wind, and probably would cause the failure of crops. That is why in v. 24 the man prefers being exposed to bad weather to being exposed to unexpected bad speech.

However, Prov. 25:25 equates the life-giving water revitalising the weary person with the spiritual remedy for a person weary from anxiety about the well-being of a situation in a distant land, while a polluted spring is equated with the righteous person that has become wicked. In an ancient world where news travelled upsettingly slowly and in a desert with scarce remote oases, the metaphor is ecologically meaningful. Polluting an oasis was seen by the Bedouins as a wicked act worthy of the death penalty. Here water is not merely a drink, but a medication (v. 25). Any behaviour leading to the pollution of a water source is simply an act of wickedness.

Two other texts, namely Prov. 8:22-31 and 3:19-20, present water as a cosmic entity presented with both life-giving and life-threatening potential. Proverbs 8:22-31 declares that the created order is made by Wisdom, but that the life-threatening waters are also part of it. By God's Wisdom the תהום can burst forth with life-giving water, whereas vv. 27-29 deal with several limitations of תהום in order to shape, secure, establish, support and stabilise the earth since the unbound תהום is a lurking danger against the created order.

In Prov. 3:19-20, God is presented as the perfect architect, sinking the pillars of the earth in the תהום (waters of chaos) in order to establish the earth as an arena of life that can survive the threatening pressure of the watery chaos. Contrary to Gen. 7:11, which uses the verb בקע to describe the beginning of a disastrous flood, Prov. 3:20a attributes a fertilising function to the cosmic deluge because it flows within limits.

7.2.2.3. Water and water-related phenomena in Qoheleth. The analysis of Qoh. 1:4-11; 2:4-6 and 11:1-6 revealed extensive ecological wisdom about water and water-related phenomena. The water-related phenomena in Qoheleth present themselves with ambiguity and unpredictability, providing them with the potential to cause life or death.

There is a kind of ambiguous relationship between human life and nature/water in the artful ambiguity of Qoh. 1:4-11. Human beings sometimes do experience nature as pointless – particularly when it is not serving their interest – but at the same time nature/water acts purposefully – in the service of the created order. The interpretation of the movement of water in Qoh. 1:7 as both wearisome and purposeful denotes water as an uneasy and puzzled entity involving unpredictable realities (romantic and life-threatening) similar to those happening in human life. The purposeful use of ambiguity in v. 7 underlines the intrinsic value of water acting on its own, whether for human interest or not.

In Qoh. 2:4-6, water is regarded as essentially life-giving. Anthropocentric readings of Qoh. 2:4-6 simply ignore the ecological significance of water in this text in favour of debates about Solomon's luxurious measure of pleasure. In an arid land, the creation of a well-watered garden was seen as an act of authority and fertility in a land of frequent droughts. It becomes clear that the control of water and the ordering of water resources for irrigation and fertilisation within the garden was an act of water management awareness.

Although Qoheleth realises that all his effort is *hebel*, the text nevertheless reflects the water management attitudes in the mind of the writer. One can read in the language of Qoh. 2:5 the idea of making the arid land fruitful by proper water management. As a great king, Hezekiah also listed his achievements in terms of making pools and conduits of water to the city (2 Kgs 20:20; Sir. 50:4-6) along with vineyards and gardens as well as the irrigation aqueducts and reservoirs.

For Qoheleth, water management is seen as positive even though it is also part of *hebel*. Qoheleth complains not about his wealth, including his parks, gardens and their waters, but the efforts he invested in acquiring them. Water is seen as having an intrinsic value since it creates life in the desert. Qoheleth's measures of water irrigation testify to his awareness of water management and sanitation as the key to making the environment fruitful and delightful.

Finally, Qoh. 11:1-6 reinforces water's ambivalent potential to cause life or death. Given that water is implied as having both life-threatening (risk) and life-giving roles – the words על־פני המים usually occur with negative connotations,[2] while bread upon the waters will at least be found

---

2. See Gen. 1:2; Job 24:18.

later – v. 2 encourages measures of security regarding potential disasters. The idea of dividing the seed into seven/eight parts (v. 2) denotes that a single sowing at what seemed the right time would not be seen as guaranteeing success given the unpredictability of nature (water) appearing with the potential to cause life or threat.

It is, therefore, not unreasonable that Crenshaw[3] has linked Qoh. 11:1-2 with the ambivalent character of the Nile inundation. The flooding of the Nile is potentially life-threatening in its scale, but it results in the fertility of the land and the supply of sufficient water to survive the dry season. The words על־פני המים in Gen. 1:2b, for instance, usually refer to the life-threatening primeval deep, but at the same time they allude to the situation prior to the 'fertility of the land' since when deeps retreated the land yielded fruits (Gen. 1:9-12). Qoheleth 11:1-2 has both ideas in mind.

Furthermore, while the clouds were a sign of life-giving water for agricultural life if occurring at the expected time (Deut. 11:14), in Qoh. 11:3-4 גשם (rain) has the potential to cause death, as it is linked with the hesitation to reap. The irony gives the impression that it will surely rain (v. 3), but quickly emphasises the uncertainty of nature (v. 4). For Qoh. 11:1-6, despite some signs of reliability, water remains a mystery capable of causing life and death, especially in an agrarian context. Humans cannot fully control nature.

7.2.2.4. Water and water-related phenomena in Sirach and Wisdom. The analysis of Sir. 24:23-34; 43:13-26; Wis. 11:2-14 and 19:1-12 revealed insightful ecological wisdom about the potential of water to cause life and death. In Sir. 24:23-34, the flowing of wisdom from the Torah is equated with the flooding water of the six rivers: four Edenic rivers (Pishon, Euphrates, Tigris and Gihon) and two renowned rivers of the ancient Near East (the Nile and the Jordan).

By comparing the Torah to these rivers, the author invites his/her listeners to keep it and to hold it tight as a valuable inheritance and source of life. In this sense, the themes of fullness, irrigation and flooding occur in vv. 25-27 as part of the water process to make the land arable and fertile in order to supply food and drink to those residing on earth. For Sir. 24:25-27, water is life and it should be regarded as such and valued for it. In this sense, vv. 28-29 depicts water as an unfathomable entity of life that should not be individualised.

---

3. James L. Crenshaw, 'A Proverb in the Mouth of a Fool', in Troxel, Friebel and Magary, eds., *Seeking the Wisdom of the Ancient*, 110.

In addition, Sir. 43:13-26 appeals for delight that is beyond an anthropocentric view of nature/water. In highlighting the sense of delight and beauty of water, Sirach wants to show that when perceived as subjects of wonder, even familiar water-related phenomena, such as snow, ice/frost or dew, look new and surprising. Sirach sees a world that is not primarily and exclusively designed for humans. In Sir. 43:13-26, it is not a matter of utilitarianism, but of contemplating water and water-related phenomena for their own value as *subjects not objects*.

The idea is reinforced in the book of Wisdom. On a first look at Wis. 11:2-14 and 19:1-12, one could deduce that God is merely using elements of creation for blessing and cursing as in Job 37:13. The anthropocentric view of nature is eloquent in the texts evaluating water and water-phenomena for the roles they play for Israel and against Egyptians. It is as if anthropocentrism is used to gauge the worth of water and water-related phenomena.

However, it is strikingly stated in Wis. 19:6 that when water-related phenomena rescued Israel or punished Egypt, they were really acting according to certain laws of nature, and complying with God's commands. In its use of the Greek principle of interchangeability, Wisdom has brought a specific contribution to eco-theology. The water-related events (water from the rock, the bleeding of the Nile, raging sea) are not seen as miraculous events, but part of the potential of water to cause life and death. In other words, both texts assert that the principle of life and death is inherent in water.

7.3. *Ecological Implications of the Study for Today*

7.3.1. *Introduction*

Having conducted an exegetical exploration of water in various wisdom texts, I am now faced with the challenge of explaining how the ecological insights of these texts can be applied to contemporary problems of water. The question is whether the message of these ancient wisdom traditions can be revelatory for today's readers.

We should explain, first, that one has to be careful not to criticise the current world on the basis of the views and principles of the ancient world. However, as we are open to the revelatory potential of the biblical texts without being captive to their limitations, we are obliged to connect with these ancient texts. Moltmann argued that: 'the earth crisis challenges us to read the Bible afresh…'[4]

---

4. Jurgen Moltmann, *God in Creation: An Ecological Doctrine of Creation* (London: SCM, 1985), xi.

We should argue that people of the ancient world, like some modern African traditions, had a more holistic view of nature than ours. The reason is that they were directly reliant on the natural world, which acted either in their favour as a life-giving entity or against them as a life-threatening one. Therefore, motivated by our ecological awareness of contemporary water problems in the present world, we should scrutinise whether some insights of the wisdom books can be used partly to address the issue of water in the present world.

7.3.2. *Implications of Texts of the Book of Job*

The simile of Job 14:11-12 and its echo in Isa. 19:5-10 have significant implications with regard to contemporary issues of water. In sub-Saharan Africa where the drying of great lakes and desertification are threatening life on the continent, the simile of Job 14:7-12 teaches the awareness of the life-giving potential of water, the relevance of a reliable water supply and the danger of the depletion of water reserves.

The current problems regarding desertification may largely be attributed to human activity rather than to divine fiat. Job 14:11 is imbued with the awareness of the possibility of withering of water reserves. Job 14:11-12 also points to the modern idea that there is no substitute for water when it compares the drying of a sea or river with human death. The simile can, thus, be used to teach about the relevance of a reliable water supply and offers an invitation to desist from activities that may weaken water supplies.

God's speech in 38:22-38 decentres human beings. For Job, humans do not control water. Water has intrinsic worth. The text invites us, humans, to restrain from viewing nature as if it were uniquely made for us. When the rain falls in the wilderness, it is not a waste as Job would claim, but part of the cosmic order. Other earth members in this remote place have the right to benefit from the rain as well. Everything has purpose: the snow and hail, for instance, are kept in treasuries and are designed to be used during specific times. To reinforce their intrinsic worth, these water-related phenomena are also called in Ps. 148:8 to celebrate 'their' Lord.

7.3.3. *Implications of Texts of Proverbs*

Proverbs 5:15-20 and 9:13-18 appeal for proper water management. It should be noted that Africa is the second driest area in the world despite holding great water supplies, and millions of Africans still suffer from water scarcity and water-related diseases. Shortages are often due not to an absolute lack of water, but mainly to issues relating to uneven distribution, management and poor maintenance checks of existing supplies that could be improved. Pointing to the necessity of good water management in South Africa, Rivonia Naidu-Hoffmeester declares:

> The mismatch between water supply and water demand, the theft of water resources, a deteriorating infrastructure, the loss of essential skills, a strangling educational pipeline, management failure, and deterioration in the quality of water, are all potential threats and key concerns [causing water scarcity in the country].[5]

Proverbs 5:15-20 would teach three facts about water: first, water should be kept clean; second, water should not be used for wrong purpose or simply wasted; third, not all water is safe for consumption. These ideas could be applied at several levels. First, at a personal level, there is a need to develop these attitudes in our homes. Second, there is a call to governments to provide clean water and proper sanitation to their peoples. The management of water resources is crucial for today's world as it is reflected in this metaphorical wisdom poem of the ancient world.

Furthermore, Prov. 25:23-26 has significant ecological wisdom for our time. The view of water not only as a drink but also as a medication in 25:25 for a thirsty person is insightful. Furthermore, 25:26 regards polluting or muddying a fountain as an act of wickedness. This should invite us to avoid attitudes that would undermine the vitality of our waters.

7.3.4. *Implications of Texts in Qoheleth*

Qoheleth 1:4-11 aims to teach that although humans do not comprehend things in nature, this does not mean that there is no regularity and purpose in the natural world. Regularity and pointlessness are human terms and concepts used in relation to the movement of water. However, both perceptions are true and part of the natural order.

Without being anachronistic, Qoh. 2:4-6 can be used to criticise the contemporary ego-centric appropriation of the resources. Qoheleth engaged in the management of water – pools and irrigation systems – not for his people, but for himself. In other words, Qoheleth was not interested in the management of public works, but projects for his 'self-pleasure'. Interestingly, Qoheleth concludes that all this was *hebel*.

By concluding with the words of deception in terms of 'all is *hebel* and chasing after wind' (v. 11), Qoheleth invites another view of wealth

---

5. See R. Naidu-Hoffmeester, 'South Africa's Water Resource Under Immense Pressure'. Available online: www.unisa.ac.za/news&media.htm (accessed 16 April 2014).

distribution. The text is indicative for contemporary readers in criticising current resource abuses, including water resources, to serve the happiness and interest of those in power or a small group of people. Water is seen to have life-giving aspects/functions although it is used for the interest/happiness of one person to the detriment of many.

Qoheleth 11 implies the unpredictability of nature. For Qoh. 11:1-6, despite some signs of reliability, water remains a mystery capable of causing life or death, especially in the context of agrarian activities. Water has intrinsic worth that is independent of human knowledge or involvement. Once more, this text, like Job 38, decentres human beings by underlining their incapacity to master water.

7.3.5. *Implications of Texts in Sirach*

For Sir. 24:23-34, water is life and moves naturally to fertilise the land. It should be regarded as such and valued for its intrinsic worth. When the Nile flooded, for instance, it was life-threatening – as people had to keep their settlements beyond the flood plains – but it was always viewed as God's providence for the renewal and re-creation of the land.

In Sirach, the streams of the six rivers that bring life-giving water to the land must not be individualised. In this sense, the unfathomable entity of water, just as in Wisdom, is expected to be community property (v. 28). That is why Ben Sirach is depicted with a dual role: as a gardener who waters the garden, and as a canal spreading the streams of water far off for the benefit of others. This is a significant ecological thought for modern users of water.

The real contemporary issue with regard to the water supply is usually not so much an absolute lack of water, but instead a lack of human willingness and wisdom to distribute water consistently for the benefit of others. An African proverb advises that *Amaghetsi syaliyak' omututu* (Nobody can individualise water).[6] Both Sir. 24:25-27 and this African wisdom underline the idea of water as a common good.

Water should flow; it should not be individualised. The image is furthered in Rev. 22:1-2, where the river of life freely flows from the throne of God, producing along its course trees and fruit for the healing of people. The insights of Sir. 24:23-29 give further awareness about what it means to practise theology in the contemporary world in which our rivers are becoming waters of death.

---

6. This proverb is from the Nande People, the main ethnic group in North Kivu Province of the Congo.

In Wis. 11:2-14, water is simultaneously acting as a life-giving and life-threatening agent. This is not regarded as a miraculous event, but as part of the natural potential/quality of water. The comments by Philo are of particular interest for modern people. With his new knowledge of the Nile basin, Philo commented that the bleeding of the Nile was a regional water crisis.[7] Although the plague concerned Egypt, from Ethiopia to the sea (Mediterranean Sea) water turned into blood, and so also did the lakes, canals, wells, springs and all other existing water supplies of Egypt This also resulted in the death of biodiversity: humans and fish suffered from the plague. The idea is that the pollution of a single water supply can cause great water crises in the neighbourhood and threaten the life of biodiversity.

7.4. *Remaining Questions for Further Research*

The abundance of texts that contain references to water and water-related phenomena in the Old Testament wisdom books invites studies that can aid in retrieving additional significant ecological wisdom based on water and water-related phenomena. Indeed, the references are so numerous that this work could not explore them all. Given that the Old Testament wisdom books are often ignored in biblical studies about water and water-related phenomena, it might be helpful to launch a series of scholarly volumes devoted to exploring nature in these works.

A separate study might also compare water in the Old Testament wisdom books and African wisdom material containing references to water and water-related phenomena. The result could well be utilised in raising ecological awareness in African societies. Such a project would also encourage African societies to recognise the inherent value of their wisdom traditions, encouraging them to take such wisdom seriously.

---

7. Colson, 'Philo on De Vita Mosis I', 327.

Appendix A:
References to Water and Water-Related Phenomena in the Old Testament Wisdom Books*

Water(s)

Job 3:24 For my sighing comes like my bread, and my groanings are poured out like waters.

Job 5:10 He gives rain on the earth and sends waters on the fields.

Job 8:11 Can papyrus grow where there is no marsh? Can reeds flourish where there is no water?

Job 11:16 You will forget your misery; you will remember it as waters that have passed away.

Job 12:15 If he withholds the waters, they dry up; if he sends them out, they overwhelm the land.

Job 14:9 Yet at the scent of water it will bud and put forth branches like a young plant.

Job 14:11 As waters fail from a lake, and a river wastes away and dries up....

Job 14:19 The waters wear away the stones; the torrents wash away the soil of the earth; so you destroy the hope of mortals.

Job 15:16 How much less one who is abominable and corrupt, one who drinks iniquity like water!

Job 22:7 You have given no water to the weary to drink, and you have withheld bread from the hungry.

* No claim of exhaustiveness is made for the following list of texts.

Job 22:11 or darkness so that you cannot see; a flood of water covers you.

Job 24:18 Swift are they on the face of the waters; their portion in the land is cursed; no treader turns toward their vineyards.

Job 24:19 Drought and heat snatch away the snow waters; so does Sheol those who have sinned.

Job 26:5 The shades below tremble, the waters and their inhabitants.

Job 26:8 He binds up the waters in his thick clouds, and the cloud is not torn open by them.

Job 26:10 He has described a circle on the face of the waters, at the boundary between light and darkness.

Job 27:20 Terrors overtake them like a flood; in the night a whirlwind carries them off.

Job 28:4 They open shafts in a valley away from human habitation; they are forgotten by travelers, they sway suspended, remote from people.

Job 28:25 When he gave to the wind its weight, and apportioned out the waters by measure.

Job 29:19 My roots spread out to the waters, with the dew all night on my branches.

Job 30:14 As through a wide breach they come; amid the crash they roll on.

Job 34:7 Who is there like Job, who drinks up scoffing like water.

Job 36:27 For he draws up the drops of water; he distills his mist in rain.

Job 37:10 By the breath of God ice is given, and the broad waters are frozen fast.

Job 38:25 Who has cut a channel for the torrents of rain, and a way for the thunderbolt.

Job 38:30 The waters become hard like stone, and the face of the deep is frozen.

Job 38:34 Can you lift up your voice to the clouds, so that a flood of waters may cover you?

Prov. 5:15 Drink water from your own cistern, flowing water from your own well.

Prov. 5:16 Should your springs be scattered abroad, streams of water in the streets?

Prov. 8:24 When there were no depths I was brought forth, when there were no springs abounding with water.

Prov. 8:29 When he assigned to the sea its limit, so that the waters might not transgress his command, when he marked out the foundations of the earth.

Prov. 9:17 Stolen water is sweet, and bread eaten in secret is pleasant.

Prov. 11:25 A generous person will be enriched, and one who gives water will get water.

Prov. 17:14 The beginning of strife is like letting out water; so stop before the quarrel breaks out.

Prov. 18:4 The words of the mouth are deep waters; the fountain of wisdom is a gushing stream.

Prov. 20:5 The purposes in the human mind are like deep water, but the intelligent will draw them out.

Prov. 21:1 The king's heart is a stream of water in the hand of the LORD; he turns it wherever he will.

Prov. 25:21 If your enemies are hungry, give them bread to eat; and if they are thirsty, give them water to drink.

Prov. 25:25 Like cold water to a thirsty soul, so is good news from a far country.

Prov. 27:19 Just as water reflects the face, so one human heart reflects another.

Prov. 30:4 Who has ascended to heaven and come down? Who has gathered the wind in the hollow of the hand? Who has wrapped up the waters in a garment? Who has established all the ends of the earth? What is the person's name? And what is the name of the person's child? Surely you know!

Prov. 30:16 Sheol, the barren womb, the earth ever thirsty for water, and the fire that never says, 'Enough'.

Qoh. 2:6 I made myself pools from which to water the forest of growing trees.

Qoh. 11:1 Send out your bread upon the waters, for after many days you will get it back.

Wis. 5:10 Like a ship that sails through the billowy water, and when it has passed no trace can be found, no track of its keel in the waves.

Wis. 5:22 And hailstones full of wrath will be hurled as from a catapult; the water of the sea will rage against them, and rivers will relentlessly overwhelm them.

Wis. 10:18 She brought them over the Red Sea, and led them through deep waters.

Wis. 11:4 When they were thirsty, they called upon you, and water was given them out of flinty rock, and from hard stone a remedy for their thirst.

Wis. 11:7 In rebuke for the decree to kill the infants, you gave them abundant water unexpectedly.

Wis. 13:2 But they supposed that either fire or wind or swift air, or the circle of the stars, or turbulent water, or the luminaries of heaven were the gods that rule the world.

Wis. 16:17 For – most incredible of all – in water, which quenches all things, the fire had still greater effect, for the universe defends the righteous.

Wis. 16:19 And at another time even in the midst of water it burned more intensely than fire, to destroy the crops of the unrighteous land.

Wis. 16:29 For the hope of an ungrateful person will melt like wintry frost, and flow away like waste water.

Wis. 17:18 Whether there came a whistling wind, or a melodious sound of birds in wide-spreading branches, or the rhythm of violently rushing water.

Wis. 19:7 The cloud was seen overshadowing the camp, and dry land emerging where water had stood before, an unhindered way out of the Red Sea, and a grassy plain out of the raging waves.

Wis. 19:19 For land animals were transformed into water creatures, and creatures that swim moved over to the land.

Wis. 19:20 Fire even in water retained its normal power, and water forgot its fire-quenching nature.

Sir. 3:30 As water extinguishes a blazing fire, so almsgiving atones for sin.

Sir. 15:3 She will feed him with the bread of learning, and give him the water of wisdom to drink.

Sir. 15:16 He has placed before you fire and water; stretch out your hand for whichever you choose.

Sir. 18:10 Like a drop of water from the sea and a grain of sand, so are a few years among the days of eternity.

Sir. 24:14 I grew tall like a palm tree in En-gedi, and like rosebushes in Jericho; like a fair olive tree in the field, and like a plane tree beside water I grew tall.

Sir. 24:30 As for me, I was like a canal from a river, like a water channel into a garden.

Sir. 24:31 I said, 'I will water my garden and drench my flower-beds'. And lo, my canal became a river, and my river a sea.

Sir. 25:25 Allow no outlet to water, and no boldness of speech to an evil wife.

Sir. 26:12 As a thirsty traveler opens his mouth and drinks from any water near him, so she will sit in front of every tent peg and open her quiver to the arrow.

Sir. 29:21 The necessities of life are water, bread, and clothing, and also a house to assure privacy.

Sir. 38:5 Was not water made sweet with a tree in order that its power might be known?

Sir. 39:13 Listen to me, my faithful children, and blossom like a rose growing by a stream of water.

Sir. 39:17 No one can say, 'What is this?' or 'Why is that?' – for at the appointed time all such questions will be answered. At his word the waters stood in a heap, and the reservoirs of water at the word of his mouth.

Sir. 39:26 The basic necessities of human life are water and fire and iron and salt and wheat flour and milk and honey, the blood of the grape and oil and clothing.

Sir. 40:16 The reeds by any water or river bank are plucked up before any grass.

Sir. 43:20 The cold north wind blows, and ice freezes on the water; it settles on every pool of water, and the water puts it on like a breastplate.

Sir. 48:17 Hezekiah fortified his city, and brought water into its midst; he tunneled the rock with iron tools, and built cisterns for the water.

Sir. 50:3 In his days a water cistern was dug, a reservoir like the sea in circumference.

Sir. 50:8 Like roses in the days of first fruits, like lilies by a spring of water, like a green shoot in Lebanon on a summer day.

2. *The Deep*

Prov. 8:27 When he established the heavens, I was there, when he drew a circle on the face of the deep.

Prov. 8:28 When he made firm the skies above, when he established the fountains of the deep.

Prov. 18:4 The words of the mouth are deep waters; the fountain of wisdom is a gushing stream.

Sir. 43:23 By his plan he stilled the deep and planted islands in it.

3. *The Sea/Ocean*

Job 3:8 Let those curse it who curse the Sea, those who are skilled to rouse up Leviathan.

Job 6:3 For then it would be heavier than the sand of the sea; therefore my words have been rash.

Job 7:12 Am I the Sea, or the Dragon, that you set a guard over me?

Job 9:8 Who alone stretched out the heavens and trampled the waves of the Sea.

Job 11:9 Its measure is longer than the earth, and broader than the sea.

Job 12:8 Ask the plants of the earth, and they will teach you; and the fish of the sea will declare to you.

Job 26:12 By his power he stilled the Sea; by his understanding he struck down Rahab.

Job 28:14 The deep says, 'It is not in me', and the sea says, 'It is not with me'.

Job 36:30 See, he scatters his lightning around him and covers the roots of the sea.

Job 38:8 Or who shut in the sea with doors when it burst out from the womb?

Job 38:16 Have you entered into the springs of the sea, or walked in the recesses of the deep?

Job 41:31 It makes the deep boil like a pot; it makes the sea like a pot of ointment.

Prov. 8:29 When he assigned to the sea its limit, so that the waters might not transgress his command, when he marked out the foundations of the earth.

Prov. 23:34 You will be like one who lies down in the midst of the sea, like one who lies on the top of a mast.

Qoh. 1:7 All streams run to the sea, but the sea is not full; to the place where the streams flow, there they continue to flow.

Wis. 5:22 And hailstones full of wrath will be hurled as from a catapult; the water of the sea will rage against them, and rivers will relentlessly overwhelm them.

Wis. 10:18 She brought them over the Red Sea, and led them through deep waters.

Wis. 10:19 But she drowned their enemies, and cast them up from the depth of the sea.

Wis. 14:3 But it is your providence, O Father, that steers its course, because you have given it a path in the sea, and a safe way through the waves.

Wis. 14:4 Showing that you can save from every danger, so that even a person who lacks skill may put to sea.

Wis. 19:7 The cloud was seen overshadowing the camp, and dry land emerging where water had stood before, an unhindered way out of the Red Sea, and a grassy plain out of the raging waves.

Wis. 19:12 For, to give them relief, quails came up from the sea.

Sir. 1:2 The sand of the sea, the drops of rain, and the days of eternity – who can count them?

Sir. 24:6 Over waves of the sea, over all the earth, and over every people and nation I have held sway.

Sir. 24:29 For her thoughts are more abundant than the sea, and her counsel deeper than the great abyss.

Sir. 24:31 I said, 'I will water my garden and drench my flower-beds'. And lo, my canal became a river, and my river a sea.

Sir. 29:18 Being surety has ruined many who were prosperous, and has tossed them about like waves of the sea; it has driven the influential into exile, and they have wandered among foreign nations.

Sir. 43:24 Those who sail the sea tell of its dangers, and we marvel at what we hear.

Sir. 44:21 Therefore the Lord assured him with an oath that the nations would be blessed through his offspring; that he would make him as numerous as the dust of the earth, and exalt his offspring like the stars, and give them an inheritance from sea to sea and from the Euphrates to the ends of the earth.

Sir. 50:3 In his days a water cistern was dug, a reservoir like the sea in circumference.

4. *Waves/Ship*

Wis. 5:10 Like a ship that sails through the billowy water, and when it has passed no trace can be found, no track of its keel in the waves.

Wis. 14:1 Again, one preparing to sail and about to voyage over raging waves calls upon a piece of wood more fragile than the ship that carries him.

Wis. 14:3 But it is your providence, O Father, that steers its course, because you have given it a path in the sea, and a safe way through the waves.

Wis. 19:7 The cloud was seen overshadowing the camp, and dry land emerging where water had stood before, an unhindered way out of the Red Sea, and a grassy plain out of the raging waves.

Sir. 24:6 Over waves of the sea, over all the earth, and over every people and nation I have held sway.

Sir. 29:18 Being surety has ruined many who were prosperous, and has tossed them about like waves of the sea; it has driven the influential into exile, and they have wandered among foreign nations.

5. *Stream(s)*

Prov. 5:16 Should your springs be scattered abroad, streams of water in the streets?

Prov. 18:4 The words of the mouth are deep waters; the fountain of wisdom is a gushing stream.

Prov. 21:1 The king's heart is a stream of water in the hand of the LORD; he turns it wherever he will.

Qoh. 1:7 All streams run to the sea, but the sea is not full; to the place where the streams flow, there they continue to flow.

Sir. 39:13 Listen to me, my faithful children, and blossom like a rose growing by a stream of water.

6. *River(s)*

Job 14:11 As waters fail from a lake, and a river wastes away and dries up.

Job 20:17 They will not look on the rivers, the streams flowing with honey and curds.

Job 28:11 The sources of the rivers they probe; hidden things they bring to light.

Job 33:18 To spare their souls from the Pit, their lives from traversing the River.

Job 40:23 Even if the river is turbulent, it is not frightened; it is confident though Jordan rushes against its mouth.

Wis. 5:22 And hailstones full of wrath will be hurled as from a catapult; the water of the sea will rage against them, and rivers will relentlessly overwhelm them.

Wis. 11:6 Instead of the fountain of an ever-flowing river, stirred up and defiled with blood

Wis. 19:10 For they still recalled the events of their sojourn, how instead of producing animals the earth brought forth gnats, and instead of fish the river spewed out vast numbers of frogs.

Sir. 4:26 Do not be ashamed to confess your sins, and do not try to stop the current of a river.

Sir. 24:30 As for me, I was like a canal from a river, like a water channel into a garden.

Sir. 24:31 I said, 'I will water my garden and drench my flower-beds'. And lo, my canal became a river, and my river a sea.

Sir. 39:22 His blessing covers the dry land like a river, and drenches it like a flood.

Sir. 40:13 The wealth of the unjust will dry up like a river, and crash like a loud clap of thunder in a storm.

Sir. 40:16 The reeds by any water or river bank are plucked up before any grass.

7. Fountain(s)

Prov. 5:18 Let your fountain be blessed, and rejoice in the wife of your youth.

Prov. 8:28 When he made firm the skies above, when he established the fountains of the deep.

Prov. 10:11 The mouth of the righteous is a fountain of life, but the mouth of the wicked conceals violence.

Prov. 13:14 The teaching of the wise is a fountain of life, so that one may avoid the snares of death.

Prov. 14:27 The fear of the LORD is a fountain of life, so that one may avoid the snares of death.

Prov. 16:22 Wisdom is a fountain of life to one who has it, but folly is the punishment of fools.

Prov. 18:4 The words of the mouth are deep waters; the fountain of wisdom is a gushing stream.

Prov. 25:26 Like a muddied spring or a polluted fountain are the righteous who give way before the wicked.

Qoh. 12:6 Before the silver cord is snapped, and the golden bowl is broken, and the pitcher is broken at the fountain, and the wheel broken at the cistern.

Wis. 11:6 Instead of the fountain of an ever-flowing river, stirred up and defiled with blood

8. *Well/Cistern*

Prov. 5:15 Drink water from your own cistern, flowing water from your own well.

Prov. 23:27 For a prostitute is a deep pit; an adulteress is a narrow well.

Qoh. 12:6 Before the silver cord is snapped, and the golden bowl is broken, and the pitcher is broken at the fountain, and the wheel broken at the cistern.

Sir. 50:3 In his days a water cistern was dug, a reservoir like the sea in circumference.

9. *Rain*

Job 5:10 He gives rain on the earth and sends waters on the fields.

Job 20:23 To fill their belly to the full God will send his fierce anger into them, and rain it upon them as their food.

Job 24:8 They are wet with the rain of the mountains, and cling to the rock for want of shelter.

Job 28:26 When he made a decree for the rain, and a way for the thunderbolt.

Job 29:23 They waited for me as for the rain; they opened their mouths as for the spring rain.

Job 36:27 For he draws up the drops of water; he distills his mist in rain.

Job 37:6 For to the snow he says, 'Fall on the earth'; and the shower of rain, his heavy shower of rain.

Job 38:25 Who has cut a channel for the torrents of rain, and a way for the thunderbolt.

Job 38:26 Go bring rain on a land where no one lives, on the desert, which is empty of human life.

Job 38:28 Has the rain a father, or who has begotten the drops of dew?

Prov. 16:15 In the light of a king's face there is life, and his favor is like the clouds that bring the spring rain.

Prov. 19:13 A stupid child is ruin to a father, and a wife's quarreling is a continual dripping of rain.

Prov. 25:14 Like clouds and wind without rain is one who boasts of a gift never given.

Prov. 25:23 The north wind produces rain, and a backbiting tongue, angry looks.

Prov. 26:1 Like snow in summer or rain in harvest, so honor is not fitting for a fool.

Prov. 28:3 A ruler who oppresses the poor is a beating rain that leaves no food.

Qoh. 11:3 When clouds are full, they empty rain on the earth; whether a tree falls to the south or to the north, in the place where the tree falls, there it will lie.

Qoh. 12:2 Before the sun and the light and the moon and the stars are darkened and the clouds return with the rain.

Wis. 16:22 Snow and ice withstood fire without melting, so that they might know that the crops of their enemies were being destroyed by the fire that blazed in the hail and flashed in the showers of rain.

Wis. 16:16 for the ungodly, refusing to know you, were flogged by the strength of your arm, pursued by unusual rains and hail and relentless storms, and utterly consumed by fire.

Sir. 1:2 The sand of the sea, the drops of rain, and the days of eternity – who can count them?

Sir. 35:26 His mercy is as welcome in time of distress as clouds of rain in time of drought.

10. *Storm(s)*

Job 21:18 How often are they like straw before the wind, and like chaff that the storm carries away?

Job 30:22 You lift me up on the wind, you make me ride on it, and you toss me about in the roar of the storm.

Prov. 1:27 When panic strikes you like a storm, and your calamity comes like a whirlwind, when distress and anguish come upon you.

Prov. 3:25 Do not be afraid of sudden panic, or of the storm that strikes the wicked.

Wis. 5:14 Because the hope of the ungodly is like thistledown carried by the wind, and like a light frost driven away by a storm; it is dispersed like smoke before the wind, and it passes like the remembrance of a guest who stays but a day.

Wis. 16:16 For the ungodly, refusing to know you, were flogged by the strength of your arm, pursued by unusual rains and hail and relentless storms, and utterly consumed by fire.

Sir. 33:2 The wise will not hate the law, but the one who is hypocritical about it is like a boat in a storm.

Sir. 40:13 The wealth of the unjust will dry up like a river, and crash like a loud clap of thunder in a storm.

Sir. 43:17 The voice of his thunder rebukes the earth; so do the storm from the north and the whirlwind. He scatters the snow like birds flying down, and its descent is like locusts alighting.

11. *Snow*

Job 6:16 That run dark with ice, turbid with melting snow.

Job 24:19 Drought and heat snatch away the snow waters; so does Sheol those who have sinned.

Job 37:6 For to the snow he says, 'Fall on the earth'; and the shower of rain, his heavy shower of rain.

Job 38:22 Have you entered the storehouses of the snow, or have you seen the storehouses of the hail.

Prov. 25:13 Like the cold of snow in the time of harvest are faithful messengers to those who send them; they refresh the spirit of their masters.

Prov. 26:1 Like snow in summer or rain in harvest, so honor is not fitting for a fool.

Wis. 16:22 Snow and ice withstood fire without melting, so that they might know that the crops of their enemies were being destroyed by the fire that blazed in the hail and flashed in the showers of rain.

Sir. 43:13 By his command he sends the driving snow and speeds the lightnings of his judgment.

Sir. 43:17 The voice of his thunder rebukes the earth; so do the storm from the north and the whirlwind. He scatters the snow like birds flying down, and its descent is like locusts alighting.

12. *Hail*

Job 38:22 Have you entered the storehouses of the snow, or have you seen the storehouses of the hail.

Wis. 16:16 For the ungodly, refusing to know you, were flogged by the strength of your arm, pursued by unusual rains and hail and relentless storms, and utterly consumed by fire.

Wis. 16:22 Snow and ice withstood fire without melting, so that they might know that the crops of their enemies were being destroyed by the fire that blazed in the hail and flashed in the showers of rain.

Sir. 39:29 Fire and hail and famine and pestilence, all these have been created for vengeance.

13. *Ice*

Job 6:16 That run dark with ice, turbid with melting snow.

Job 37:10 By the breath of God ice is given, and the broad waters are frozen fast.

Job 38:29 From whose womb did the ice come forth, and who has given birth to the hoarfrost of heaven?

Wis. 16:22 Snow and ice withstood fire without melting, so that they might know that the crops of their enemies were being destroyed by the fire that blazed in the hail and flashed in the showers of rain.

Sir. 43:20 The cold north wind blows, and ice freezes on the water; it settles on every pool of water, and the water puts it on like a breastplate.

14. *Dew*

Job 29:19 My roots spread out to the waters, with the dew all night on my branches.

Job 29:22 After I spoke they did not speak again, and my word dropped upon them like dew.

Job 38:28 Has the rain a father, or who has begotten the drops of dew?

Prov. 3:20 By his knowledge the deeps broke open, and the clouds drop down the dew.

Prov. 19:12 A king's anger is like the growling of a lion, but his favor is like dew on the grass.

Wis. 11:22 Because the whole world before you is like a speck that tips the scales, and like a drop of morning dew that falls on the ground.

Sir. 18:16 Does not the dew give relief from the scorching heat? So a word is better than a gift.

Sir. 43:22 A mist quickly heals all things; the falling dew gives refreshment from the heat.

15. *Mist*

Job 36:27 For he draws up the drops of water; he distills his mist in rain.

Wis. 2:4 Our name will be forgotten in time, and no one will remember our works; our life will pass away like the traces of a cloud, and be scattered like mist that is chased by the rays of the sun and overcome by its heat.

Sir. 24:3 I came forth from the mouth of the Most High, and covered the earth like a mist.

Sir. 43:22 A mist quickly heals all things; the falling dew gives refreshment from the heat.

16. *Drink*

Job 1:4 His sons used to go and hold feasts in one another's houses in turn; and they would send and invite their three sisters to eat and drink with them.

Job 21:20 Let their own eyes see their destruction, and let them drink of the wrath of the Almighty.

Job 22:7 You have given no water to the weary to drink, and you have withheld bread from the hungry

Prov. 4:17 For they eat the bread of wickedness and drink the wine of violence.

Prov. 5:15 Drink water from your own cistern, flowing water from your own well.

Prov. 9:5 Come, eat of my bread and drink of the wine I have mixed.

Prov. 20:1 Wine is a mocker, strong drink a brawler, and whoever is led astray by it is not wise.

Prov. 23:7 For like a hair in the throat, so are they. 'Eat and drink!' they say to you; but they do not mean it.

Prov. 23:35 'They struck me', you will say, 'but I was not hurt; they beat me, but I did not feel it. When shall I awake? I will seek another drink'.

Prov. 25:21 If your enemies are hungry, give them bread to eat; and if they are thirsty, give them water to drink.

Prov. 31:4 It is not for kings, O Lemuel, it is not for kings to drink wine, or for rulers to desire strong drink.

Prov. 31:5 Or else they will drink and forget what has been decreed, and will pervert the rights of all the afflicted.

Prov. 31:6 Give strong drink to one who is perishing, and wine to those in bitter distress.

Prov. 31:7 Let them drink and forget their poverty, and remember their misery no more.

Qoh. 2:24 There is nothing better for mortals than to eat and drink, and find enjoyment in their toil. This also, I saw, is from the hand of God.

Qoh. 3:13 Moreover, it is God's gift that all should eat and drink and take pleasure in all their toil.

Qoh. 5:18 This is what I have seen to be good: it is fitting to eat and drink and find enjoyment in all the toil with which one toils under the sun the few days of the life God gives us; for this is our lot.

Qoh. 8:15 So I commend enjoyment, for there is nothing better for people under the sun than to eat, and drink, and enjoy themselves, for this will go with them in their toil through the days of life that God gives them under the sun.

Qoh. 9:7 Go, eat your bread with enjoyment, and drink your wine with a merry heart; for God has long ago approved what you do.

Sir. 9:10 Do not abandon old friends, for new ones cannot equal them. A new friend is like new wine; when it has aged, you can drink it with pleasure.

Sir. 15:3 She will feed him with the bread of learning, and give him the water of wisdom to drink.

Sir. 24:21 Those who eat of me will hunger for more, and those who drink of me will thirst for more.

Sir. 29:25 You will play the host and provide drink without being thanked, and besides this you will hear rude words like these:

Sir. 50:15 He held out his hand for the cup and poured a drink offering of the blood of the grape; he poured it out at the foot of the altar, a pleasing odor to the Most High, the king of all.

17. *Moisture*

Job 21:24 his loins full of milk and the marrow of his bones moist.

Job 37:11 He loads the thick cloud with moisture; the clouds scatter his lightning.

18. *Lake/Evaporate*

Job 14:11 As waters fail from a lake, and a river wastes away and dries up.

19. *Marsh*

Job 8:11 Can papyrus grow where there is no marsh? Can reeds flourish where there is no water?

Job 40:21 Under the lotus plants it lies, in the covert of the reeds and in the marsh.

20. *Wash*

Job 9:30 If I wash myself with soap and cleanse my hands with lye.

Job 14:19 The waters wear away the stones; the torrents wash away the soil of the earth; so you destroy the hope of mortals.

21. *Flood/Deluge*

Job 22:11 Or darkness so that you cannot see; a flood of water covers you.

Job 22:16 They were snatched away before their time; their foundation was washed away by a flood.

Job 27:20 Terrors overtake them like a flood; in the night a whirlwind carries them off.

Job 38:34 Can you lift up your voice to the clouds, so that a flood of waters may cover you?

Wis. 18:5 When they had resolved to kill the infants of your holy ones, and one child had been abandoned and rescued, you in punishment took away a multitude of their children; and you destroyed them all together by a mighty flood.

Sir. 21:13 The knowledge of the wise will increase like a flood, and their counsel like a life-giving spring.

Sir. 39:22 His blessing covers the dry land like a river, and drenches it like a flood.

Sir. 40:10 All these were created for the wicked, and on their account the flood came.

Sir. 44:17 Noah was found perfect and righteous; in the time of wrath he kept the race alive; therefore a remnant was left on the earth when the flood came.

Sir. 44:18 Everlasting covenants were made with him that all flesh should never again be blotted out by a flood.

22. *Wet*

Job 24:8 They are wet with the rain of the mountains, and cling to the rock for want of shelter.

23. *Plunge*

Job 9:31 Yet you will plunge me into filth, and my own clothes will abhor me.

24. *Drench*

Sir. 24:31 I said, 'I will water my garden and drench my flower-beds'. And lo, my canal became a river, and my river a sea.

Sir. 39:22 His blessing covers the dry land like a river, and drenches it like a flood.

25. *Pool*

Sir. 43:20 The cold north wind blows, and ice freezes on the water; it settles on every pool of water, and the water puts it on like a breastplate.

26. *Leviathan*

Job 3:8 Let those curse it who curse the Sea, those who are skilled to rouse up Leviathan.

Job 41:1 Can you draw out Leviathan with a fishhook, or press down its tongue with a cord?

27. *Rahab*

Job 9:13 God will not turn back his anger; the helpers of Rahab bowed beneath him.

Job 26:12 By his power he stilled the Sea; by his understanding he struck down Rahab.

28. *Behemoth*

Job 40:15 Look at Behemoth, which I made just as I made you; it eats grass like an ox.

29. *Drought*

Job 24:19 Drought and heat snatch away the snow waters; so does Sheol those who have sinned.

30. *Dry Land*

Job 12:15 If he withholds the waters, they dry up; if he sends them out, they overwhelm the land.

Wis. 19:7 The cloud was seen overshadowing the camp, and dry land emerging where water had stood before, an unhindered way out of the Red Sea, and a grassy plain out of the raging waves.

Sir. 39:22 His blessing covers the dry land like a river, and drenches it like a flood.

Job 13:25 Will you frighten a windblown leaf and pursue dry chaff?

Job 18:16 Their roots dry up beneath, and their branches wither above.

Job 30:3 Through want and hard hunger they gnaw the dry and desolate ground.

Prov. 17:1 Better is a dry morsel with quiet than a house full of feasting with strife.

Wis. 4:19 Because he will dash them speechless to the ground, and shake them from the foundations; they will be left utterly dry and barren, and they will suffer anguish, and the memory of them will perish.

Wis. 19:7 The cloud was seen overshadowing the camp, and dry land emerging where water had stood before, an unhindered way out of the Red Sea, and a grassy plain out of the raging waves.

Sir. 39:22 His blessing covers the dry land like a river, and drenches it like a flood.

Sir. 40:13 The wealth of the unjust will dry up like a river, and crash like a loud clap of thunder in a storm.

Job 14:11 As waters fail from a lake, and a river wastes away and dries up.

Prov. 17:22 A cheerful heart is a good medicine, but a downcast spirit dries up the bones.

31. *Fish*

Job 12:8 Ask the plants of the earth, and they will teach you; and the fish of the sea will declare to you.

Qoh. 9:12 For no one can anticipate the time of disaster. Like fish taken in a cruel net, and like birds caught in a snare, so mortals are snared at a time of calamity, when it suddenly falls upon them.

Wis. 19:10 For they still recalled the events of their sojourn, how instead of producing animals the earth brought forth gnats, and instead of fish the river spewed out vast numbers of frogs.

32. *Jordan*

Job 40:23 Even if the river is turbulent, it is not frightened; it is confident though Jordan rushes against its mouth.

Sir. 24:26 It runs over, like the Euphrates, with understanding, and like the Jordan at harvest time.

33. *Euphrates*

Sir. 44:21 Therefore the Lord assured him with an oath that the nations would be blessed through his offspring; that he would make him as numerous as the dust of the earth, and exalt his offspring like the stars, and give them an inheritance from sea to sea and from the Euphrates to the ends of the earth.

34. *Water Creatures*

Wis. 19:19 For land animals were transformed into water creatures, and creatures that swim moved over to the land.

35. *Flow/Flowing/Overflowing*

Prov. 4:23 Keep your heart with all vigilance, for from it flow the springs of life.

Qoh. 1:7 All streams run to the sea, but the sea is not full; to the place where the streams flow, there they continue to flow.

Wis. 16:29 For the hope of an ungrateful person will melt like wintry frost, and flow away like waste water.

Job 20:17 They will not look on the rivers, the streams flowing with honey and curds.

Prov. 5:15 Drink water from your own cistern, flowing water from your own well.

Sir. 46:8 And these two alone were spared out of six hundred thousand infantry, to lead the people into their inheritance, the land flowing with milk and honey.

Sir. 47:14 How wise you were when you were young! You overflowed like the Nile with understanding.

36. *Thirsty*

Job 5:5 The hungry eat their harvest, and they take it even out of the thorns; and the thirsty pant after their wealth.

Wis. 11:4 When they were thirsty, they called upon you, and water was given them out of flinty rock, and from hard stone a remedy for their thirst.

Appendix B:
References to the Life-Giving and Life-Threatening Potential of Water and Water-Related Phenomena

It should be noted that this selection is the researcher's own classification and might not be exhaustive and comprehensive regarding all wisdom texts containing water and water-related phenomena with life-giving or life-threatening potential in the Old Testament wisdom books.

1. References to water and water-related phenomena with life-giving potential:
   - Humans and the rest of nature are dependent on water: Job 8:11; 14:7-12; Prov. 25:13;
   - Sir. 24:23-29 depicts the dependence on water in terms of the six ancient Near Eastern rivers compared to the wisdom flowing from the Torah.
   - Prov. 5:15-20; Sir. 29:21 and 26:12 concern human dependence on water.

2. References to water and water-related phenomena with life-threatening potential:
   - God's use of water: Job 12:15 contains the notion of God using water to destroy earth, while Job 38:22-24; Wis. 10:18-19; 16:16; 18:5; Sir. 39:28-29 concern God's use of water for the destruction or judgment of the wicked.
   - Humans are affected by water: Job 29:19; 24:18-20; Wis. 5:22-23 and Prov. 9:13-18 portray the threats related to water.

3. Water and water-related phenomena as life-giving and life-threatening:
   - While God is involved in the use of water to harm or heal in Job 38:22-38 and Sir. 39:22-23, in Wis. 11:6-14 and 19:1-9 water follows natural laws to fight for the righteous and punish the wicked.

- Qoh. 1:4-11 and 11:1-6 bear elements of unpredictability of water that makes it a vehicle of life or death. The same is visible in Prov. 25:23-26.
- Job 36:26–37:13 contains the notion of God's use of water for good and harm, while Sir. 43:13-26 appeals for wonder and contemplation of water-related phenomena.

4. Water management and responsible use of water:
   - Qoh. 2:4-6; Prov. 5:15-20; Sir. 48:17 and 50:3-5 deal with infrastructures related to water.
   - God's management of water: Job 28:25-26; 38:8-11, 16-17; Prov. 3:19-20; 8:22-31 and Sir. 39:17-21 show God establishing order/limit to the waters.
   - Qoh. 11:1-6 and Prov. 21:1 portray the agricultural use of water.
   - Sir. 38:4-5 assumes water treatment to make it safe for consumption.
   - Water as a human right is implied in Job 22:7; Prov. 11:25; 25:21 and Sir. 39:26 contain the notion of liberality in relation to water.

Bibliography

Agam, Ninari, and Pedro R. Berliner. 'Dew Formation and Water Vapor Absorption in Semi-arid Environments – A Review'. *Journal of Arid Environments* 65 (2006): 572–90.
Albright. William F. 'The Etymology of Še'ôl'. *AJSL* 34 (1918): 210.
Alter, Robert. *The Pleasures of Reading in an Ideological Age*. New York: Simon & Schuster, 1990.
Amnesty International. *Troubled Waters – Palestinians denied fair access to water: Israel-Occupied Palestinian Territories.* London: Amnesty International Publications, 2009.
Anderson, Bernhard W. 'Water'. *IDB* 4:806–10.
Ansari, Mojtaba. *Principles of Islamic Traditional Architectural Design*. Tehran: Tarbiat Modares University Press, 1989.
Ansberry, Christopher B. *Be Wise, my Son, and Make my Heart Glad: An Exploration of the Courtly Nature of the Book of Proverbs*. Berlin: de Gruyter, 2011.
Anthonioz, Stéphanie. *L'eau, Enjeux Politiques et Théologiques, de Sumer à la Bible*. Leiden/Boston: Brill, 2009.
Bagnall, Roger S. *The Administration of the Ptolemaic Possessions Outside Egypt*. Leiden: Brill, 1976.
Balentine, Samuel E. *Smyth & Helwys Bible Commentary: Job*. Macon: Smyth & Helwys, 2006.
Balogh, Csaba. *The Stele of YHWH in Egypt: The Prophecies of Isaiah 18–20 Concerning Egypt and Kush*. Leiden/Boston: Brill, 2011.
Barbour, Jennie. *The Story of Israel in the Book of Qoheleth: Ecclesiastes as Cultural Memory*. Oxford: Oxford Academic, 2012.
Batto, Bernard F. 'The Reed Sea: Requiescat in Pace'. *JBL* 102, no. 1 (1983): 27–35.
Ben Zvi, Ehud, and Christoph Levin, eds. *Thinking of Water in the Early Second Temple Period*. Berlin/Boston: de Gruyter, 2014.
Ben Zvi, Ehud. 'Thinking of Water in Late Persian/Early Hellenistic Judah: An Exploration'. In *Thinking of Water in the Early Second Temple Period*, edited by Ehud Ben Zvi and Christoph Levin, 11–28. Berlin/Boston: de Gruyter, 2014.
Bergant, Dianne. 'The Wisdom of Solomon'. In *Reading from the Perspective of Earth*, edited by Norman C. Habel, 138–50. Sheffield: Sheffield Academic; Cleveland: Pilgrim, 2000.
Bickerman, Elias J. *The Jews in the Greek Age*. Cambridge, MA: Harvard University Press, 1988.
Bimson, John J. 'Has the Rain a Father? A Biblical Theology of Water'. *EMJ* 42 (2012): 1–9.
Boer, R [s. a.]. *Keeping it Literal: The Economy of the Song of Songs*, http://jhsonline.org/cocoon/jhs/a067.html (accessed 26 August 2013).

Boorer, Suzanne. 'Job's Hope: A Reading of the Book of Job from the Perspective of Hope'. *Colloquium* 30, no. 2 (1998): 101–22.
Bowes, D. R. 'Water'. In *The Zondervan Pictorial Encyclopedia of the Bible*, edited by M. C. Tenney, 5:902–6. Grand Rapids: Zondervan, 1975.
Brenner, Athalya. 'God's Answer to Job'. *VT* 31 (1981): 130–7.
Brown, William P. *The Ethos of the Cosmos: The Genesis of Moral Imagination in the Bible*. Grand Rapids/Cambridge: Eerdmans, 1999.
Brown, William P. *The Seven Pillars of Creation: The Bible, Science, and the Ecology of Wonder*. Oxford: Oxford University Press, 2010.
Bryce, Glendon E. 'Another Wisdom-"Book" in Proverbs'. *JBL* 91 (1972): 145–57.
Caleb, Sunil M. 'The Use of Water as a Metaphor and Symbol in Biblical Theology: An Exploration'. In *Water Struggle*, edited by V. J. John, 69–79. Kolkata: Bishop's College, 2007.
Cheon, Samuel. *The Exodus Story in the Wisdom of Solomon: A Study in Biblical Interpretation*. Sheffield: Sheffield Academic, 1997.
Chisholm Jr, Robert B. 'Drink Water from Your Own Cistern: A Literary Study of Proverbs 5:15–23'. *BS* 157 (2000): 397–409.
Clifford, Richard J. 'The Theology of Creation in Proverbs 8:22–31'. In *Creation in the Biblical Traditions*, edited by Richard J. Clifford and John J. Collins, 85–96. Washington: CBAA, 1992.
Clifford, Richard J. *Creation Accounts in the Ancient Near East and in the Bible*. Washington, DC: CBAA, 1994.
Clifford, Richard J. *Proverbs: A Commentary*. Louisville: Westminster John Knox, 1999.
Clines, David J. A. *Job 1–20*. Dallas: Word, 1989.
Clines, David J. A. *Job 38–42*. Nashville: Thomas Nelson, 2011.
Collins, John J. 'Cosmos and Salvation: Jewish Wisdom and Apocalyptic in the Hellenistic Age'. *History of Religions* 17, no. 2 (1977): 121–42.
Collins, John J. *Jewish Wisdom in the Hellenistic Age*. Louisville: John Knox, 1997.
Colson, F. H. 'Philo, Moses I and II (*De Vita Mosis*)'. In *Philo in Ten Volumes and Two Supplementary Volumes*, edited by F. H. Colson, 274–596. London: William Heinemann, 1935.
Conradie, Ernest. 'What on Earth is an Ecological Hermeneutics? Some Broad Parameters'. In *Ecological Hermeneutics: Biblical, Historical and Theological Perspectives*, edited by D. G. Horrell, C. Hunt and C. Southgate, 295–313. New York: T&T Clark, 2010.
Conradie, Ernest. *Christianity and Ecological Theology: Resources for Further Research*. Stellenbosch: Sun, 2006.
Cook, Johann. *The Septuagint of Proverbs Jewish and/or Hellenistic Proverbs: Concerning the Hellenistic Colouring of LXX Proverbs*. Leiden: Brill, 1997.
Coote, Robert B. 'The Tell Siran Bottle Inscription'. *BASOR* 240 (1980): 93.
Cregg, John Allen F. *The Wisdom of Solomon*. Cambridge: Cambridge University Press, 1909.
Crenshaw, James L. 'A Proverb in the Mouth of a Fool'. In *Seeking the Wisdom of the Ancient: Essays Offered to Honour Michael V. Fox on the Occasion of his Sixty-Fifth Birthday*, edited by Roland L. Troxel, Kelvin G. Friebel and Dennis R. Magary, 105–16. Winona Lake, IN: Eisenbrauns, 2005.
Crenshaw, James L. 'Prolegomenon'. In *Studies in Ancient Israelite Wisdom*, edited by James L. Crenshaw, 1–60. New York: Ktav.

Crenshaw, James L. 'Nothing New Under the Sun: Ecclesiastes 1:4–11'. In *Reflecting with Solomon: Selected Studies on the Book of Ecclesiastes*, edited by Roy B. Zuck, 241–8. Grand Rapids, MI: Baker House, 1994.
Crenshaw, James L. 'The Book of Sirach'. *NIB* 5:601–868.
Crenshaw, James L. *Ecclesiastes*. London: SCM, 1988.
Crenshaw, James L. *Reading Job: A Literary and Theological Commentary*. Macon: Smyth & Helwys, 2011.
Cross, Frank M. 'Oldest Manuscripts from Qumran'. *JBL* 74, no. 3 (1955): 147–72.
Dahood, Mitchell J. 'Eblaite Ì-du and Hebrew ƆĒd, Rain Cloud'. *CBQ* 43 (1981): 534–8.
Dahood, Mitchell J. 'Zacharia 9:1, *'Ên 'Ādām*'. *CBQ* 25 (1963): 123–4.
Davis, Ellen F. *Proverbs, Ecclesiastes, and the Song of Songs*. Louisville: John Knox, 2000.
De Savignac, Jean. 'Proverbs'. *VT* 4 (1954): 429–32.
Delitzsch, Franz. *Biblical Commentary on the Proverbs of Solomon*, vol. 2, translated by M. G. Easton. Grand Rapids: Eerdmans, 1950.
Delitzsch, Franz. *Commentary on Song of Songs and Ecclesiastes*, translated by M. G. Easton. Grand Rapids: Eerdmans, 1968.
Dell, Katharine J. *The Book of Proverbs in Social and Theological Context*. New York: Cambridge University Press, 2006.
Donner, Herbert and Wolfgang Röllig, eds. *Kanaanäische und Aramamäische Inschriften*. Wiesbaden: Harrassowitz, 1964.
Driver, Godfrey R. 'Two Astronomical Passages in the Old Testament'. *JTS* 7 (1956): 1–11.
Eidevall, Göran. *Grapes in the Desert: Metaphors, Models, and Themes in Hosea 4–14*. Stockholm: Almqvist & Wiksell International, 1996.
Emerton, John A. 'Spring and Torrent in Psalm 74:15'. *VTSup* 15 (1966): 122–33.
Fejo, Wali. 'The Voice of the Earth: An Indigenous Reading of Genesis 9'. In *The Earth Story in Genesis*, edited by Norman C. Habel and Shirley Wurst, 140–6. Sheffield: Sheffield Academic, 2000.
Feliks, Yehuda. 'Agriculture in the Land of Israel'. In *Encyclopaedia Judaica*, 2:382–98. 16 vols. Jerusalem, 1972
Fontaine, Carol R. 'Proverb Performance in the Hebrew Bible'. In *Wise Words: Essays on the Proverbs*, edited by Wolf Mieder, 393–414. New York: Garland, 1994.
Fontaine, Carol R. 'Visual Metaphors and Proverbs 5:15–20: Some Archaeological Reflections on Gendered Iconography'. In *Seeking the Wisdom of the Ancient: Essays Offered to Honour Michael V. Fox on the Occasion of his Sixty-Fifth Birthday*, edited by R. Troxel, K. G. Friebel and D. R. Magary, 185–202. Winona Lake: Eisenbrauns, 2005.
Fox, Michael V. 'Aging and Death in Qohelet 12'. *JSOT* 42 (1988): 55–77.
Fox, Michael V. 'Joseph and Wisdom'. In *The Book of Genesis: Composition, Reception and Interpretation*, edited by C. A. Evans, J. N. Lohr and D. L. Petersen, 231–62. Leiden/Boston: Brill, 2012.
Fox, Michael V. 'The Use of Indeterminacy'. *Semeia* 71 (1995): 173–92.
Fox, Michael V. *Proverbs 1–9*. New York: Doubleday, 2000.
Fox, Michael V. *Qoheleth and his Contradictions*. Sheffield: Almond, 1989.
Gadamer, Hans G. *Truth and Method*. New York: Seabury, 1975.
Gardner, Anne. 'Ecojustice: A Study of Genesis 6:11–13'. In *The Earth Story in Genesis*, edited by Norman C. Habel and Shirley Wurst, 117–30. Sheffield: Sheffield Academic, 2000.

Gilead, M., and N. Rosenan. 'Ten Years of Dew Observation in Israel'. *IEJ* 4, no. 2 (1954): 120–23.
Good, Edwin M. 'The Unfilled Sea: Style and Meaning in Ecclesiastes 1:2–11'. In *Israelite Wisdom: Theological and Literary Essays in Honour of Samuel Terrien*, edited by John G. Gammie, Walter A. Brueggemann, W. L. Humphreys and James M. Ward, 59–73. Missoula: Scholars Press, 1978.
Grave, Cecilia. 'The Etymology of Northwest Semitic *ṣapānu*'. *UF* 12 (1980): 221–9.
Green, Douglas. 'When the Gardener Returns: An Ecological Perspective on Adam's Dominion'. In *Keeping God's Earth: The Global Environment in Biblical Perspective*. Edited Noah J. Toly and Daniel I. Block, 267–75. Downers Grove: InterVarsity; Nottingham: Apollos, 2010.
Grünfeld, Joseph. 'Étude Critique: Kittay's Theory of Metaphor'. *Science et Esprit* 44 (1992): 83–9.
Gunkel, Hermann. *Creation and Chaos in the Primeval Era and the Eschaton: A Religion-Historical Study of Genesis 1 and Revelation 12*, translated by K. W. Grand Rapids: Eerdmans, 2006.
Habel, Norman, C., and Peter Trudinger, eds. *Water: A Matter of Life and Death*. Adelaide: ATF Theology, 2011.
Habel, Norman C. 'Introduction: Water: A Matter of Life and Death'. In *Water: A Matter of Life and Death*, edited by Norman C. Habel and Peter Trudinger, 1–8. Adelaide: ATF Theology, 2011.
Habel, Norman C. 'Introducing Ecological Hermeneutics'. In *Exploring Ecological Hermeneutics*, edited by Norman C. Habel and Peter Trudinger, 1–8. Atlanta: SBL, 2008.
Habel, Norman C. 'Earth First: Inverse Cosmology in Job'. In *The Earth Story in Wisdom Traditions*, edited by Norman C. Habel and Shirley Wurst, 65–77. Sheffield: Sheffield Academic; Cleveland: Pilgrim, 2001.
Habel, Norman C. *Job: A Commentary*. London: SCM, 1985.
Hadas, Moses. *Aristeas to Philocrates (Letter of Aristeas)*. New York: Harper, 1951.
Harris, Robert L. 'The Meaning of the Word Sheol as Shown by Parallels in Poetic Text'. *BETS* 4, no. 4 (1961): 129–35.
Haupt, Paul. 'The Original Meaning of Sheol'. *JBL* 36, no. 3–4 (1917): 258.
Hembrom, Timotheas. 'Significance of Water in the Old Testament'. In *Water Struggle*, edited by V. J. John, 49–56. Kolkata: Bishop's College, 2007.
Hertzberg, Hans W. *Der Prediger*. Gütersloh: Gerd Mohn, 1963.
Hess, Richard S. 'Eden'. *Bible Review* (1991): 28–33.
Hillel, Daniel. *The Natural History of the Bible: An Environmental Exploration of the Hebrew Scriptures*. New York: Columbian University Press, 2006.
Hobgood-Oster, L. 'For Out of that Well the Flocks were Watered: Stories of Wells in Genesis'. In *The Earth Story in Genesis*, edited by Norman C. Habel and Shirley Wurst, 187–99. Sheffield: Sheffield Academic; Cleveland: Pilgrim, 2000.
Hopkins, David C. *The Highlands of Canaan: An Agricultural Life in the Early Iron Age*. Sheffield: Almond, 1985.
Horne, Milton P. *Smyth & Helwys Bible Commentary: Proverbs-Ecclesiastes*. Macon: Smyth & Helwys, 2003.
Hubbard, David A. 'Principles of Financial Investment: Ecclesiastes 11:1–8'. In *Reflecting with Solomon: Selected Studies on the Book of Ecclesiastes*, edited by Roy B. Zuck, 341–6. Grand Rapids: Baker, 1994.

Hurvitz, Avi. 'The Date of the Prose Tale of Job Linguistically Recognised'. *HTR* 67 (1974): 17–34.
Ikram, Salima. *Ancient Egypt: An Introduction*. Cambridge: Cambridge University Press, 2010.
Israeli Water Law and Water Authorities of 1959. 'Water Law 5719–1959'. Available online: http://www.sviva.gov.il/English/Legislation/Documents/Water%20Laws%20 and%20Regulations/WaterLaw1959-Excerpts.pdf (accessed 16 September 2018).
Issar, A. S. *Water Shall Flow from the Rock: Hydrogeology and Climate in the Land of the Bible*. Berlin: Springer-Verlag, 1990.
Jaussen, Antonin. 'Le coq et la pluie dans la tradition palestinienne'. *RB* 33 (1924): 574–82.
Jenney, Timothy P. 'Water'. In *Eerdmans Dictionary of the Bible*, edited by David N. Freedman, 1367–9. Grand Rapids: Eerdmans, 2000.
Johnston, Philip. 'The Underworld and the Dead in the Old Testament'. *Tyndale Bulletin* 45, no. 2 (1994): 415–19.
Jonker, Louis. 'Manasseh in Paradise? The Influence of ANE Palace Garden Imagery in LXX 2 Chronicles 33:20'. In *Thinking of Water in the Early Second Temple Period*, edited by Ehud Ben Zvi and Christophe Levin, 339–58. Berlin: de Gruyter, 2014.
Kadish, Gerald E. 'Seasonality and the Name of the Nile'. *JARCE* 25 (1988): 185–94.
Kahn, Charles. *Anaximander and the Origins of Greek Cosmology*. New York: Colombia University Press, 1960.
Kang, Shin T. 'Irrigation in Ancient Mesopotamia'. *AWRA* 8, no. 3 (1972): 619–24.
Kee, Min Suc. 'A Study on the Dual Form of Mayim, Water'. *JBQ* 40, no. 3 (2012): 183–7.
King, Philip and Lawrence E. Stager. *Life in Biblical Israel*. Louisville: John Knox, 2001.
Klopper, Frances. 'Aspects of Creation: The Water in the Wilderness motif in the Psalms and the Prophets'. *OTE* 18, no. 2 (2005): 253–64.
Klopper, Frances. 'The Rhetoric of Conflicting Metaphors: A Fountain Desired in the Song of Songs but Abhorred in Leviticus'. *OTE* 15, no. 3 (2002): 675–86.
Koh, Yee-Von. *Royal Autobiography in the Book of Qoheleth*. Berlin: de Gruyter, 2006.
Köhlenberger III, J. R. *The NRSV Concordance Unabridged: Including the Apocryphal/ Deuterocanonical Books*. Grand Rapids: Zondervan, 1991.
Köhler, Ludwig. 'Der Jordan'. *ZDPV* 62 (1939): 115–20.
Kolarcik, Michael. 'The Book of Wisdom'. *NIB* 5:435–600.
Kolarcik, Michael. *The Ambiguity of Death in the Book of Wisdom 1–6: A Study of Literary Structure and Interpretation*. Rome: Pontificio Istituto Biblico, 1991.
Komano, Naoto. *Cosmology and Character: Qoheleth's Pedagogy from a Rhetorical-Critical Perspective*. Berlin: de Gruyter, 2001.
Kruger, Paul A. 'Promiscuity or Marriage Fidelity? A Note on Proverbs 5:15–18'. *JNSL* 13 (1987): 61–8.
Krüger, Thomas. *Qoheleth: A Commentary*. Translated by O. C. Dean Jr. Minneapolis: Fortress, 2004.
Kuhrt, Amélie. *The Persian Empire: A Corpus of Sources from Achaemenid Period*. London: Routledge, 2010.
Landy, Francis. 'Fluvial Fantasies'. In *Thinking of Water in the Early Second Temple Period*, edited by Ehud Ben Zvi and Christophe Levin, 436–55. Berlin/Boston: de Gruyter, 2014.

Levin, Christophe. 'Drought and Locust Plague in Joel 1–2'. In *Thinking of Water in the Early Second Temple Period*, edited by Ehud Ben Zvi and Christophe Levin, 197–228. Berlin/Boston: de Gruyter, 2014.
Lichtheim, Miriam. *Ancient Egyptian Literature*, Vol. 3. Berkeley: University of California Press, 1980.
Loader, James A. 'Image and Order: Old Testament Perspectives on the Ecological Crisis'. In *Are We Killing God's Earth? Ecology and Theology*, edited by W. S. Vorster, 6–29. Pretoria: UNISA, 1987.
Loader, James A. *Polar Structures in the Book of Qohelet*. Berlin/New York: de Gruyter, 1979.
Loew, Cornelius. *Myth, Sacred History and Philosophy*. New York: Harcourt, Brace & Brothers, 1967.
Lohfink, Norbert. *Qohelet: A Continental Commentary*. Minneapolis: Fortress, 2003.
Longman III, Tremper. *Proverbs*. Grand Rapids: Baker, 2006.
Longman III, Tremper. *The Book of Ecclesiastes*. Grand Rapids: Eerdmans, 1998.
Luc, Alex. 'Storm and the Message of Job'. *JSOT* 87 (2000): 111–23.
Malbim, Meir L. *The Commentary of Rabbi Meir Leibush Malbim on the Book of Proverbs*. Jerusalem: Feldeim, 1973.
Manser, Martin H. *The Facts on File Dictionary of Proverbs: Meaning and Origins of More than 1,700 Popular Sayings*. New York: Facts on File, 2007.
Marlow, Hilary. 'The Lament over the River Nile – Isaiah xix:5–10 in its Wider Context'. *VT* 57 (2007): 229–42.
May, Herbert G. 'Some Cosmic Connotations of Mayim Rabbîm, Many Waters'. *JBL* 74 (1955): 9–21.
Mazzinghi, L. 'The Antithetical Pair "to Punish" and "to Benefit" (κολάζω and εὐεργετέω) in the Book of Wisdom'. In *Wisdom for Life: Essays Offered to Honor Prof. Maurice Gilbert, SJ on the Occasion of His Eightieth Birthday*, edited by N. Calduch-Benages, 237–49. Berlin: de Gruyter, 2014.
McCann, Clinton Jr. 'Between Text and Sermon Psalm 104'. *Interpretation* 66, no. 1 (2012): 67–9.
McCarter, Peter K. 'The River Ordeal in Israelite Literature'. *HTR* 66 (1973): 403–12.
McKane, William. *Proverbs: A New Approach*. London: SCM, 1970.
Metzger, B. M., ed. *The NRSV Exhaustive Concordance: Completed and Unabridged*. Nashville: Thomas Nelson, 1991.
Michel, Walter L. *Job: In Light of Northwest Semitic*. Rome: Biblical Institute, 1987.
Migliore, Daniel. *Faith Seeking Understanding: An Introduction to Christian Theology*. Grand Rapids: Eerdmans, 1991.
Millard, Alan R. 'The Etymology of Eden'. *VT* 34 (1984): 103–6.
Min, Young-Jin. 'How Do the Rivers Flow (Ecclesiastes 1:7)'. *BT* 42 (1991): 226–31.
Moltmann, Jurgen. *God in Creation: An Ecological Doctrine of Creation*. London: SCM, 1985.
Morgan, Ruth A., and James L. Smith. 'Premodern Streams of Thought in Twenty-First-Century Water Management'. *Radical History Review* 116 (2013): 105–29.
Morris, Paul. 'Exiled From Eden: Jewish Interpretations of Genesis'. In *A Walk in the Garden: Biblical, Iconographical and Literary Images of Eden*, edited by Paul Morris and D. Sawyer, 117–67. Sheffield: JSOT, 1992.

Murphy, Roland E. 'The Interpretation of Old Testament Wisdom Literature'. *Interpretation* 23 (1969): 289–301.

Murphy, Roland E. *The Tree of Life: An Exploration of Biblical Wisdom Literature*. 3rd edn. Grand Rapids: Eerdmans, 1990.

Naidu-Hoffmeester, R. 'South Africa's Water Resource Under Immense Pressure'. Available online: www.unisa.ac.za/news&media.htm (accessed 16 April 2014).

Newsom, Carol A. 'The Book of Job'. *NIB* 4:317–638.

Newsom, Carol A. *The Book of Job: A Contest of Moral Imaginations*. Oxford: Oxford University Press, 2003.

Nõmmik, Urmas. 'Thinking of Water in the Book of Job: A Fluvial Introduction to the Job Literature'. In *Thinking of Water in the Early Second Temple Period*, edited by Ehud Ben Zvi and Christophe Levin, 279–98. Berlin/Boston: de Gruyter, 2014.

Obermann, Julian. 'Wind, Water, and Light in an Archaic Inscription from Shechem'. *JBL* 57, no. 3 (1938): 239–53.

Ogden, Graham S. *Qoheleth*. Sheffield: JSOT, 1987.

Orni, Efraim, and Elisha Efrat. *Geography of Israel*. Philadelphia: Jewish Publication Society, 1973.

Patai, Raphael. 'The Control of Rain in Ancient Palestine: A Study in Comparative Religion'. *HUCA* 14 (1939): 251–86.

Patrick, D. 'Divine Creative Power and the Decentring of Creation: The Subtext of the Lord's Addresses to Job'. In *The Earth Story in Wisdom Traditions*, edited by Norman C. Habel and Shirley Wurst, 103–15. Sheffield: Sheffield Academic; Cleveland: Pilgrim, 2001.

Pedersen, Johannes. *Israel, its Life and Culture (parts I-II)*. London: Oxford University Press, 1940.

Perdue, Leo G. *Proverbs: Interpretation. A Bible Commentary for Teaching and Preaching*. Louisville: John Knox, 2000.

Perdue, Leo G. *Wisdom and Creation: The Theology of Wisdom Literature*. Nashville: Abingdon, 1994.

Perdue, Leo G. *Wisdom Literature: A Theological History*. London: Westminster John Knox, 2007.

Perry, Theodore A. *Dialogue with Kohelet: The Book of Ecclesiastes, Translation and Commentary*. Pennsylvania: Pennsylvania State University Press, 1993.

Perry, Theodore A. *Wisdom Literature and the Structure of Proverbs*. Pennsylvania: Pennsylvania State University Press, 1993.

Peters, John P. 'The Cock in the Old Testament'. *JBL* 33, no. 2 (1914): 152–6.

Petrova, Roumyana. 'Comparing Proverbs as Cultural Texts'. *Proverbium: Yearbook of International Proverb Scholarship* 20 (2003): 331–44.

Prinsloo, Gert T. M. 'Historical Reality and Mythological Metaphor in Psalm 124'. *OTE* 18, no. 3 (2003): 790–810.

Propp, W. H. *Water in the Wilderness: A Biblical Motif and its Mythological Background*. Atlanta: Scholars Press, 1987.

Rad, Gerhard von. 'The Theological Problem of the Old Testament Doctrine of Creation'. In *The Problem of The Hexateuch and Other Essays*, 131–43, translated by E. W. Dicken. London: SCM, 1984.

Rad, Gerhard von. *Wisdom in Israel*, translated by J. D. Martin. London: SCM, 1972.

Rasmussen, Carl. *The Zondervan NIV Atlas of the Bible*. Grand Rapids: Zondervan Publishing, 1989.

Reese, James M. 'Plan and Structure in the Book of Wisdom'. *CBQ* 27 (1965): 391–9.
Reymond, Philippe. *L'eau, sa Vie et sa Signification dans l'Ancien Testament*. Leiden: Brill, 1958.
Ricoeur, Paul. 'Biblical Hermeneutics'. *Semeia* 4 (1975): 29–145.
Ricoeur, Paul. *Interpretation Theory: The Surplus of Meaning*. Fort Worth: Texas Christian University Press, 1976.
Rogers, Jessie F. 'Wisdom and Creation in Sirach 24'. *JNSL* 22, no. 2 (1996): 141–56.
Ross, M. M. 'Water for Life, Water of Life and Water as Life: Meaning and Symbol in Theology'. In *Water Struggle*, edited by V. J. John, 80–101. Kolkata: Bishop's College, 2007.
Rudman, Dominic. *Determinism in the Book of Ecclesiastes*. Sheffield: Sheffield Academic, 2001.
Rudman, Dominic. 'The Use of Water Imagery in Descriptions of Sheol'. *ZAW* 113 (2001): 240–4.
Sachs, Gerardo. 'Why Shamayim as Sky'. *JBQ* 34, no. 2 (2006): 130.
Samet, Nili. 'Qohelet 1,4 and the Structure of the Book's Prologue'. *ZAW* 126 (2014): 92–100.
Schifferdecker, Kathryn. *Out of the Whirlwind: Creation Theology in the Book of Job*. Cambridge, MA: Harvard University Press, 2008.
Schökel, L. A., and J. L. Díaz. *Job: Commentario Teológico Y Literario*. Madrid: Cristiandad, 1983.
Seow, Choon-Leon. 'Hope in Two Keys: Musical Impact and the Poetics of Job 14'. In *Congress Volume Ljubljana 2007*, edited by André Lemaire, 495–510. Leiden, Boston: Brill, 2010.
Seow, Choon-Leong. *Ecclesiastes: A New Translation with Introduction and Commentary*. New Haven/London: Yale University Press, 1997.
Sharp, Carolyn J. 'Ironic Representation, Authorial Voice, and Meaning in Qohelet,' *Biblical Interpretation* 12 (2004): 37–68.
Shavit, Yaakov, and Mordechai Eran. *The Hebrew Bible Reborn: From Scripture to the Book of Books*. Berlin: de Gruyter, 2007.
Sheppard, Gerald T. *Wisdom as a Hermeneutical Construct: A Study in the Sapientializing of the Old Testament*. Berlin: de Gruyter, 1980.
Simkins, Ronald A. *Yahweh's Activity in History and Nature in the Book of Joel*. Lewiston: Edwin Mellen, 1991.
Sinnott, Alice M. 'Job 12: Cosmic Devastation and Social Turmoil'. In *The Earth Story in Wisdom Traditions*, edited by Norman C. Habel and Shirley Wurst, 78–91. Sheffield: Sheffield Academic, 2001.
Skehan, Patrick, and Alexander A. Di Lella. *The Wisdom of Ben Sira*. New Haven: Yale University Press, 1987.
Skehan, Patrick W. 'Proverbs 5:15–19 and 6:20–24'. *CBQ* 8 (1946): 290–7.
Skehan, Patrick W. 'Structure in Poems on Wisdom: Proverbs 8 and Sirach 24'. *CBQ* 41 (1979): 365–79.
Snaith, John G. *Ecclesiasticus or the Wisdom of Jesus Son of Sirach*. Cambridge: Cambridge University Press, 1974.
Spangenberg, Izak. 'Irony in the Book of Qoheleth'. *JSOT* 72 (1996): 57–69.
Sutcliffe, Edmund F. 'The Clouds as Water-Carriers in Hebrew Thought'. *VT* 3 (1953): 99–103.

Sweeney, Marvin A. *TANAK: A Theological and Critical Introduction to the Jewish Bible*. Minneapolis: Fortress, 2012.

Sylva, Dennis. 'The Rising נהרות of Psalm 93: The Chaotic Order'. *JSOT* 36 (2012): 471–82.

The Earth Bible Team. 'Guiding Ecojustice Principles'. In *Reading from the Perspective of Earth*, edited by Norman C. Habel, 38–53. Sheffield: Sheffield Academic, 2000.

Thompson, Henry, and Fawzi Zayadine. 'The Tell Siran Inscription'. *BASOR* 212 (1973): 5–11.

Tsumura, David Toshio. 'A Biblical Theology of Water: Plenty, Food and Drought in the Created Order'. In *Keeping God's Earth: The Global Environment in Biblical Perspective*, edited by Noah J. Toly and Daniel I. Block, 165–84. Downers Grove: InterVarsity; Nottingham: Apollos, 2010.

Tsumura, David Toshio. *The Earth and the Waters in Genesis 1 and 2: A Linguistic Investigation*. Sheffield: JSOT, 1989.

Tur-Sinai, Naftali H. *The Book of Job*. Jerusalem: Kiriath Sepher, 1967.

UNESCO. Water Issues. Available online: http://www.unesco.org/water/water_links/Water_Issues/ (accessed 6 June 2013).

Van der Ploeg, Johannes Petrus M. 'Prov. 25:23'. *VT* 3 (1953): 189–91.

Van Heerden, S. W. 'Norman Habel se Interpretasie van Genesis 1:1–2:4a binne die Raamwerk van die Earth Bible Project'. *OTE* 18, no. 2 (2005): 371–93.

Van Leeuwen, Raymond C. 'The Book of Proverbs'. *NIB* 5:17–264.

Van Leeuwen, Raymond C. *Context and Meaning in Proverbs 25–27*. Atlanta: Scholar Press, 1988.

VanGemeren, Willem A., ed. *New International Dictionary of Old Testament Theology & Exegesis*, 5 vols. Grand Rapids: Zondervan, 1997.

Vawter, Bruce. 'Proverbs 8:22: Wisdom and Creation'. *JBL* 99 (1980): 205–16.

Verheij, Arian. 'Paradise Retried: On Qohelet 2:4–6'. *JSOT* 50 (1991): 113–15.

Walls, C. 'Wash, Water & Unclean: Water, Drink, Fountain, Sea & Wash'. In *A Theological Word Book*, edited by Alan Richardson, 279–81. London: SCM, 1957.

Waltke, Bruce K., and Michael O'Connor. *An Introduction to the Hebrew Syntax*. Winona Lake: Eisenbrauns, 1990.

Waltke, Bruce K. *The Book of Proverbs: Chapters 1–15*. Grand Rapids, MI: Eerdmans, 2004.

Waltke, Bruce K. *The Book of Proverbs: Chapters 15–31*. Grand Rapids: Eerdmans, 2005.

Waters, Larry J. 'The Authenticity of the Elihu Speeches in Job 32–37'. *BS* 156 (1999): 28–41.

Watson, R. S. *Chaos Uncreated: A Reassessment of the Theme*. Berlin: de Gruyter, 2005.

Westermann, Claus. *The Structure of the Book of Job*. Philadelphia: Fortress, 1981.

White, Lynn. 'The Historical Roots of Our Ecological Crisis'. *Science* 155 (1967): 1203–7.

Whitwell, Christopher. 'The Variation of Nature in Ecclesiastes 11'. *JSOT* 34 (2009): 81–98.

Whybray, Roger N. *Ecclesiastes*. Grand Rapids: Eerdmans, 1989.

Whybray, Roger N. 'Ecclesiastes 1:5–7 and the Wonders of Nature'. *JSOT* 41 (1988): 105–12.

Whybray, Roger N. 'Qoheleth, Preacher of Joy'. *JSOT* 23 (1982): 87–98.

Whybray, Roger N. *The Composition of the Book of Proverbs*. Sheffield: Sheffield Academic, 1994.

Willis, John T. 'Alternating (ABA'B') Parallelism in the Old Testament'. In *Directions in Biblical Hebrew Poetry*, edited by Elaine R. Follis, 49–76. Sheffield: JSOT, 1987.

Wilson, Lindsay. 'Artful Ambiguity in Ecclesiastes 1:1–11'. In *Qoheleth in the Context of Wisdom*, edited by Antoon Schoors, 357–66. Leuven: Uitgeverij Peeters, 1998.
Wilson, Lindsay. *Job*. Grand Rapids: Eerdmans, 2015.
Winston, David. *The Book of Wisdom of Solomon*. New York: Doubleday, 1979.
Wolde, Ellen van. 'Facing the Earth: Primeval History in a New Perspective'. In *The World of Genesis: Persons, Places*, edited by Philip R. Davies and David J. A. Clines, 22–47. Sheffield: Sheffield Academic, 1998.
Yee, Gale A. '"I Have Perfumed My Bed with Myrrh": The Foreign Woman in Proverbs 1–9'. *JSOT* 43 (1989): 53–68

Index of References

Hebrew Bible/ Old Testament		2:15	125, 134	9:25	55
		3:19	86	14:19	166
Genesis		6–9	52, 85	15:8	75, 85
1–11	31	7:11	56, 57, 99,	15:27	95
1–9	2		100, 131,	16:14	153
1	100, 104,		173	17:1-6	93, 94
	166	7:35	85	20:21	94
1:1–2:4	103, 104	8:2	57, 131	24:1	94
1:1-2	101	8:4-12	104		
1:2–2:4	122	13:10	142	Leviticus	
1:2	29, 103,	15:18	146	20:10	78
	133, 134,	16:12	48	26:4	92
	154, 166,	21:17-20	20		
	175	21:25-34	20	Numbers	
1:6-10	75	21:30	74	20:11	94
1:6	48, 51, 63,	22:4	94	21:18	73
	100	25:8	34	33:9	95
1:9-12	134, 175	25:29	94		
1:11-12	59, 166	26:13-14	34	Deuteronomy	
1:11	125	26:17-22	20	1:7	142
1:14-18	62, 66	26:18	83	6:11	74
1:14-16	62	26:25	74	8:7	95, 103
1:20-25	167	27:28	60, 154	8:15	161
1:20-21	155	27:39	154	10:11-17	60
1:28	141	30:29-30	34	11:8-15	127, 146
1:31	122, 126	33:19	34	11:10-15	162
2–3	122	35:29	34	11:10-11	162
2	122, 148	37:4	94	11:11	162
2:4	99, 103, 122	37:5	84	11:13-15	48
2:5-6	52	37:20	75	11:14	92, 131, 134
2:5	48			22:22	78
2:6	17, 47	Exodus		28:12	55
2:7	86	2:3	143	32:2	60
2:8	125	2:4	94	32:18	92
2:10-14	141, 147,	7:1-24	157		
	148	7:5	161	Joshua	
2:10-13	147	7:21	163	10:1	55
2:10	140, 147	9:19	55	10:12	159
2:11-14	138	9:22-26	55	15:19	76

15:34	76	*Nehemiah*		12	24, 119
15:62	76	3:15	122	12:1-6	35
17:11	76	4:15	62	12:7-8	64
19:21	76	10:39	55	12:8	187, 201
		11:29	76	12:12	42
Judges				12:15	24, 35, 58,
4:21	94	*Esther*			181, 200,
5:20	159	10:13	92		204
6:38	60			13:1-2	35
16:9	39	*Job*		13:25	201
		1:1–2:13	9, 34	14	23, 36, 37,
1 Samuel		1:3	34		39
3:8	64	1:4	196	14:1-6	36, 38
12:17	60	1:10	34	14:1	40
17:17	130	2:3	34	14:6	39
26:13	94	3–37	34	14:7-22	36, 38
		3–31	34	14:7-12	12, 22, 33,
2 Samuel		3:1–42:6	9, 34		36, 37, 39,
1:21	60	3:3	42		42, 67, 171,
14:14	61	3:8	186, 200		177, 204
17:12	60	3:24	181	14:7-9	36–9, 67,
17:19	74	3:26	49		171
17:29	94	4–27	39	14:7-8	37, 38
22:17	85	4:7-12	170	14:7	39
23:4	48	5:5	203	14:8-9	40
		5:10	60, 181, 191	14:9	37–9, 43,
1 Kings		5:26	39		181
1:38	144	6:3	186	14:10-12	37, 38, 40,
18:5	95	6:15-17	39		42, 43, 79,
		6:16-17	61		171
2 Kings		6:16	194, 195	14:10	37-39
6:2	143	7:2	116, 118	14:11-12	37, 38, 42,
18:17	57	7:9	42, 85		171, 177
18:31	74, 83	7:12	186	14:11	37, 43, 177,
19:24	51	7:21	42		181, 189,
20:20	127, 174	8:11-13	39		198, 201
		8:11	181, 198,	14:12	42
1 Chronicles			204	14:13-17	37
12:16	142	9:6	100	14:13	42
		9:8	186	14:17	39
2 Chronicles		9:13	200	14:18-22	37
11:11	55	9:17	58	14:19	181, 198
32:2-5	73	9:30	198	15:2	56
32:2-4	144	9:31	199	15:16	181
32:3-4	95	11:9	187	17:13	84
32:4	52	11:16	181	18:16	201
32:30	144	12–14	36, 37	20:11	42

Job (cont.)

20:17	189, 202	34:2-37	45	37:8-10	46
20:23	191	34:7	182	37:8	50, 51
21:18	193	35:2-16	45	37:9-11	52
21:20	196	36–37	21	37:9	51, 91
21:24	198	36:1–37:24	45	37:10	52, 182,
21:26	42	36:1–37:13	45		195
22:7	94, 181,	36:1-21	45	37:11-13	46
	196, 205	36:22–37:24	45	37:11	198
22:11	182, 198	36:26–37:13	12, 22, 23,	37:12	171
22:16	198		33, 43–6,	37:13	45, 52, 67,
24:8	192, 199		52, 63, 67,		167, 168,
24:18-20	204		171, 205		176
24:18	133, 182	36:26-29	46	37:17	151
24:19	182, 194,	36:26-28	12, 46, 48	37:18	52
	200	36:26	21, 46, 47	38–42	2, 5
26:5	182	36:27-29	46	38–41	35, 53, 54
26:8	51, 182	36:27-28	36, 46–8,	38	12, 23, 24,
26:10-13	16		50, 52, 57,		35, 151
26:10	182		59, 66, 67	38:1–42:6	34
26:11	100	36:27	8, 16, 17,	38:1–40:2	54
26:12	154, 187,		116, 152,	38:1-21	54
	200		182, 192,	38:8-11	16, 24, 52,
26:27	48		196		53, 154,
27:20	182, 198	36:28	47, 48, 99,		205
28	102		171	38:8	187
28:4	182	36:29–37:5	49	38:16-17	61, 85, 205
28:9-11	17	36:29-30	50	38:16	154, 187
28:11	189	36:29	49, 50, 64	38:22-38	12, 22, 33,
28:14	154, 187	36:30-33	46		53, 54, 67,
28:24-25	56	36:30	49, 50, 187		171, 177,
28:24	56	36:31-33	49		204
28:25-26	205	36:31-32	50	38:22-30	53
28:25	182	36:31	46, 50, 52	38:22-27	23, 35
28:26	192	37:1-4	46	38:22-24	24, 55, 56,
29:19	182, 195,	37:1	46		204
	204	37:2-5	49	38:22-23	36, 56, 66
29:22	195	37:2	49, 52, 171	38:22	55, 194
29:23	192	37:4	49	38:23-38	171
30:3	58, 59, 201	37:5-13	46	38:23	24, 55
30:14	182	37:5-7	46	38:24-25	66
30:22	193	37:6-13	21, 36	38:25-27	57
32–37	35, 45	37:6-12	50	38:25	24, 57, 58,
32:6-22	45	37:6-8	36		182, 192
33:1-33	45	37:6-7	21, 47, 48,	38:26-27	24, 36, 58
33:18	189		51–3	38:26	48, 58, 161,
		37:6	51, 192,		192
			194		

38:27	58, 59	40:3	87	2:1-22	70
38:28-30	59	51:7	153	2:16-19	80
38:28-29	59–61	65:9-13	47	2:17	81
38:28	60, 61, 192, 195	65:12	99	2:18	81
		69:1-3	85	3:1–4:27	71
38:29-30	61	69:3	85	3:1-12	70
38:29	59, 195	69:15-16	86	3:13-35	70
38:30	182	72:6	48	3:13-20	97
38:31-33	62	74:13-14	155	3:13-18	97
38:31	62	78:16	75	3:13-17	97
38:32	62	78:23	57	3:18	97
38:33	63	78:44	75	3:19-20	12, 22, 28, 68, 96–9, 101, 105, 106, 172, 173, 205
38:34-38	63, 66	78:47	55, 61, 152		
38:34-35	63	78:48	55		
38:34	64, 182, 199	88:4-6	84		
		88:7	85		
38:35	64	89:9-10	154	3:19	97-99, 101
38:36	63-65	104	2, 114, 151, 155	3:20	74, 98–100, 173, 195
38:37-38	63				
38:37	65	104:10-16	119	3:25	193
38:38	65	104:10-11	95	4:1-9	70
38:39–40:2	54	104:13	50	4:10-19	70
39:10-12	53	104:24	99	4:17	196
40–41	53	104:25-26	155	4:20-27	70
40:3-5	54	104:27	50	4:23	202
40:6–41:26	54	104:35	96	5:1–6:35	71
40:15	200	105	120	5:1-23	70, 80
40:21	198	105:44	111	5:1-20	71
40:23	190, 202	107:23	154	5:1	71
41:1	200	110:31	60	5:2-14	71
41:31	187	119:13	116	5:5	81, 85
42:7-17	9, 34	119:131	118	5:6	81
42:11	34	133:3	61	5:9-13	78
42:17	34	135:7	55, 57	5:9-10	78
48	59	136:6	99	5:9	78
		148:8	56, 152, 177	5:10	78
				5:11-13	78
Psalms				5:12	69
1	141			5:15-20	1, 10, 12, 22, 25–7, 68, 70–2, 79, 80, 82, 83, 94, 105, 172, 177, 178, 204, 205
1:3	48, 141	*Proverbs*			
1:6	40	1–9	28, 70, 71, 81, 82, 89, 97, 138		
18:5	85				
22:15	61				
24:2	99	1:8-19	70		
29:3-11	50	1:12	85		
30:2	87	1:20-33	70		
33:7	55	1:20	77		
38:12	94	1:27	193	5:15-18	71

Proverbs (cont.)

Ref	Pages
5:15	16, 68, 69, 71, 72, 74, 75, 82, 83, 87, 94, 172, 183, 191, 196, 202
5:16-18	72, 75, 77, 79
5:16-17	77, 81
5:16	68, 69, 71, 76–8, 183, 189
5:17-18	71, 82
5:17	69, 79, 82
5:18-20	71, 74, 172
5:18	72, 79, 190
5:19-20	72, 79
5:19	72, 75, 172
5:20	26
5:21-23	71
6:1-19	70, 71
6:20-35	70, 81
6:26	81
6:30	83
7:1-27	70, 81
7:10-21	81
7:18	83
7:20	77
7:26-27	85
7:27	81
8	102
8:1-36	70
8:4-21	102
8:21	55
8:22-36	105
8:22-31	5, 12, 16, 22, 28, 68, 87, 96, 101–6, 138, 172, 173, 205
8:22-23	102
8:22	103
8:23	103
8:24-29	102
8:24-26	102, 103
8:24-25	103
8:24	103, 104, 183
8:25	104
8:26	103, 104
8:27-29	102–4, 173
8:27-28	105
8:27	186
8:28	104, 186, 190
8:29	103, 104, 183, 187
8:30-31	102
8:32-36	102
9:1-18	81
9:1-6	81
9:1-3	81
9:4	81
9:5	82, 196
9:11	81
9:13-18	12, 22, 27, 68, 80, 81, 105, 172, 177, 204
9:13-14	81
9:13	81
9:17-18	80
9:17	16, 29, 79, 81–3, 183
9:18	80, 81, 83–7
10:11	96, 190
11:25	183, 205
13:14	96, 191
14:27	96, 191
15:15-20	172
15:16-17	172
15:16	55
16:15	131, 192
16:22	96, 191
17:1	201
17:14	183
17:22	201
18:4	86, 183, 186, 189, 191
18:10	96
18:18	87
19:12	195
19:13	192
20:1	196
20:5	86, 183
20:17	29
21:1	183, 189, 205
23:7	196
23:27	75, 82, 191
23:34	187
23:35	197
25–27	88
25	88
25:1	88
25:2-27	88, 89
25:2-5	88
25:2-3	88, 89
25:4-5	88, 89
25:6-15	89
25:13	56, 95, 194, 204
25:14	92, 192
25:16-26	89
25:17	89
25:21	93, 183, 197, 205
25:23-26	12, 22, 27, 68, 87–90, 105, 106, 153, 172, 173, 178, 205
25:23-24	27, 87, 89, 90, 93
25:23	87, 89–93, 173, 192
25:24	89, 90, 93, 173
25:25-26	27, 28, 87, 89, 90
25:25	76, 89, 90, 93–5, 106, 173, 178, 183
25:26	89, 90, 95, 96, 106, 148, 178, 191

25:27	89	1:7	110, 112–14,		133–5, 173–
26:1-12	88		116–20, 174,		5, 179, 205
26:1	93, 192, 194		187, 189,	11:1-2	129, 130,
26:13-16	88		202		132, 134,
26:17-28	88	1:8-11	113		175
27:1-22	88	1:8	114, 115,	11:1	29, 128, 129,
27:19	183		119		131, 184
27:23-27	88	1:9	113	11:2-6	128
27:29	16	1:11	110, 178	11:2-4	29
28:3	192	1:12–2:26	122	11:2	129, 133,
30:4	51, 183	1:12–2:11	122		134, 175
30:14	48	1:13	122	11:3-6	131, 132
30:16	183	2	122	11:3-4	131, 133,
30:27	152, 153	2:1	126		134, 175
31:4	197	2:3	107	11:3	129, 131,
31:5	197	2:4-11	121, 122,		132, 134,
31:6	197		134		152, 175,
31:7	197	2:4-9	123		192
		2:4-6	12, 22, 30,	11:4-6	132
Qohelet			107, 121–6,	11:4	129, 132,
1:1–2:26	121		134, 173,		134, 175
1:1-11	112		174, 178,	11:5	129, 133
1:1	110		205	11:6	129, 131,
1:2-11	111	2:4	127		132
1:2	111, 112,	2:5	127, 134,	11:7–12:7	129
	114		174	11:9–12:14	112
1:3	111, 113,	2:6	184	12	128
	114, 118,	2:7-9	122	12:2	192
	152	2:10	126	12:6	191
1:4-11	12, 22, 107,	2:11	124	12:7	86
	110, 112–14,	2:24-26	122	12:8	112, 113
	117, 120,	2:24	197	19:10	130
	133, 134,	3:5	29	24:23-27	141
	173, 174,	3:13	197	24:25-27	141
	178, 205	4:1-3	124	24:25	141
1:4-8	111	5:18	197	24:26	141
1:4-7	111, 113–15	6:12	110	24:28-29	141
1:4-6	117	8:15	197	43:14	55
1:4-5	115	9:1	109		
1:4	113–15, 118	9:7	197	*Song of Songs*	
1:5-8	115	9:9	110	2:12	48
1:5-7	113, 115	9:12	201	4:12-15	40, 122
1:5	113, 116,	10:10	110	4:13	127
	118	11	179	4:15	74, 75
1:6	113, 116,	11:1-6	5, 12, 22, 29,		
	118		107, 128–30,		

Isaiah

3:7	142
6:8	64
7:3	57
8:6	142
13:5	94
14:11	84
19	42
19:1-4	42
19:5-10	38, 40–3, 67, 161, 171, 177
19:5-7	41
19:5-6	41
19:6	143
19:8	41
19:9-10	41
19:11-14	42
20:22	100
24:18	57, 131
24:22	75
26:19	61
28:17	55
29:6	152
30:30	55
32:20	29, 48, 128
34:9	117
36:16	79, 83
37:25	51
38:18	84
40:26	62
41:4	115
41:17-18	77
42:14	118
43:2	86
44:3	75
46:11	94
47:13	63
51:1	74
51:2	92
51:9-10	154
51:9	115
51:10	86
51:33	100
55:10-11	55, 153
55:10	153
57:13	110
59:9	94

Jeremiah

1:5	86
2:13	74
2:18	139, 143
5:24	92
6:7	74
6:20	94
10:13	55
14:6	118
14:22	60
18:14	51, 153
23:19	152
23:23	94
32:30	48
50:25	55
51:16	55
51:36	142

Lamentations

4:7	56

Ezekiel

1:26	58
13:11	55
23:40	94
27:1	154
28:2	155
32:2	95
34:19	95
34:26	92
34:27	48
47:1-12	40, 144
47:10	76

Daniel

4:25	154

Hosea

2:24	48
6:3	61
14:6	61

Joel

1:1-4	153
2:23	47

Amos

5:24	118, 119
9:2-3	100

Jonah

2:2-6	42
2:2-3	85
2:6	103

Micah

5:7	61

Zephaniah

1:15	58

Haggai

2:17	55

Zechariah

2:10	51
9:11	75
12:1	86
13:5	48
14:6	152

Malachi

3:10	57

NEW TESTAMENT

Matthew

2:15	166
26:27	166

Mark

16:3	166

Luke

12:4	91, 173
17:24	143

Acts

17:33	166
28:23	143

1 Corinthians
4:3	143
15:2	27

Galatians
3:13	166

Colossians
1:22-23	27

2 Timothy
2:12	27

1 Peter
3:20	166

Revelation
14:13	166
16:14	143
22:1-2	179

SEPTUAGINT
Wisdom of Solomon
1:1–11:1	158
2:1	42
2:4	196
4:19	201
5:10	184, 188
5:14	152, 193
5:19-23	158
5:22-23	31, 204
5:22	184, 187, 190
7:5	157
8:21	157
9:7-8	157
10:1-21	158
10:18-19	31, 204
10:18	184, 187
10:19	187
11:2–19:22	158–60, 164
11:2-14	12, 22, 30, 67, 136, 156–61, 166–9, 175, 176, 180
11:2-11	157
11:2-7	161
11:2	161
11:4-7	30
11:4	160, 161, 184, 203
11:5	157
11:6-14	159–61, 204
11:6-10	162
11:6-7	161
11:6	161, 190, 191
11:7	184
11:8-10	162
11:11-14	163
11:12	163
11:13	161, 163
11:15–16:15	159
11:15-16	157
11:22	195
13:2	184
14:1	188
14:3	187, 189
14:4	188
15:7	158
16:15-29	159
16:16	193, 194, 204
16:17	184
16:19	184
16:22	193-95
16:24	158
16:25	166
16:29	184, 202
17:1–18:4	159
17:18	184
18:5–19:22	159, 164
18:5	199, 204
19:1-12	12, 22, 31, 136, 163, 164, 166–9, 175, 176
19:1-9	67, 158–60, 164, 204
19:1-5	164, 167
19:4-6	165
19:6-12	164
19:6-8	166
19:6	159, 165, 168, 169, 176
19:7	166, 184, 188, 189, 200, 201
19:10-12	164
19:10	167, 190, 201
19:12	167, 188
19:18-22	165
19:19	165, 168, 169, 184, 202
19:20	165, 185

Sirach
1–24	137, 138
1:2	188, 193
1:4-11	28
1:7	28
1:9	99
2:4-6	28
3:15	152
3:30	185
4:26	190
9:10	197
11:1-6	28
11:1	28
15:3	185, 197
15:16	185
18:10	185
18:16	196
21:13	199
21:23	96
24	138, 146
24:1-22	138
24:3	196
24:5-6	145
24:6	188, 189
24:8	146
24:14	185
24:21	197
24:23-34	10, 12, 31, 136–8, 147, 175, 179

Wisdom of Solomon (cont.)		29:21	185, 204	43:19	152, 153
		29:22	190	43:20	149, 153, 154, 186, 195, 200
24:23-29	138–40, 146, 147, 168, 179, 204	29:25	198		
		33:2	193		
		35:26	193	43:21-22	151, 154, 156
		38:4-5	205		
24:23-25	138	38:5	185	43:21	154
24:23-24	22	39:13	185, 189	43:22	151, 154, 196
24:23	138, 140	39:17-21	205		
24:24	139	39:17	185	43:23-26	151, 154, 156
24:25-29	148	39:22-23	204		
24:25-27	138–40, 143, 148, 175, 179	39:22	199–201	43:23	186
		39:26	186, 195, 205	43:24	156, 188
				43:25-26	155, 156
24:25-26	168	39:27–44:71	137	43:25	154, 155
24:25	140	39:27–43:30	149	43:26	150, 156
24:26	140, 142, 143, 202	39:28-29	204	43:27-31	150
		40:10	199	43:30	149
24:27	139, 140, 143, 144	40:13	190, 193, 201	43:32-33	150
				44–51	138
24:28-34	138	40:16	186, 190	44:17	199
24:28-29	119, 138, 145, 148, 175	41:15–43:33	138	44:18	199
		42:15–43:33	45, 138, 149, 150	44:21	188, 202
				46:3-26	168
24:28	140, 145, 179	42:15-25	150	46:8	202
24:29	5, 140, 145, 188	42:22	150	46:13-26	168
		43	155	46:23-26	145
24:30-34	138, 146, 147, 149, 168	43:1-12	150	47:14	202
		43:13-46	12	48:17	186, 205
		43:13-26	22, 31, 136–8, 149–51, 155, 156, 175, 176, 205	50:3-5	205
24:30-31	146, 147			50:3	186, 188, 191
24:30	185, 190				
24:31	146, 185, 188, 190, 199			50:4-6	127, 174
				50:8	186
		43:13-20	156	50:15	198
24:32-34	31	43:13-17	150–2	51:13-20	138
24:32-33	146, 147	43:13	194		
24:32	139	43:14	152	**INSCRIPTIONS**	
24:34	146	43:15	152	*KAI*	
25–43	137	43:16	152	181 line 23	123
25:25	185	43:17-20	151, 152	181 line 9	123
26:12	185, 204	43:17	152, 153, 194		
27:27	90				
29:18	188, 189				

Index of Authors

Agam, N. 60
Albright, W. F. 84
Alter, R. 112
Anderson, B. W. 16
Ansari, M. 126
Ansberry, C. B. 70, 81
Anthonioz, S. 18

Bagnall, R. S. 108
Balentine, S. F. 40
Balogh, C. 41
Barbour, J. 113
Batto, B. F. 85
Ben Zvi, E. 3, 10, 18, 37
Bergant, D. 2, 160, 165
Berliner, P. R. 60
Bickerman, E. J. 108
Bimson, J. 43, 47, 91
Boer, R. 10
Boorer, S. 37
Bowes, D. R. 15
Brenner, A. 23, 24, 36
Brown, W. P. 72, 74, 79, 81, 98, 105, 110, 111, 114
Bryce, G. E. 89

Caleb, S. M. 18, 41
Cheon, S. 157
Chisholm, R. B. 68
Clifford, R. J. 28, 86, 96, 102
Clines, D. J. A. 23, 56, 62
Collins, J. J. 138, 158, 165
Colson, F. H. 162, 166, 180
Conradie, E. 7
Cook, J. 86
Coote, R. B. 124
Cregg, J. A. F. 162, 163, 166
Crenshaw, J. L. 5, 28, 48, 50, 130, 145, 151, 175
Cross, F. M. 108

Dahood, M. J. 47, 48
Davis, E. F. 26
De Savignac, J. 103
Delitzsch, F. 91, 107
Dell, K. J. 70, 72, 78, 82, 104
Di Lella, A. A. 31, 137, 141, 143, 147
Díaz, J. L. 60
Donner, H. 123
Driver, G. R. 62

Efrat, E. 76
Eidevall, G. 10
Emerton, J. A. 100, 101
Eran, M. 148, 159

Fabry, H.-J. 16
Fejo, W. 20
Feliks, Y. 76
Fontaine, C. R. 9, 25, 26, 74
Fox, M. V. 4, 26, 27, 70, 71, 81, 83, 109, 111, 112, 128

Gadamer, H. G. 7, 9
Gardner, A. 20
Gilead, M. 60
Good, E. M. 111
Grave, C. 91
Green, D. 123, 127
Grisanti, M. A. 16
Grünfeld, J. 10
Gunkel, H. 19

Habel, N. 2, 21, 32, 35, 36, 38, 40, 42, 46, 49, 54, 56, 60
Hadas, M. 108, 118
Hamilton, R. W. 73, 116
Harris, R. L. 85
Haupt, P. 87
Hembrom, T. 17
Hertzberg, H. W. 122
Hess, R. S. 125

Hillel, D. 51, 65, 73, 83, 91, 144, 152
Hobgood-Oster, L. 20
Hopkins, D. C. 73, 76, 77, 91, 96, 131, 132
Horne, M. P. 27, 28
Hubbard, D. A. 29, 130, 133
Hurvitz, A. 33, 34

Ikram, S. 143, 144
Issar, A. S. 17

Jaussen, A. 64
Jenney, T. P. 15
Johnston, P. 84–6
Jonker, L. 126

Kadish, G. E. 131
Kahn, C. 159
Kaiser, W. C. 16
Kang, S. T. 126
Kee, M. S. 63
King, P. 73, 92, 131
Klopper, F. 19, 21, 76
Köhlenberger, J. R. 11
Köhler, L. 142
Koh, Y.-V. 30, 108, 121, 123
Kolarcik, M. 9, 31, 157, 158, 164, 167
Krüger, P. A. 69, 108, 114, 124, 130, 132
Kuhrt, A. 125

Landy, F. 120
Levin, C. 3, 18, 133
Lichtheim, M. 29, 130
Loader, J. A. 2, 5, 122, 130
Loew, C. 158
Lohfink, N. 117
Longman, T. 27, 114
Luc, A. 24, 50

Malbim, M. L. 28, 93
Manser, M. H. 78
Marlow, H. 42
May, H. G. 19, 84
Mazzinghi, L. 167
McCann, C. 156
McCarter, P. K. 84, 86
McKane, W. 95
Metzger, B. M. 11
Michel, W. L. 39
Migliore, D. 150, 151

Millard, A. R. 125
Min, Y.-J. 113
Moltmann, J. 176
Morgan, R. A. 78
Morris, P. 127
Murphy, R. E. 22, 30

Naidu-Hoffmeester, R. 178
Newsom, C. A. 9, 23, 45, 150, 155, 156
Nõmmik, U. 25

O'Connor, M. 49
Obermann, J. 56
Ogden, G. S. 110, 116
Orni, E. 76

Patai, R. 60
Patrick, D. 23
Pedersen, J. 84
Perdue, L. G. 8, 26, 28, 31, 97, 99, 100, 108, 109, 112, 113, 121, 137, 138, 145, 155, 157, 165
Perry, T. A. 29, 90
Peters, J. P. 64
Petrova, R. 5
Prinsloo, G. T. M. 19
Propp, W. H. 17

Rad, G. von 23, 98, 102
Rasmussen, C. 141
Reese, J. M. 159
Reymond, P. 17, 41, 43, 58, 73, 78, 85, 86, 103, 118, 142
Ricoeur, P. 7
Röllig, W. 123
Rogers, J. F. 137
Rosenan, N. 60
Ross, M. M. 18
Rudman, D. 19, 84, 86, 127

Sachs, G. 58
Samet, N. 117
Schifferdecker, K. 24, 34, 59
Schökel, L. A. 60
Seow, C.-L. 29, 39, 132
Sharp, C. J. 112
Shavit, Y. 148, 159
Sheppard, G. T. 31, 140, 146
Simkins, R. A. 153
Sinnott, A. M. 24

Skehan, P. 31, 69, 137, 140, 141, 143, 147
Smith, J. L. 78
Snaith, J. G. 142
Spangenberg, I. 112
Stager, L. E. 73, 92, 131
Sutcliffe, E. F. 47, 57, 58, 65
Sweeney, M. A. 109
Sylva, D. 19

Thompson, H. 124
Trudinger, P. 2, 21
Tsumura, D. T. 17, 21, 47, 84, 148
Tur-Sinai, N. H. 51

Van Leeuwen, R. C. 27, 28, 88, 89
Van der Ploeg, J. P. M. 87, 91
VanGemeren, W. 999
Vawter, B. 103
Verheij, A. 125, 126

Walls, C. 15
Waltke, B. 26–8, 49, 71, 89, 92, 94, 99
Waters, L. J. 45
Watson, R. S. 25
Westermann, C. 24
White, L. 167
Whitwell, C. 130
Whybray, R. N. 28, 98, 110, 111, 116–18
Willis, J. T. 38, 72, 98
Wilson, L. 37, 111, 120
Winston, D. 166, 167
Wolde, E. van 63

Yee, G. A. 82

Zayadine, F. 124

www.ingramcontent.com/pod-product-compliance
Lightning Source LLC
Chambersburg PA
CBHW050327020526
44117CB00031B/1834